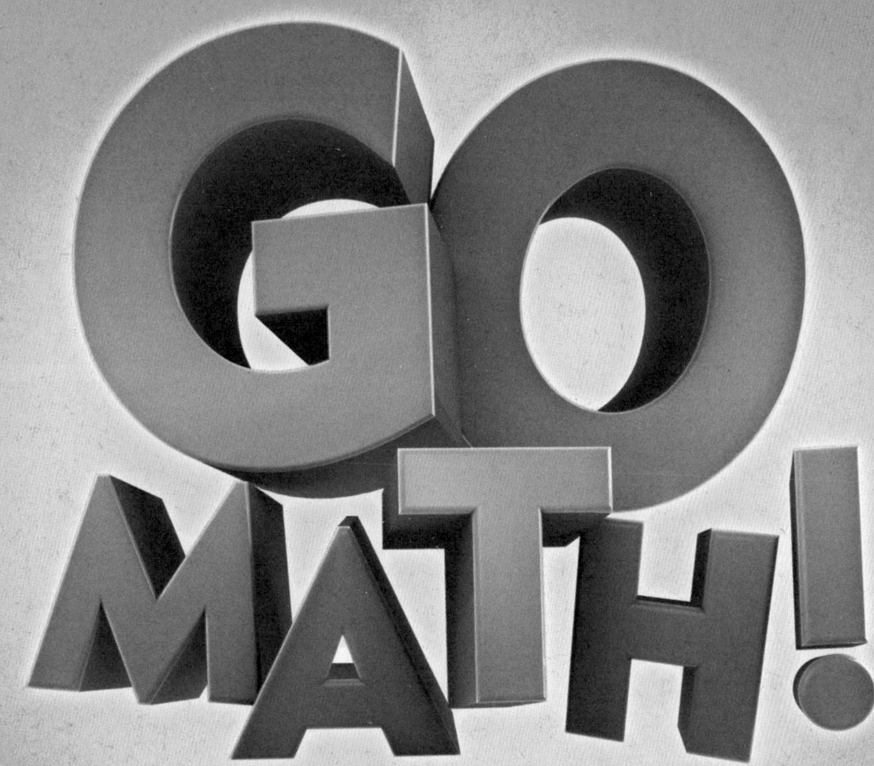

Volume 2

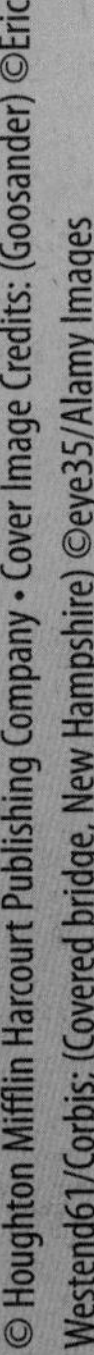

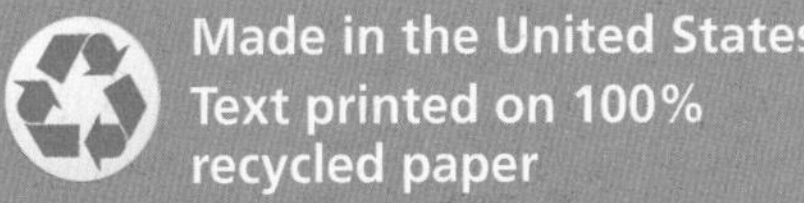
Made in the United States
Text printed on 100%
recycled paper

Houghton
Mifflin
Harcourt

2017 Edition

Printed in the U.S.A.

ISBN 978-0-544-71057-3

14 15 16 0607 24 23 22 21

4500842366 D E F G

Dear Students and Families,

Welcome to **Go Math!**, Grade 2! In this exciting mathematics program, there are hands-on activities to do and real-world problems to solve. Best of all, you will write your ideas and answers right in your book. In **Go Math!**, writing and drawing on the pages helps you think deeply about what you are learning, and you will really understand math!

By the way, all of the pages in your **Go Math!** book are made using recycled paper. We wanted you to know that you can Go Green with **Go Math!**

Sincerely,

The Authors

Made in the United States
Text printed on 100% recycled paper

Authors

Juli K. Dixon, Ph.D.
Professor, Mathematics Education
University of Central Florida
Orlando, Florida

Edward B. Burger, Ph.D.
President, Southwestern University
Georgetown, Texas

Steven J. Leinwand
Principal Research Analyst
American Institutes for Research (AIR)
Washington, D.C.

Matthew R. Larson, Ph.D.
K-12 Curriculum Specialist for Mathematics
Lincoln Public Schools
Lincoln, Nebraska

Martha E. Sandoval-Martinez
Math Instructor
El Camino College
Torrance, California

Contributor

Rena Petrello
Professor, Mathematics
Moorpark College
Moorpark, CA

English Language Learners Consultant

Elizabeth Jiménez
CEO, GEMAS Consulting
Professional Expert on English Learner Education
Bilingual Education and Dual Language
Pomona, California

VOLUME 1

Number Sense and Place Value

Big Idea Extend conceptual understanding of number relationships and place value.

Number Concepts 9

Big Idea

GO DIGITAL

Go online! Your math lessons are interactive. Use *i*Tools, Animated Math Models, the Multimedia *e*Glossary, and more.

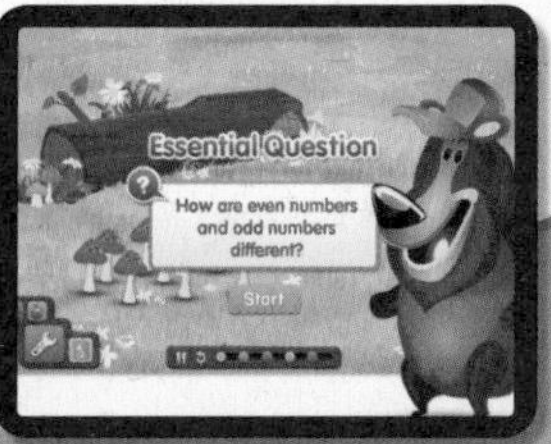

Chapter 1 Overview

In this chapter, you will explore and discover answers to the following **Essential Questions**:

- How do you use place value to find the values of numbers and describe numbers in different ways?
- How do you know the value of a digit?
- What are some different ways to show a number?
- How do you count by 1s, 5s, 10s, and 100s?

Personal Math Trainer
Online Assessment and Intervention

Chapter 2 Overview

In this chapter, you will explore and discover answers to the following **Essential Questions**:

- How can you use place value to model, write, and compare 3-digit numbers?
- How can you use blocks to show a 3-digit number?
- How can you write a 3-digit number in different ways?
- How can place value help you compare 3-digit numbers?

Practice and Homework

Lesson Check and Spiral Review in every lesson

2 Numbers to 1,000 71

Addition and Subtraction

Big Idea Develop fluency with addition and subtraction within 100. Solve addition and subtraction problems within 1,000.

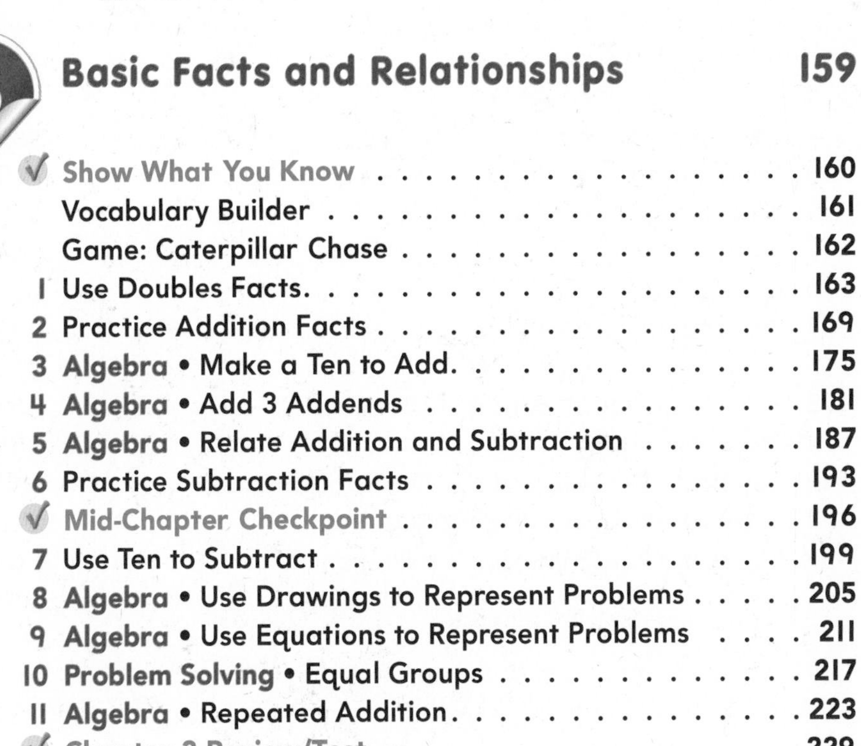

Big Idea

GO DIGITAL

Go online! Your math lessons are interactive. Use *i*Tools, Animated Math Models, the Multimedia *e*Glossary, and more.

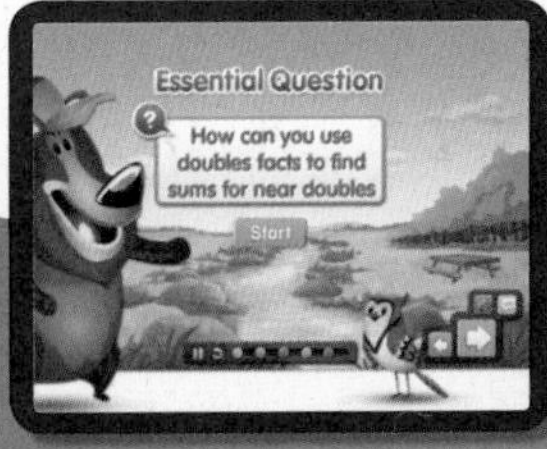

Chapter 3 Overview

In this chapter, you will explore and discover answers to the following **Essential Questions**:

- How can you use patterns and strategies to find sums and differences for basic facts?
- What are some strategies for remembering addition and subtraction facts?
- How are addition and subtraction related?

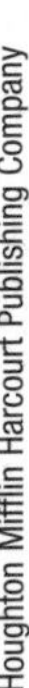

Chapter 4 Overview

In this chapter, you will explore and discover answers to the following **Essential Questions**:

- How do you use place value to add 2-digit numbers, and what are some different ways to add 2-digit numbers?
- How do you make an addend a ten to help solve an addition problem?
- How do you record the steps when adding 2-digit numbers?
- What are some ways to add 3 numbers or 4 numbers?

Practice and Homework

Lesson Check and Spiral Review in every lesson

2-Digit Addition 233

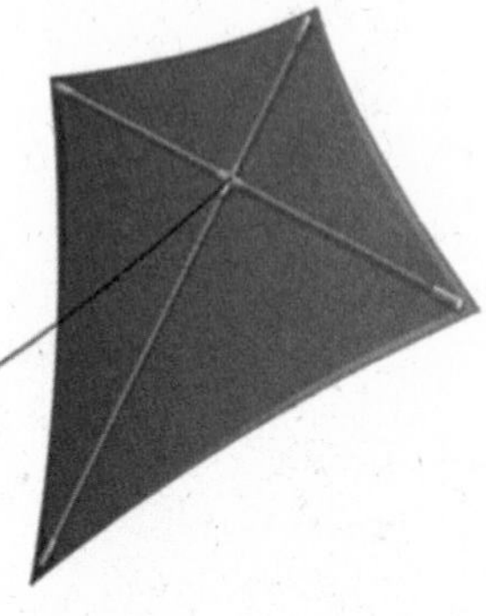

5 2-Digit Subtraction 313

Chapter 5 Overview

In this chapter, you will explore and discover answers to the following **Essential Questions**:

- How do you use place value to subtract 2-digit numbers with and without regrouping?
- How can you break apart numbers to help solve a subtraction problem?
- What are the steps you use when you solve 2-digit subtraction problems?
- What are some different ways to model, show, and solve subtraction problems?

6 3-Digit Addition and Subtraction 387

Chapter 6 Overview

In this chapter, you will explore and discover answers to the following **Essential Questions**:

- What are some strategies for adding and subtracting 3-digit numbers?
- What are the steps when finding the sum in a 3-digit addition problem?
- What are the steps when finding the difference in a 3-digit subtraction problem?
- When do you need to regroup?

Big Idea

GO DIGITAL

Go online! Your math lessons are interactive. Use *i*Tools, Animated Math Models, the Multimedia *e*Glossary, and more.

Chapter 7 Overview

Essential Questions:

- How do you use the values of coins and bills to find the total value of a group of money, and how do you read times shown on analog and digital clocks?
- What are the names and values of the different coins?
- How can you tell the time on a clock by looking at the clock hands?

Chapter 8 Overview

Essential Questions:

- What are some of the methods and tools that can be used to estimate and measure length?
- What tools can be used to measure length and how do you use them?
- What units can be used to measure length and how do they compare with each other?
- How can you estimate the length of an object?

VOLUME 2

Measurement and Data

Big Idea Use standard units of measure and extend conceptual understanding of time, data, and graphs. Develop a conceptual understanding of money.

9 Length in Metric Units 599

10 Data 649

Chapter 9 Overview

In this chapter, you will explore and discover answers to the following **Essential Questions**:

- What are some of the methods and tools that can be used to estimate and measure length in metric units?
- What tools can be used to measure length in metric units and how do you use them?
- What metric units can be used to measure length and how do they compare with each other?
- If you know the length of one object, how can you estimate the length of another object?

Practice and Homework

Lesson Check and Spiral Review in every lesson

Chapter 10 Overview

In this chapter, you will explore and discover answers to the following **Essential Questions**:

- How do tally charts, picture graphs, and bar graphs help you solve problems?
- How are tally marks used to record data for a survey?
- How is a picture graph made?
- How do you know what the bars in a bar graph stand for?

Big Idea

GO DIGITAL

Go online! Your math lessons are interactive. Use *i*Tools, Animated Math Models, the Multimedia *e*Glossary, and more.

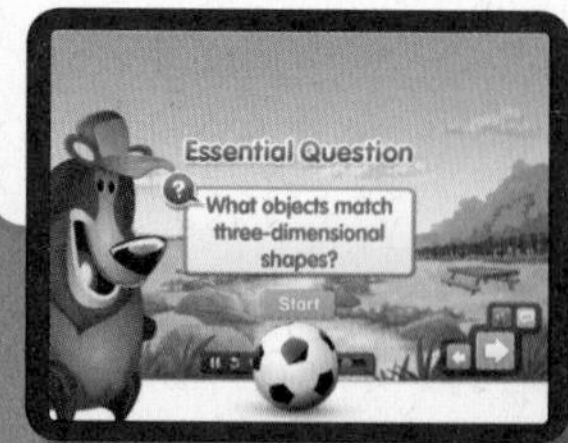

Chapter 11 Overview

In this chapter, you will explore and discover answers to the following **Essential Questions**:

- What are some two-dimensional shapes and three-dimensional shapes, and how can you show equal parts of shapes?
- How can you describe some two-dimensional and three-dimensional shapes?
- How can you describe equal parts of shapes?

Personal Math Trainer
Online Assessment and Intervention

Geometry and Fractions

Big Idea Describe, analyze, and draw two- and three-dimensional shapes. Develop a conceptual understanding of fractions.

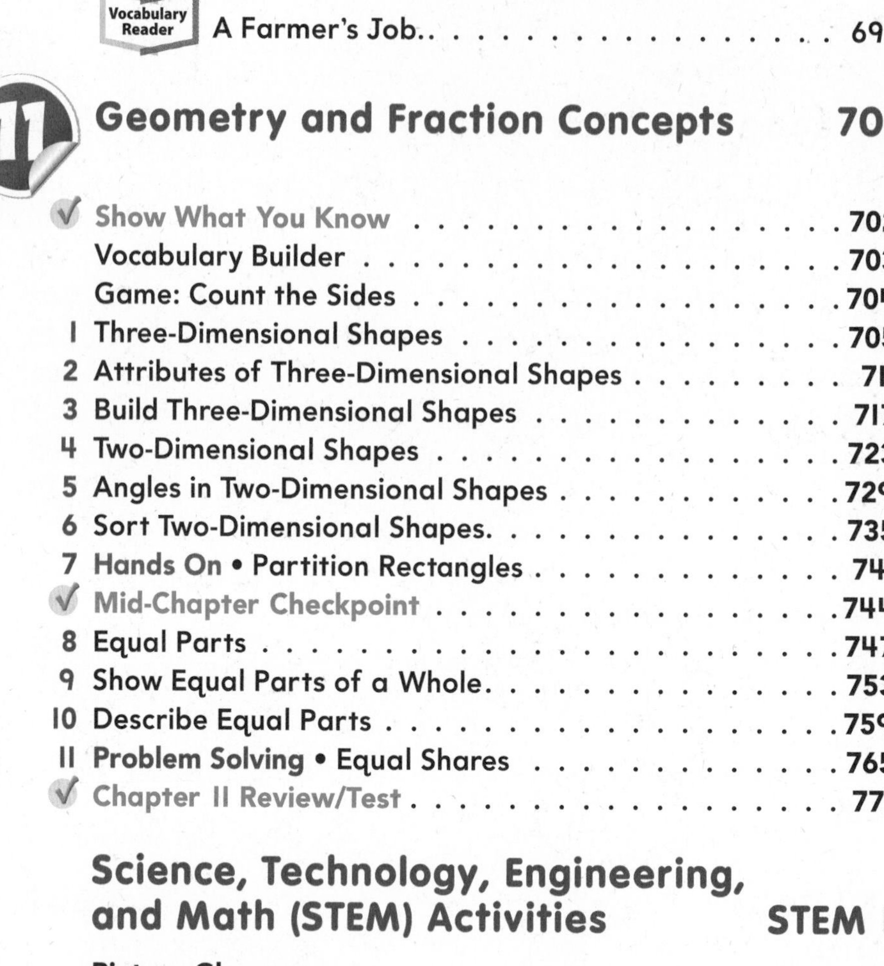

Making a Kite

by Kathryn Krieger and Christine Ruiz

BIG IDEA Use standard units of measure and extend conceptual understanding of time, data, and graphs. Develop a conceptual understanding of money.

Ellie and Mike get the materials to make a kite. Then they make the body of the kite.

Materials

paper kite pattern
tape
straw
10 small paper clips
scissors
hole punch
string
3 sheets of paper
streamer paper

1 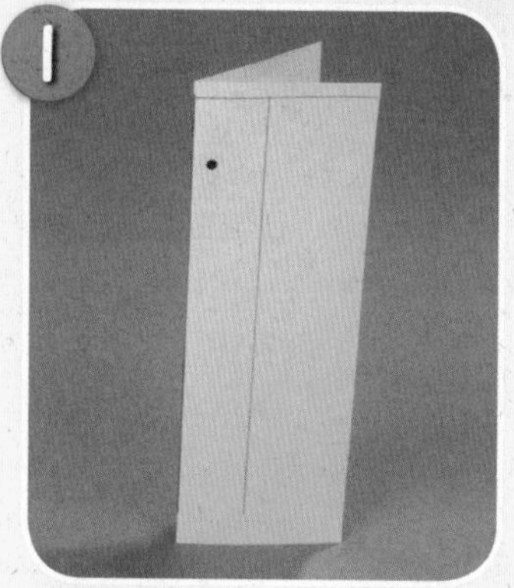
Fold the pattern in half.

2 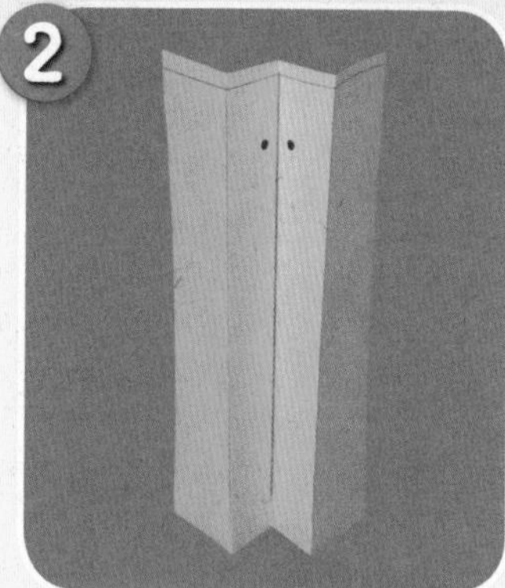
Fold along both dashed lines.

3  
Tape on each end.

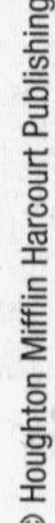

Science

What are the parts of a kite?

Mike does not want the front of the kite to bend too much. He uses a straw to make the kite stronger.

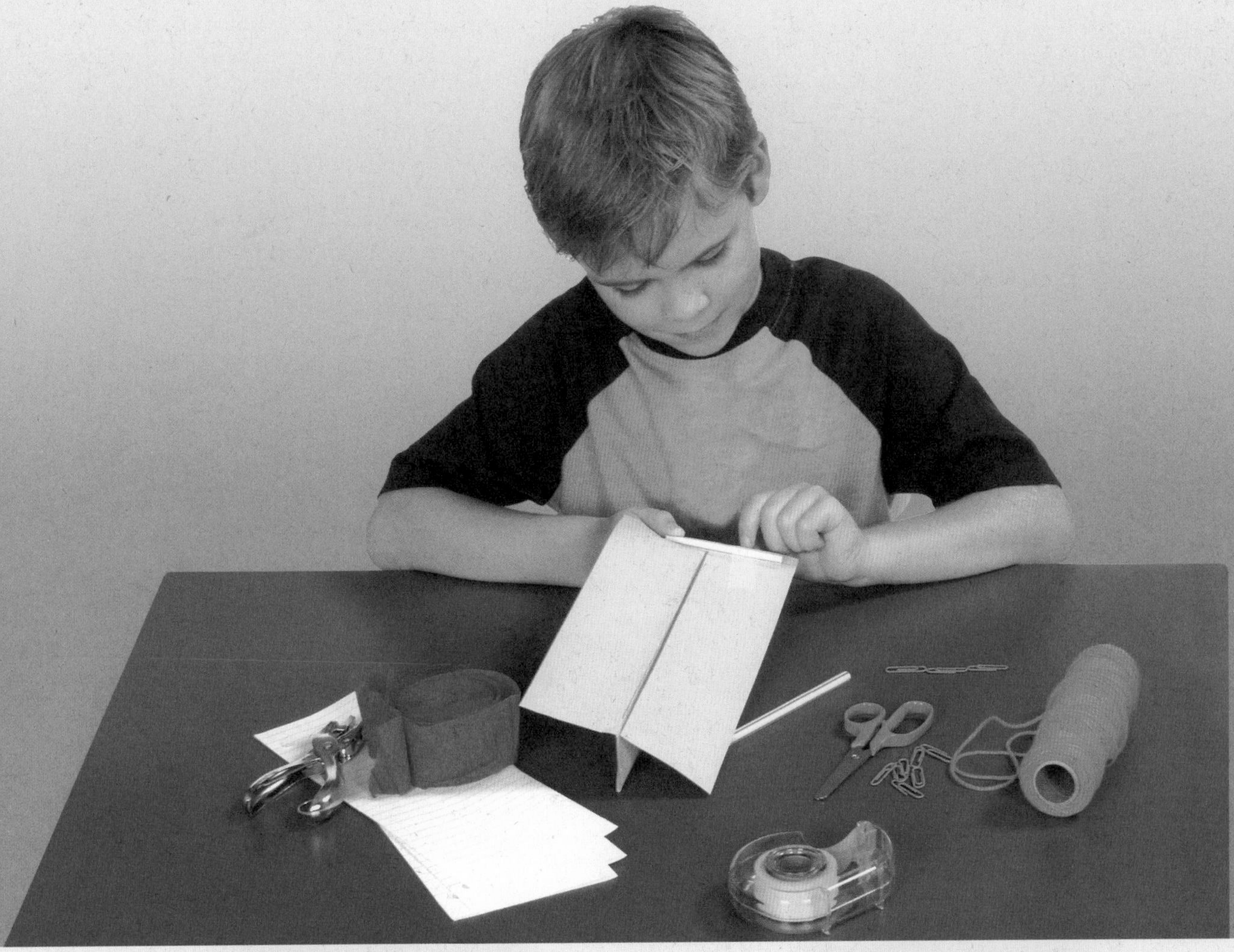

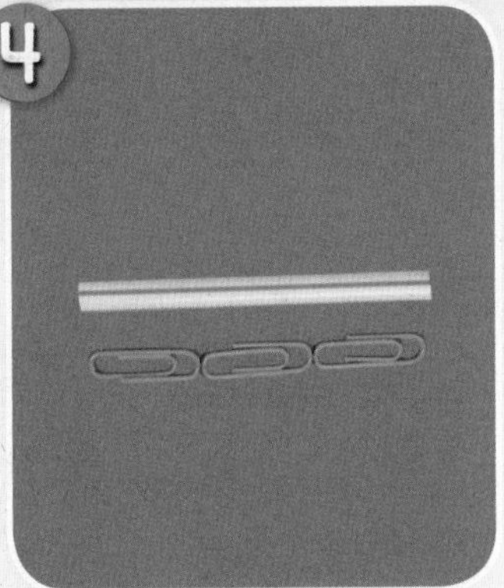

4 Measure 3 paper clips long. Cut.

5 Tape the straw on the line.

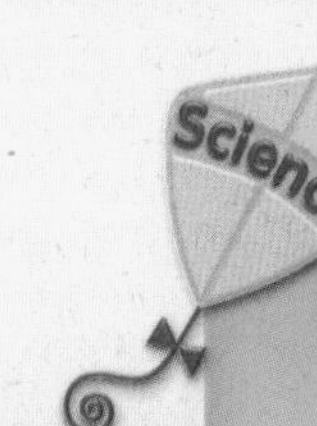

Why is a straw used as part of the kite?

The kite must have a string for Ellie or Mike to hold. If the kite does not have a string, it will blow away. Ellie will tie the string onto the kite.

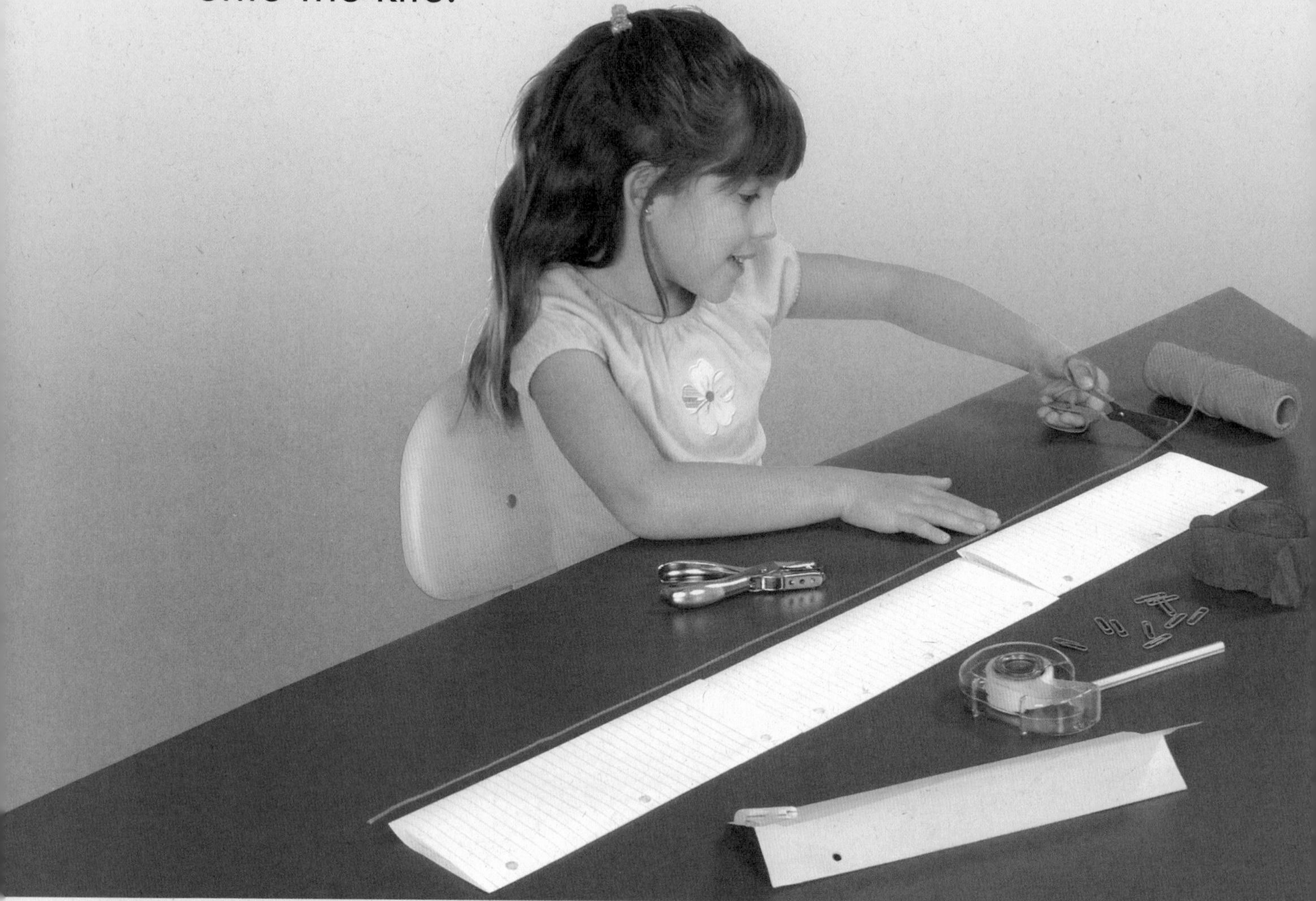

Punch one hole.

Measure 3 paper-lengths of string. Cut.

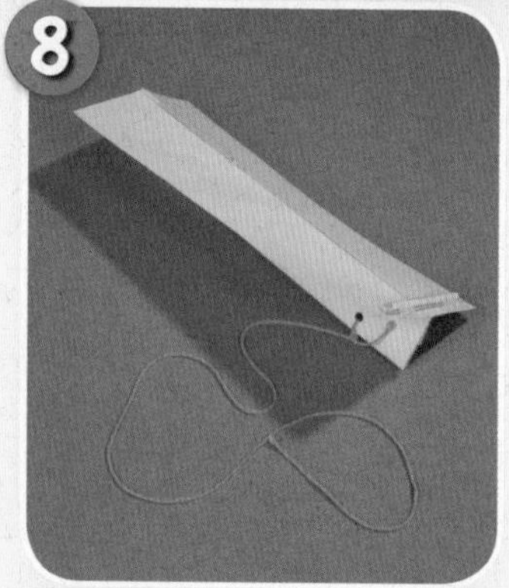

Put the string through the hole and tie it.

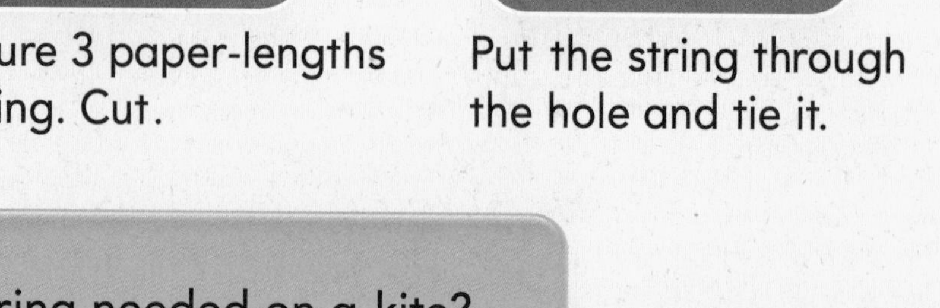

Why is a string needed on a kite?

A tail will help the kite fly straight. Mike measures streamer paper and will tape it to the kite. Then the kite will be finished!

9

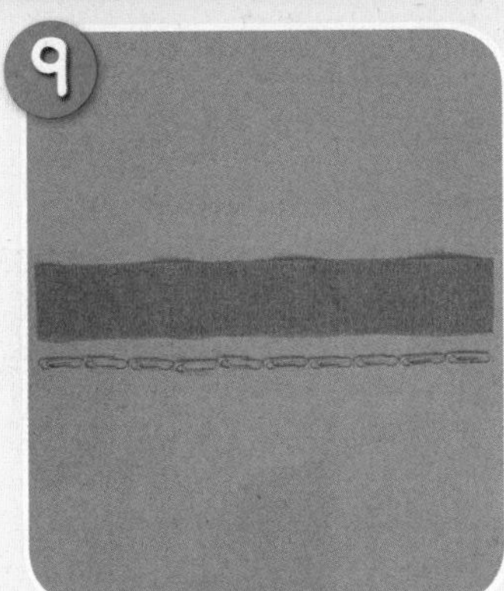

Measure 10 paper-clip-lengths of streamer paper. Cut.

10

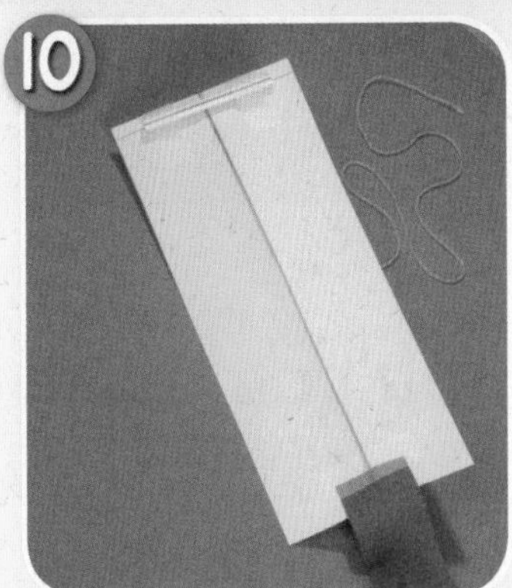

Tape the streamer to the kite as a tail.

Science

Why is a tail needed on a kite?

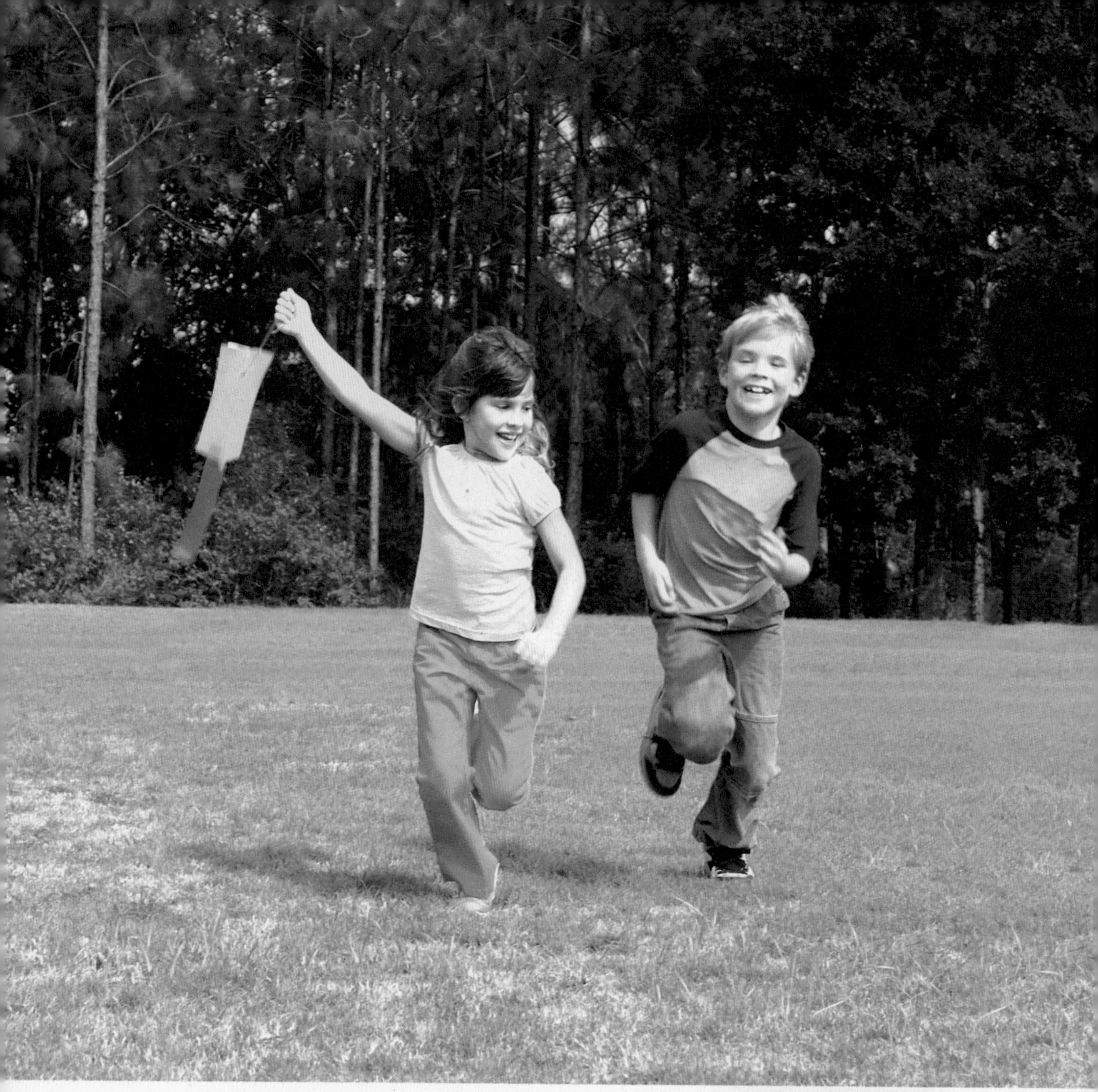

You can make a kite too. Start at the beginning of this story. Follow the steps.

How do all of the parts help the kite fly?

Name ______________________________

Write About the Story

Draw and write a story about making a kite. Explain how to measure the parts of the kite in your story.

Vocabulary Review

measure

length

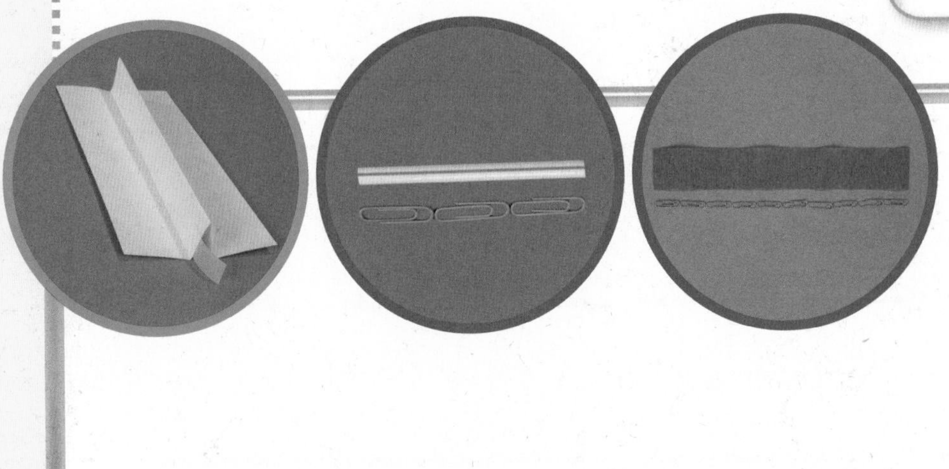

WRITE Math

____

____

____

____

____

What is the length?

Estimate the length of each straw. Then measure the length of each straw using small paper clips.

1. Estimate: about _____ paper clips long

Measure: about _____ paper clips long

2. Estimate: about _____ paper clips long

Measure: about _____ paper clips long

3. Estimate: about _____ paper clips long

Measure: about _____ paper clips long

Look around the classroom. Find other objects to measure. Measure the length of each object using small paper clips.

Money and Time

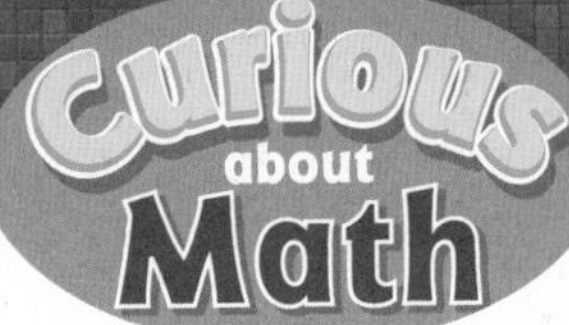

A sundial shows the time using the position of the sun. It has numbers around it, like a clock face. What numbers are on a clock face?

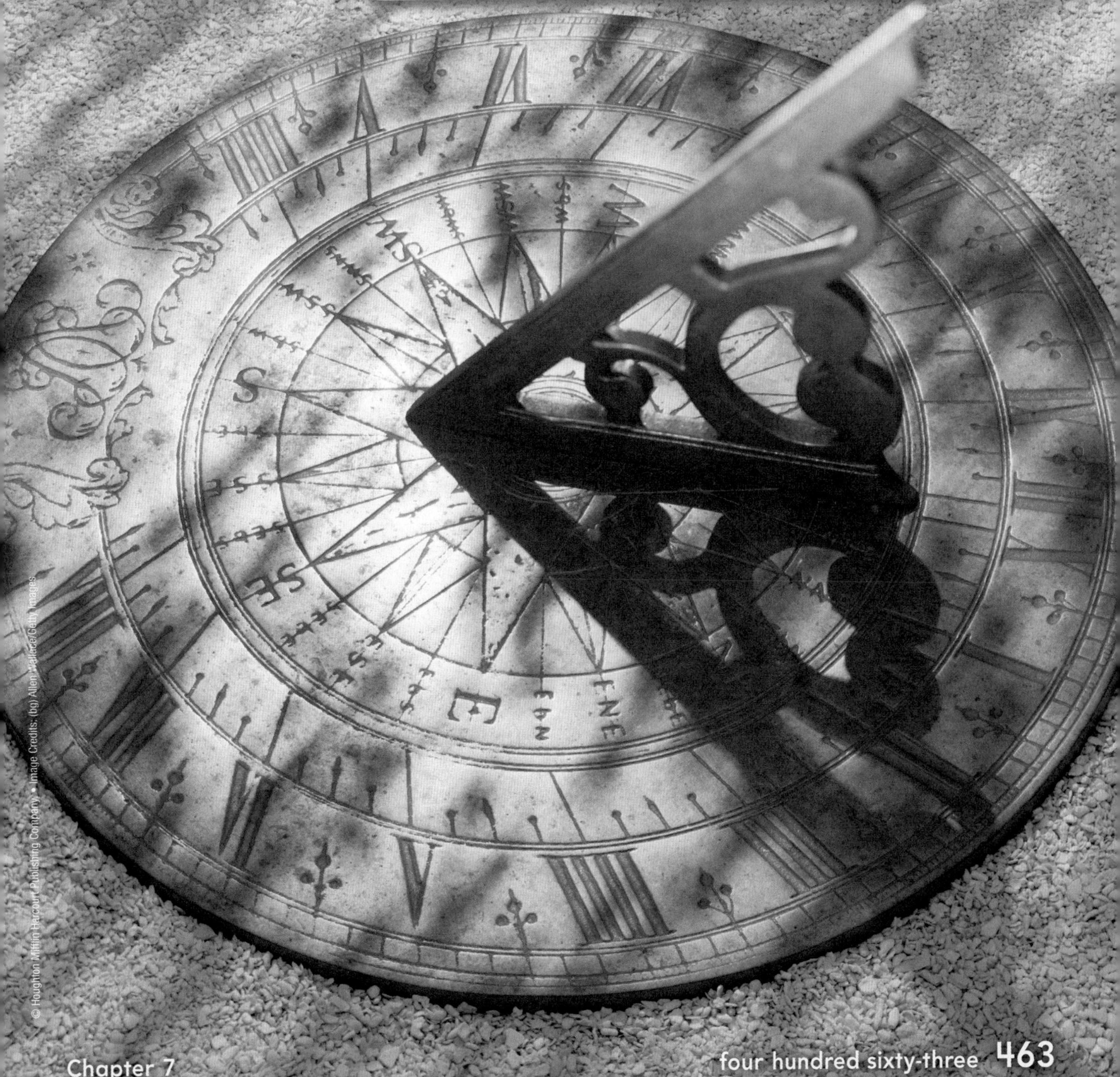

Name ____________________

Order Numbers to 100 on a Number Line

Write the number that is just before, between, or just after.

1. 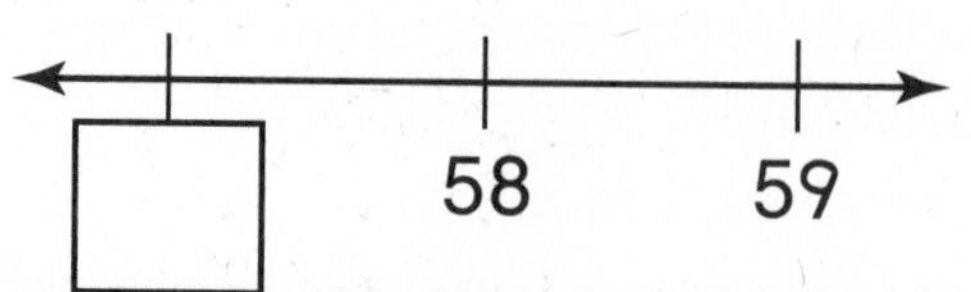

2. 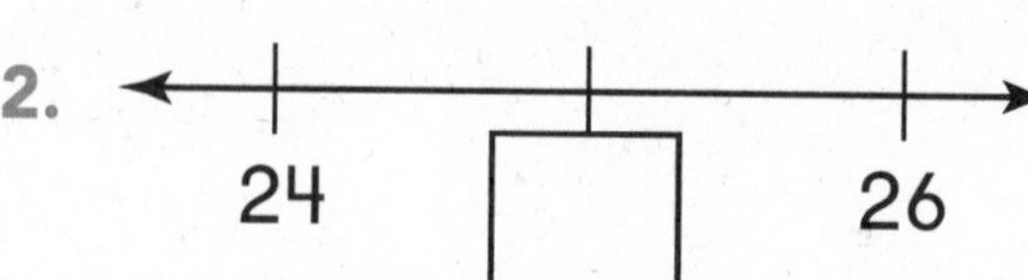

Skip Count by Fives and Tens

3. Count by fives. Write how many in all.

____________________ ______ paints in all

4. Count by tens. Write how many in all.

____________________ ______ paints in all

Time to the Hour

Write the time shown on the clock.

5. 

6.  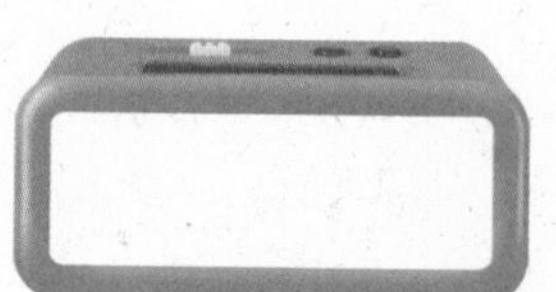

This page checks understanding of important skills needed for success in Chapter 7.

Name ______________________________

Review Words
count
pattern
count on

Vocabulary Builder

Visualize It

Fill in the graphic organizer.
Show ways to **count on**.

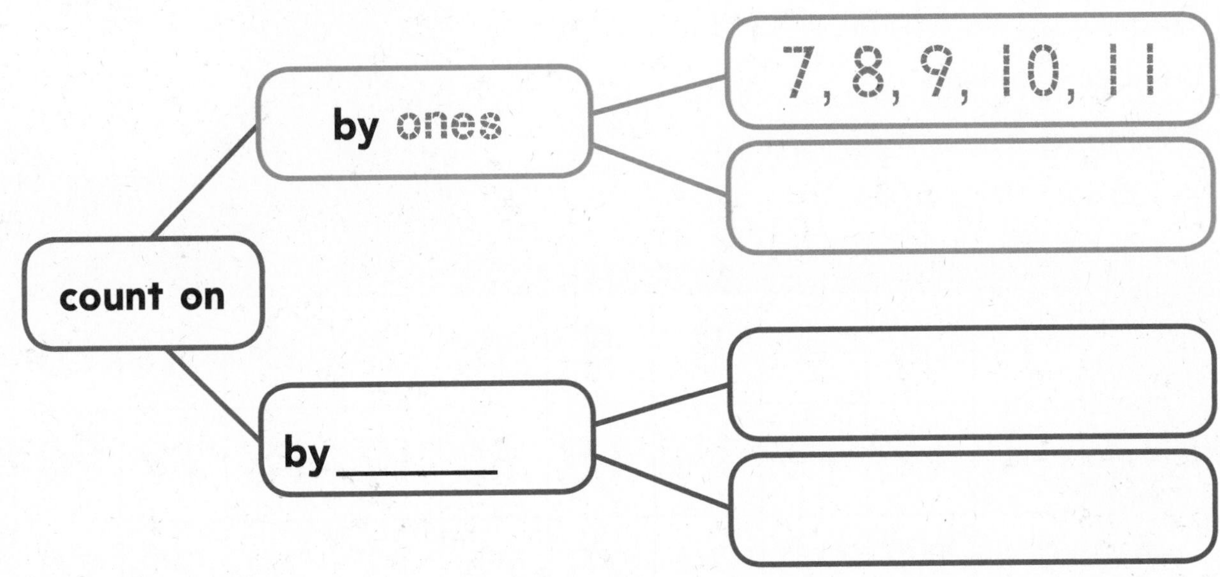

Understand Vocabulary

Write the missing numbers in each counting **pattern.**

1. **Count** by ones. 40, ____, ____, ____, 44, ____, 46, ____

2. **Count** by fives. 10, 15, ____, ____, ____, 35, ____, ____

3. **Count** by tens. 20, ____, ____, 50, ____, ____, 80, ____

• Interactive Student Edition
• Multimedia eGlossary

Chapter 7

Game

5 and 10 Count

Materials • 1 cube • 1 cube • spinner

Play with a partner.

1. Spin the pointer on the spinner for your starting number. Put your cube on that number.
2. Spin the pointer. Count on by that number two times.
3. Take turns. The first player to get to 100 wins. Play again.

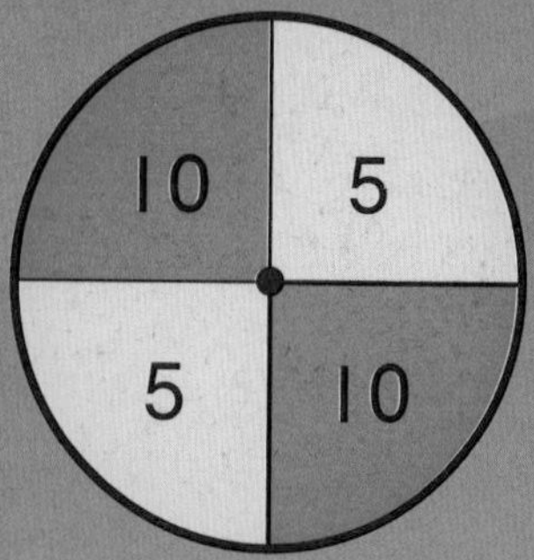

10	5
5	10

1	2	3	4	**5**	6	7	8	9	**10**
11	12	13	14	**15**	16	17	18	19	**20**
21	22	23	24	**25**	26	27	28	29	**30**
31	32	33	34	**35**	36	37	38	39	**40**
41	42	43	44	**45**	46	47	48	49	**50**
51	52	53	54	**55**	56	57	58	59	**60**
61	62	63	64	**65**	66	67	68	69	**70**
71	72	73	74	**75**	76	77	78	79	**80**
81	82	83	84	**85**	86	87	88	89	**90**
91	92	93	94	**95**	96	97	98	99	**100**

Chapter 7 Vocabulary

a.m.

a.m.

2

cent sign

símbolo de centavo

5

decimal point

punto decimal

13

dime

moneda de 10¢

16

dollar

dólar

17

dollar sign

símbolo de dólar

18

hour

hora

30

midnight

medianoche

40

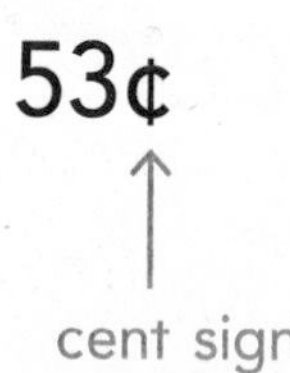

53¢

cent sign

Times after midnight and before noon are written with **a.m.**

A **dime** has a value of 10 cents.

$1.00

decimal point

$2.00

dollar sign

One **dollar** is worth 100 cents.

Midnight is 12:00 at night.

There are 60 minutes in 1 **hour**.

minute

minuto

41

nickel

moneda de 5¢

42

noon

mediodía

43

penny

moneda de 1¢

46

p.m.

p.m.

50

quarter

moneda de 25¢

52

quarter past

y cuarto

54

A **nickel** has a value of 5 cents.

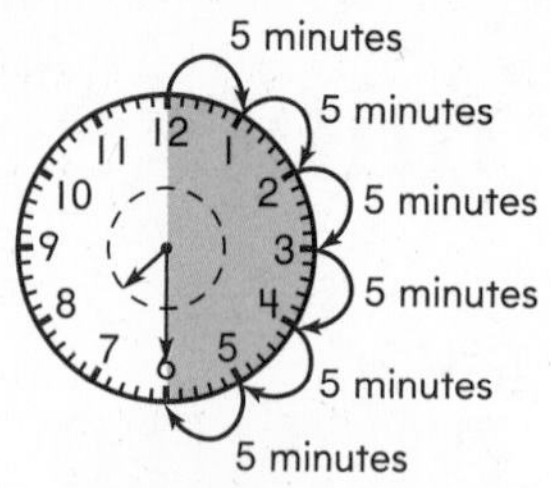

There are 30 **minutes** in a half hour.

A **penny** has a value of I cent.

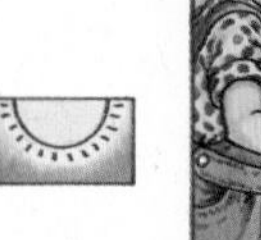

Noon is I2:00 in the daytime.

A **quarter** has a value of 25 cents.

Times after noon and before midnight are written with **p.m.**

I5 minutes after 8

quarter past 8

Going to Los Angeles

Word Box
- a.m.
- cent sign (¢)
- decimal point
- dime
- dollar
- dollar sign ($)
- midnight
- minute
- nickel
- noon
- p.m.
- penny
- quarter
- quarter past

For 2 to 4 players

Materials

• 1 [connecting cube] • 1 [connecting cube] • 1 [connecting cube] • 1 [connecting cube] • 1 [number cube] • Clue Cards

How to Play

1. Take turns to play.
2. To take a turn, toss the [number cube]. Move that many spaces.
3. If you land on this space:

   Blue Space Use a math word to name the picture or symbol you see. If you name it correctly, move ahead 1.

   Red Space The player to your right takes a Clue Card from the pile and reads you the question. If you answer correctly, move ahead 1.
   Return the Clue Card to the bottom of the pile.

   Green Space Follow the directions in the space.
4. The first player to reach FINISH wins.

DIRECTIONS 2 to 4 players. Take turns to play. • To take a turn, toss the numbered cube. Move that many spaces • Follow the directions for the space you land on. • First player to reach FINISH wins.

MATERIALS 1 connecting cube per player • 1 number cube • 1 set of clue cards

START

See art at the Getty Center. Move ahead 1.

CLUE CARD

Ride the Ferris Wheel at Santa Monica Pier. Go Back 1.

CLUE CARD

Listen to music on Olvera Street. Take another turn.

CLUE CARD

FINISH

CLUE CARD

Spot a movie star in Hollywood. Trade places with another player.

Get lost on the freeway. Lose 1 turn.

CLUE CARD

$

Get stuck at La Brea tarpits. Lose 1 turn.

CLUE CARD

The Write Way

Reflect

Choose one idea. Write about it in the space below.

- Write and draw to explain the following amount as if you were talking to a young child. Use another sheet of paper for your drawing.

$1.36

- What time is it now? Use at least **three** of these words in your answer.

a.m. midnight minute noon p.m. quarter past

- Write at least **three** things you know about money.

Name ______________________________

Dimes, Nickels, and Pennies

Essential Question How do you find the total value of a group of dimes, nickels, and pennies?

Learning Objective You will find the value of a collection of dimes, nickels, and pennies.

Listen and Draw

Real World

Hands On

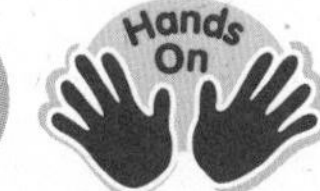

Sort the coins. Then draw the coins.

Math Talk Math Processes and Practices 1

Analyze Relationships
A nickel has the same value as how many pennies? Explain.

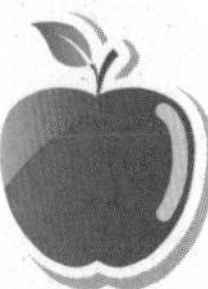

FOR THE TEACHER • Distribute play coins of dimes, nickels, and pennies and discuss their values. Have children sort the coins and draw them inside the three circles. Have children label the drawings with the numbers *1*, *5*, or *10* to indicate the cent value of each coin drawn.

Model and Draw

10 cents
10¢

dime

5 cents
5¢

nickel

1 cent
1¢

penny

¢ is the **cent sign**.

Count dimes by tens.

10¢, 20¢, 30¢

Count nickels by fives.

5¢, 10¢, 15¢

Count by tens. Count by fives. Count by ones.

10¢, 20¢, 25¢, 30¢, 31¢, 32¢

32¢
total value

Share and Show

Count on to find the total value.

1.

____

total value

2.

____

total value

Name ____________________

Remember:
Write the cent sign after the number.

On Your Own

Count on to find the total value.

3. 

____

☐ total value

4. 

____

☐ total value

5. 

☐ total value

6. 

☐ total value

7. THINKSMARTER Maggie had 5 nickels. She gave 2 nickels to her sister. What is the total value of the nickels that Maggie has now?

____

Problem Solving • Applications

Solve. Write or draw to explain.

8. Math Processes and Practices 1 **Analyze** Jackson has 4 pennies and 3 dimes. He buys an eraser that costs 20¢. How much money does Jackson have now?

____

9. Math Processes and Practices 4 **Use Models** Draw two ways to show 25¢. You can use dimes, nickels, and pennies.

10. THINK SMARTER Sue has 40¢. Circle coins to show this amount.

TAKE HOME ACTIVITY • Draw pictures of five coins, using dimes, nickels, and pennies. Ask your child to find the total value.

Name ___________________________

Dimes, Nickels, and Pennies

Learning Objective You will find the value of a collection of dimes, nickels, and pennies.

Count on to find the total value.

1. 

____

total value

2. 

____

total value

3. 

____

total value

Problem Solving

Solve. Write or draw to explain.

4. Aaron has 5 dimes and 2 nickels. How much money does Aaron have?

____

5. WRITE Math Draw three dimes, 1 nickel, and 2 pennies. Describe how to count on to find the total value of this group of coins.

____

Lesson Check

1. What is the total value of this group of coins?

____

Spiral Review

2. Hayden is building toy cars. Each car needs 4 wheels. How many wheels will Hayden use to build 3 toy cars?

_______ wheels

3. What is the value of the underlined digit?

<u>4</u>29

____

4. Lillian is counting by fives. What numbers did she say next?

40, ____, ____, ____, ____

5. Sophie has 12 grapes in her lunch bag. She shared 7 grapes with her sister. How many grapes does she have?

12 − 7 = _______

FOR MORE PRACTICE GO TO THE Personal Math Trainer

Name ______________________________

Quarters

Essential Question How do you find the total value of a group of coins?

Learning Objective You will find the value of a collection of quarters, dimes, nickels, and pennies.

Listen and Draw

Sort the coins. Then draw the coins.

Math Processes and Practices 6

Describe how the value of a quarter is greater than the value of a dime.

FOR THE TEACHER • Distribute play coins of quarters, dimes, and nickels and discuss their values. Have children sort the coins and draw them inside the three boxes. Have them label the drawings with *5¢*, *10¢*, or *25¢*.

Model and Draw

A **quarter** has a value of 25 cents.

25¢

Count by twenty-fives. Count by tens. Count by ones.

25¢, 50¢, 60¢, 70¢, 71¢, 72¢

72¢

total value

Share and Show

Remember:
¢ is the cent sign.

Count on to find the total value.

1.  

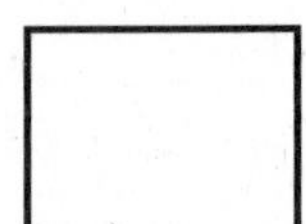

____

total value

2.     

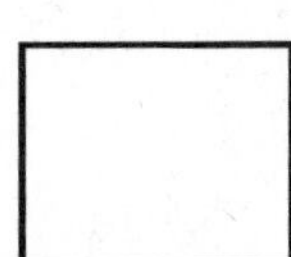

____

total value

3.     

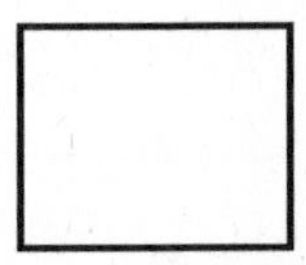

____

total value

Name ____________________

On Your Own

Count on to find the total value.

4. 

____________________ total value

5. 

____________________ total value

6. 

total value

7. 

total value

Draw and label a coin to solve.

8. THINK SMARTER Ed's coin has the same value as a group of 5 pennies and 4 nickels. What is his coin?

Problem Solving • Applications

Math Processes and Practices 6 **Make Connections**

Read the clue. Choose the name of a coin from the box to answer the question.

nickel	dime
quarter	penny

9. I have the same value as 5 pennies.

   What coin am I?

   ____

10. I have the same value as 25 pennies.

    What coin am I?

    ____

11. I have the same value as 2 nickels.

    What coin am I?

    ____

12. I have the same value as a group of 5 nickels.

    What coin am I?

    ____

13. THINKSMARTER Tom gives these coins to his brother.

Circle the value of the coins to complete the sentence.

Tom gives his brother

25¢
65¢
80¢

.

TAKE HOME ACTIVITY • Have your child draw two quarters, two dimes, and two nickels, and then find the total value.

Name ______________________________

Quarters

Learning Objective You will find the value of a collection of quarters, dimes, nickels, and pennies.

Count on to find the total value.

1.

____

[ ] total value

2.

____

[ ] total value

Problem Solving

Read the clue. Choose the name of a coin from the box to answer the question.

nickel	dime
quarter	penny

3. I have the same value as a group of 2 dimes and 1 nickel. What coin am I?

____

4. WRITE Math Draw coins to show 39¢. Describe how to count to find the total value of this group of coins.

____

____

Lesson Check

1. What is the total value of this group of coins?

____

Spiral Review

2. Circle the odd number.

8 14 17 22

3. Kai scored 4 points and Gail scored 7 points. How many points did they score altogether?

$4 + 7 =$ _______ points

4. There were 382 chairs in the music hall. Write a number greater than 382.

____

5. Write the number 61 using words.

____

FOR MORE PRACTICE GO TO THE Personal Math Trainer

Name ______________________________

Count Collections

Essential Question How do you order coins to help find the total value of a group of coins?

Learning Objective You will order coins in a collection by value and then find the total value.

Listen and Draw

Line up the coins from greatest value to least value. Then draw the coins in that order.

greatest least

greatest least

Math Processes and Practices 6

Describe how the values of the different kinds of coins compare.

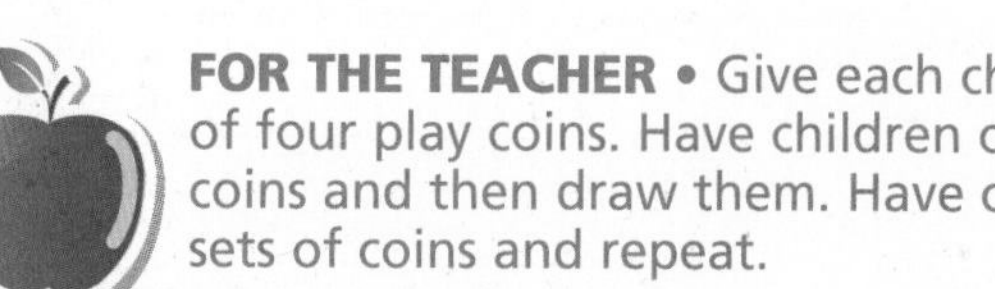

FOR THE TEACHER • Give each child a mixture of four play coins. Have children order their coins and then draw them. Have children trade sets of coins and repeat.

Model and Draw

Order the coins from greatest value to least value.
Then find the total value.

Count the cents.
25, 50, 60, 61, 62

____
total value

Share and Show 

Remember: Write the cent sign.

Draw and label the coins from greatest to least value. Find the total value.

1. 

____

2. 

____

3. 

____

Name ____________________________________

On Your Own

Draw and label the coins from greatest to least value. Find the total value.

4. 

______

5. 

______

6. 

______

7. 

______

8. GO DEEPER Andy buys a 75¢ juice box using only quarters and nickels. Show the amount he spent in two ways.

______ quarter ______ nickels

______ quarters ______ nickels

Problem Solving • Applications

Solve. Write or draw to explain.

9. THINK SMARTER Paulo had these coins.

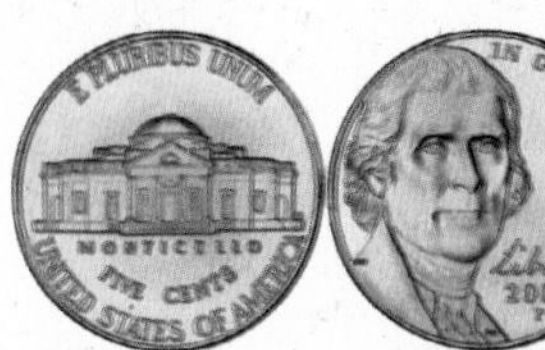

He spent 1 quarter. How much money does he have now? ________

10. Rachel has 2 quarters, 3 dimes, and 1 nickel. She wants to buy a book that costs 90¢. How much more money does she need?

____

11. GO DEEPER Blake has only nickels and dimes. He has double the number of nickels as dimes. The total value of his coins is 60¢. What coins does Blake have?

________ nickels ________ dimes

12. THINK SMARTER Malik has these coins in his pocket. What is the total value of the coins?

____

TAKE HOME ACTIVITY • Have your child draw and label coins with a total value of 32¢.

Name ______________________

Count Collections

Learning Objective You will order coins in a collection by value and then find the total value.

Draw and label the coins from greatest to least value. Find the total value.

1.

______

2.

______

Problem Solving 

Solve. Write or draw to explain.

3. Rebecca has these coins. She spends 1 quarter. How much money does she have left?

______

4. WRITE Math Draw 2 dimes, 1 nickel, and 2 quarters. Describe how to order and then count to find the total value of the coins.

____

Lesson Check

1. What is the total value of this group of coins?

______

Spiral Review

2. What number is 100 more than 562?

______

3. Describe 58 as a sum of tens and ones.

______

4. Pete helps his grandmother gather pecans. He finds 6 pecans on his left and 3 on his right. How many pecans did Pete find altogether?

$6 + 3 =$ ____ pecans

5. What number do the blocks show?

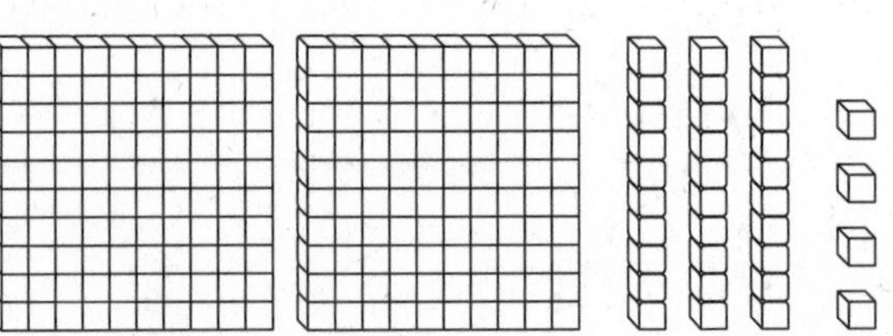

______

Name ___________________________

HANDS ON
Lesson 7.4

Show Amounts in Two Ways

Essential Question How do you choose coins to show a money amount in different ways?

Learning Objective You will show a money amount less than a dollar using two different collections of coins.

Listen and Draw

Real World

Hands On

Show the amount with coins. Draw the coins. Write the amount.

FOR THE TEACHER • Distribute play coins. Tell children to use coins to show 27 cents. Then have them draw the coins and write the amount. Repeat the activity for 51 cents.

Math Processes and Practices 

Can you show 10¢ with 3 coins? **Explain** how you know.

Model and Draw

Here are two ways to show 30¢.

Look at Matthew's way. If you trade 2 dimes and 1 nickel for 1 quarter, the coins will show Alicia's way.

Count the cents.
Start with the dimes.

Count the cents.
Start with the quarter.

Share and Show

Use coins. Show the amount in two ways. Draw and label the coins.

✓ 1. 61¢

✓ 2. 36¢

Name ______________________

On Your Own

Use coins. Show the amount in two ways. Draw and label the coins.

3. 55¢

4. 90¢

5. 75¢

6. THINK SMARTER Teresa has 42¢. She has no dimes. Draw to show what coins she might have.

Problem Solving • Applications

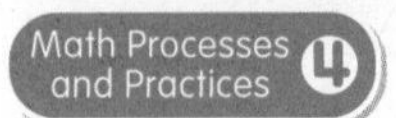

Model with Mathematics

Use coins to solve.

7. Lee buys a pen for 50¢. Draw coins to show two different ways to pay 50¢.

8. Math Processes and Practices 1 **Make Sense of Problems**
   Delia used 4 coins to buy a book for 40¢. Draw coins to show two ways to pay 40¢ with 4 coins.

9. THINK SMARTER Fill in the bubble next to all the groups of coins with a total value of 30¢.
   - ○ 6 dimes
   - ○ 1 quarter and 1 nickel
   - ○ 2 nickels and 2 dimes
   - ○ 3 nickels and 5 pennies

TAKE HOME ACTIVITY • With your child, take turns drawing different collections of coins to show 57¢.

Name ______________________

Show Amounts in Two Ways

Learning Objective You will show a money amount less than a dollar using two different collections of coins.

Use coins. Show the amounts in two ways. Draw and label the coins.

1. 39¢		
2. 70¢		

Problem Solving Real World

3. Madeline uses fewer than 5 coins to pay 60¢. Draw coins to show one way she could pay 60¢.

4. WRITE Math Draw coins in two ways to show 57¢. Describe how to chose the coins for each way.

____

____

Lesson Check

1. Circle the group of coins that has the same total value.

Spiral Review

2. Write the number 31 in tens and ones.

2 tens ____ ones

3. Write 13 tens as hundreds and tens.

____ hundreds ____ tens

4. What is the value of the underlined digit?

2<u>8</u>

____

5. Baylie's softball team scored 5 runs in the first inning and 6 runs in the second inning. How many runs did her team score?

$5 + 6 =$ ____ runs

FOR MORE PRACTICE GO TO THE Personal Math Trainer

Name ______________________________

One Dollar

Essential Question How can you show the value of one dollar with coins?

Learning Objective You will show the value of one dollar with different collections of coins.

Listen and Draw (Real World)

Draw the coins. Write the total value.

______

______

Math Processes and Practices 6

How many pennies have the same value as 80¢? **Explain.**

FOR THE TEACHER • In the first box, have children draw eight nickels and then count to find the total value. In the second box, have children draw eight dimes and then count to find the total value.

Model and Draw

One **dollar** has the same value as 100 cents.

$1.00 = 100¢

dollar sign — **decimal point**

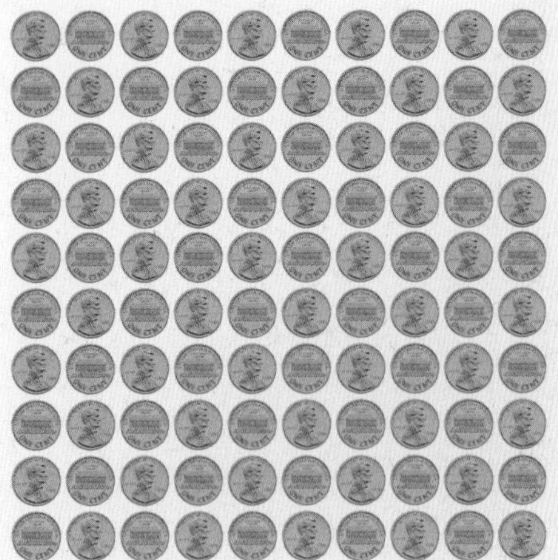

The decimal point separates the dollars from the cents.

Share and Show

Count 100 cents for one dollar.

Draw the coins to show $1.00. Write the total value.

1. nickels

$1.00

2. quarters

______

3. dimes

______

Name ______________________________

On Your Own

Circle coins to make $1.00.
Cross out the coins you do not use.

4.

5.

6. GO DEEPER Warren has $1.00. He saves 2 quarters, and uses the rest to buy a pencil. Draw and label the coins he uses to buy the pencil.

7. THINK SMARTER Sara has these coins. Draw more coins to show $1.00.

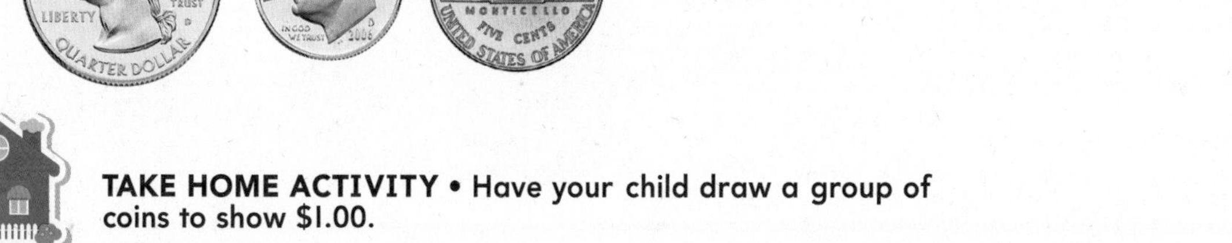

TAKE HOME ACTIVITY • Have your child draw a group of coins to show $1.00.

Name ________________________________

Mid-Chapter Checkpoint

Concepts and Skills

Count on to find the total value.

1. 

total value

2. 

total value

Use coins. Show the amount in two ways.
Draw and label the coins.

3. 

4. THINKSMARTER Mary used these coins to buy a folder. What is the total value of these coins?

total value

Name ______________________________

One Dollar

Learning Objective You will show the value of one dollar with different collections of coins.

Circle coins to make $1.00.
Cross out the coins you do not use.

1.

2.

Problem Solving

3. Draw more coins to show $1.00 in all.

4. WRITE Math Draw coins to show one way to make $1.00 using only nickels and quarters.

Lesson Check

1. Which group of coins has a value of $1.00?

Spiral Review

2. Write 692 using words.

____

3. Keith ate 7 almonds, and then ate 7 more. Is the total number of almonds even or odd?

7 + 7 = ____ almonds

______

4. What is the total value of 1 quarter and 3 nickels?

______

5. Kristin is counting by tens. What numbers does she say next?

230, ______,

______, ______

FOR MORE PRACTICE GO TO THE Personal Math Trainer

Name ______________________________

Amounts Greater Than $1

Essential Question How do you show money amounts greater than one dollar?

Learning Objective You will find the value for money amounts greater than one dollar.

Listen and Draw Real World

Draw and label the coins.
Write the total value.

____
total value

Math Processes and Practices 7

Look for Structure
Explain how you found the total value of the coins in the coin bank.

FOR THE TEACHER • Read the following problem: Dominic has 1 quarter, 2 dimes, 3 nickels, and 1 penny in his coin bank. How much money is in Dominic's bank? Have children draw and label coins to help them solve the problem.

Model and Draw

When you write amounts greater than one dollar, use a dollar sign and a decimal point.

$1.00

$1.27
total value

$1.50
total value

Share and Show

Circle the money that makes $1.00. Then write the total value of the money shown.

1.     

____

2.       

____

Name ______________________________

On Your Own

Circle the money that makes $1.00. Then write the total value of the money shown.

3.

______

4.

______

5.

______

6. THINK SMARTER Martin used 3 quarters and 7 dimes to pay for a kite. How much money did he use?

______

Problem Solving • Applications

7. GO DEEPER Pam has fewer than 9 coins. The coins have a total value of $1.15. What coins could she have?

Draw the coins. Then write a list of her coins.

____

____

Personal Math Trainer

8. THINK SMARTER+ Jason put this money in his bank.

Circle the amount to complete the sentence.

Jason put a total of [$1.10 / $1.15 / $1.35] in his bank.

TAKE HOME ACTIVITY • With your child, take turns drawing coins or a $1 bill and coins with a total value of $1.23.

Name ______________________

Amounts Greater Than $1

Learning Objective You will find the value for money amounts greater than one dollar.

Circle the money that makes $1.00. Then write the total value of the money shown.

1.

______

2.

______

Problem Solving Real World

Solve. Write or draw to explain.

3. Grace has $1.10. She spends 75¢ on a toy. How much change did she get back?

______

4.  Write about how to use the dollar sign and decimal point to show the total value of 5 quarters.

______

Lesson Check

1. Julie has this money in her bank. What is the total value of this money?

______

Spiral Review

2. There are 79 squash plants and 42 pepper plants in Julia's garden. How many vegetable plants are in Julia's garden altogether?

$$\begin{array}{r} 79 \\ +\ 42 \\ \hline \end{array}$$

3. What is the difference?

$$\begin{array}{r} 61 \\ -\ 27 \\ \hline \end{array}$$

4. What number is 100 less than 694?

______

5. Write an addition fact that has the same sum as 6 + 5.

10 + ______

FOR MORE PRACTICE GO TO THE **Personal Math Trainer**

Name ________________________________

Problem Solving • Money

Essential Question How does acting it out help when solving problems about money?

Learning Objective You will use play bills and coins and the strategy *act it out* to solve problems about money.

Kendra gave 2 dimes, 2 nickels, 1 quarter, and two $1 bills to her sister. How much money did Kendra give her sister?

Unlock the Problem

What do I need to find?

how much money
Kendra gave her
sister

What information do I need to use?

Kendra gave her sister
2 dimes, ________________
____
____

Show how to solve the problem.

Draw to show the money that Kendra used.

Kendra gave her sister ________.

HOME CONNECTION • Your child used play money to act out the problem. Representing problems with materials can be a useful strategy for children to use to solve problems.

Try Another Problem

Use play coins and bills to solve.
Draw to show what you did.

- What do I need to find?
- What information do I need to use?

1. Jacob has two $1 bills, 2 dimes, and 3 pennies in his pocket. How much money does Jacob have in his pocket? ________

2. Amber used 2 quarters, 1 nickel, and three $1 bills to buy a toy. The toy costs $1.05. How much money does Amber have left? ________

Math Processes and Practices 

Explain how you found the amount of money in Jacob's pocket.

Name ________________________________

Share and Show 

Use play coins and bills to solve.
Draw to show what you did.

3. Val used 3 quarters, 2 nickels, 2 pennies, and one $1 bill to buy a book. How much money did Val use to buy the book? ____________

4. Derek has two $1 bills, 2 quarters, and 6 dimes. How much money does he have? ____________

5. THINKSMARTER Katy has 3 quarters, 2 nickels, 2 dimes, and 3 pennies. How many more pennies does she need to have $1.10?

_________ more pennies

Problem Solving • Applications

6. Math Processes and Practices 1 **Make Sense of Problems** Victor saves 75¢ on Monday and $1.25 on Tuesday. Then he spends $1.00 to rent a movie. Draw and label how much money Victor has left.

7. THINKSMARTER Ross used 3 quarters, 4 dimes, 3 nickels, and 5 pennies to buy a card. How much money did Ross use to buy the card? Draw to show how you solve the problem.

____

TAKE HOME ACTIVITY • Ask your child to explain how he or she solved one problem in this lesson.

Name ______________________

Problem Solving • Money

Learning Objective You will use play bills and coins and the strategy *act it out* to solve problems about money.

Use play coins and bills to solve. Draw to show what you did.

1. Sara has 2 quarters, 1 nickel, and two $1 bills. How much money does Sara have? ______

2. Brad has $1.65. He spends 75¢ to buy a card. How much change does he get back? ______

3. Mr. Morgan gives 1 quarter, 3 nickels, 4 pennies, and one $1 bill to the clerk. How much money does Mr. Morgan give the clerk? ______

4. WRITE Math Write or draw to explain how you would find the total value of two $1 bills and 3 quarters.

____

Lesson Check

1. Lee has two $1 bills and 4 dimes. How much money does Lee have?

   ____

2. Dawn has 2 quarters, 1 nickel, and one $1 bill. How much money does Dawn have?

   ____

Spiral Review

3. What is the value of the underlined digit?

   5<u>6</u>

   ____

4. Cecilia collected 342 pennies for her class's penny drive. Marked collected 243 pennies. Use <, >, or = to compare. Who collected more?

   342 ____ 243

   ____________ collected more.

5. Brooke's dog has 15 treats. Then he ate 8 of them. How many treats does he have left?

   $15 - 8 =$ ____________

6. What is the next number in this pattern?

   225, 325, 425, 525, ______

FOR MORE PRACTICE GO TO THE **Personal Math Trainer**

Name ____________________________

Time to the Hour and Half Hour

Essential Question How do you tell time to the hour and half hour on a clock?

Learning Objective You will tell and write time to the hour and half hour.

Listen and Draw Real World

Draw the hour hand to show each time.

FOR THE TEACHER • Call out times to the hour and to the half hour. Begin with 3:00. Have children draw the hour hand to show the time. Repeat the activity for half past 5:00, 11:00, and half past 8:00.

Math Processes and Practices 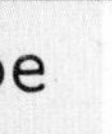

Communicate Describe where the hour hand points to show half past 4:00.

Model and Draw

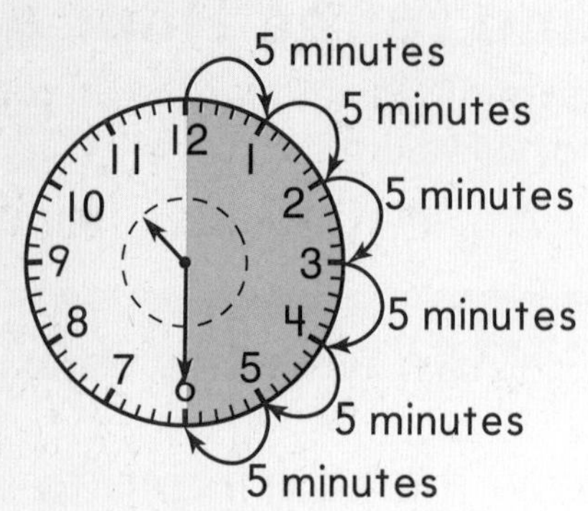

It takes 5 **minutes** for the minute hand to move from one number to the next number on a clock face.

The clock hands on these clocks show 4:00 and 4:30. Write the times below the clocks.

The 30 tells you that the time is 30 minutes after the hour.

Share and Show

Look at the clock hands. Write the time.

1.

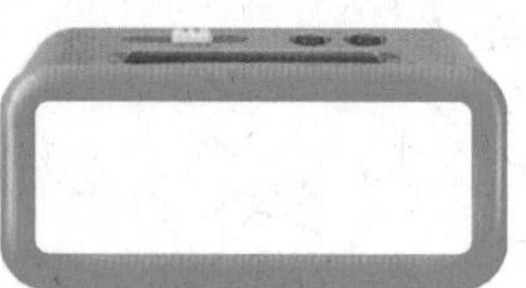

2.

3.

Name ______________________________

On Your Own

Look at the clock hands. Write the time.

4. 

5. 

6. 

7. 

8. 

9. 

10. THINK SMARTER Look at the time. Draw the hour hand and the minute hand to show the same time.

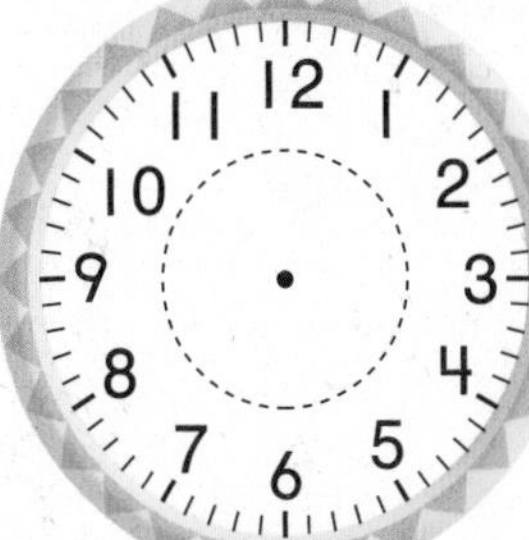

2:00

11:00

Problem Solving • Applications Real World

11. Math Processes and Practices 6 **Make Connections**
Allie eats lunch when the hour hand points halfway between the 11 and the 12, and the minute hand points to the 6. When does Allie eat lunch? Show the time on both clocks.

How do you know what time to write in the digital clock? Explain.

____

____

____

12. THINKSMARTER Match the clocks that show the same time.

9:30

TAKE HOME ACTIVITY • Have your child describe what he or she knows about a clockface.

Name ______________________________

Time to the Hour and Half Hour

Learning Objective You will tell and write time to the hour and half hour.

Look at the clock hands. Write the time.

1.

2.

3.

Problem Solving

4. Amy's music lesson begins at 4:00. Draw hands on the clock to show this time.

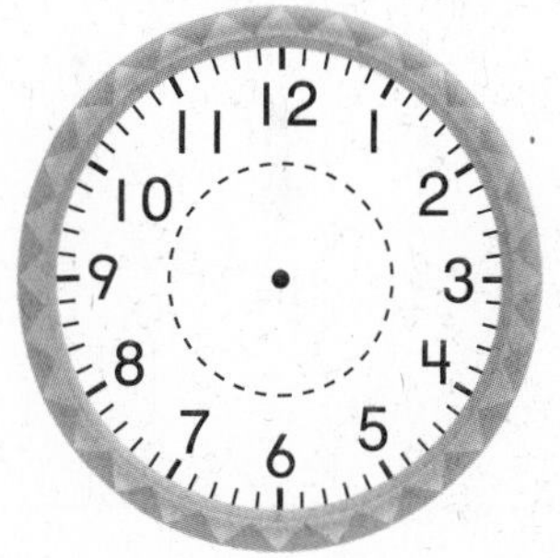

5. WRITE Math Draw a clock to show the time as 2:30. Describe how you decided where the clock hands should point.

____

____

____

Lesson Check

1. What is the time on this clock?

____

2. What is the time on this clock?

____

Spiral Review

3. Rachel has one $1 bill, 3 quarters, and 2 pennies. How much money does Rachel have?

____

4. Write <, >, or = to compare 260 and 362.

260 ____ 362

5. What number is shown with these blocks?

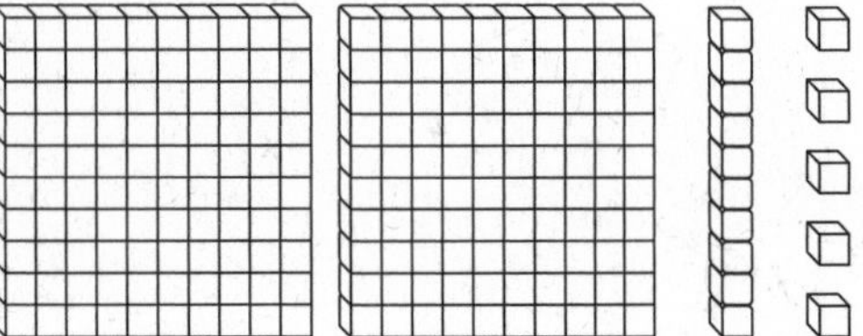

____

6. Circle any even numbers.

1 3 4 5

FOR MORE PRACTICE GO TO THE **Personal Math Trainer**

Name ______________________________

Time to 5 Minutes

Essential Question How do you tell and show time to five minutes?

Learning Objective You will tell and write time to the nearest five minutes.

Listen and Draw Real World

Draw the hour hand and the minute hand to show the time.

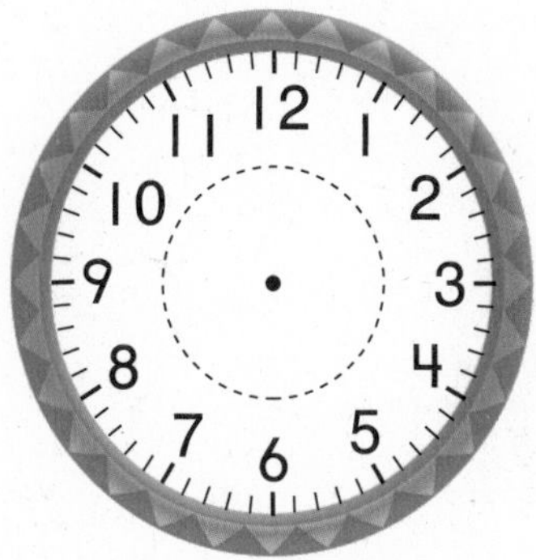

Math Processes and Practices

Describe where the minute hand points to show half past the hour.

FOR THE TEACHER • Read the following story and have children draw the hour and minute hands to show each time. Sofia goes to music at 10:30. She goes to the playground at 11:00. She eats lunch at 11:30. Show the times Sofia does these things.

Model and Draw

What does it mean when the minute hand points to the 7?

Count by fives until you reach the 7.

Remember:
The minute hand moves from one number to the next in 5 minutes.

The hour hand points between the 10 and the 11. The minute hand points to the 7.

There are 60 minutes in 1 **hour**.

The time is 

.

Share and Show

MATH BOARD

Look at the clock hands. Write the time.

1.

2.

3.

4.

✓5.

✓6.

Name ______________________________

On Your Own

Look at the clock hands. Write the time.

7.

8.

9.

10.

11.

12.

Math Processes and Practices 4 **Use Models** Look at the time. Draw the minute hand to show the same time.

13.

14.

15.

5:05

Problem Solving • Applications

Draw the clock hands to show the time.
Then write the time.

16. THINKSMARTER My hour hand points between the 8 and the 9.
In 35 minutes it will be the next hour. What time is it?

17. GO DEEPER Mr. Brady fixes broken computers. Look at the start and finish times for his work on one computer. How many minutes did he work on the computer?

Start

Finish

_______ minutes

18. THINKSMARTER Angel eats lunch at 12:45. Angel spent 10 minutes eating lunch. Draw the minute hand on the clock to show when Angel finished eating. Write the time.

_____ : _____

TAKE HOME ACTIVITY • Have your child draw a large blank clock face and use two pencils as clock hands to show some different times.

Name ______________________________

Time to 5 Minutes

Practice and Homework
Lesson 7.9

Learning Objective You will tell and write time to the nearest five minutes.

Look at the clock hands. Write the time.

1.

2.

3.

Problem Solving

Draw the minute hand to show the time. Then write the time.

4. My hour hand points between the 4 and the 5. My minute hand points to the 9. What time do I show?

5. WRITE Math Draw a clock showing 2:50. Explain how you know where the clock hands point.

____

____

____

Lesson Check

1. What is the time on this clock?

____

2. What is the time on this clock?

____

Spiral Review

3. What is the sum?

$1 + 6 + 8 = \_\_\_$

4. Which number has the same value as 30 tens?

____

5. Steven has 3 rows of toys. There are 4 toys in each row. How many toys are there?

____ toys

6. Jill has 14 buttons. She buys 8 more buttons. How many buttons does Jill have?

$$\begin{array}{r} 14 \\ +\ 8 \\ \hline \end{array}$$

buttons

Name ____________________

Practice Telling Time

Essential Question What are the different ways you can read the time on a clock?

Learning Objective You will write and tell times to the nearest five minutes in different ways.

Listen and Draw Real World

Write the times on the digital clocks.
Then label the clocks with the children's names.

____

____

____

____

Math Processes and Practices 

Where would the minute hand point to show 15 minutes after the hour? **Explain.**

FOR THE TEACHER • First have children write the time for each analog clock. Then write *Luke, Beth, Ivy,* and *Rohan* on the board. Tell children to listen for each name to label the different times with. Luke plays football at 3:25. Beth eats lunch at 11:45. Ivy reads a book at 6:10. Rohan eats breakfast at 7:15.

Model and Draw

These are different ways to write and say the time.

15 minutes after 8
quarter past 8

30 minutes after 8
half past 8

Share and Show

Draw the minute hand to show the time. Write the time.

1. 15 minutes after 1

2. half past 9

3. quarter past 5

4. quarter past 10

5. 40 minutes after 3

6. half past 7

Name ______________________________

On Your Own

Draw the minute hand to show the time.
Write the time.

7. 15 minutes after 11

8. quarter past 4

9. 25 minutes after 8

10. 10 minutes after 6

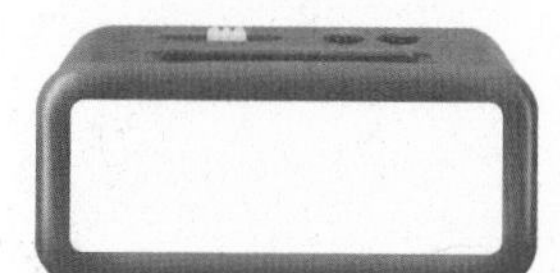

11. half past 2

12. 45 minutes after 3

13. 5 minutes after 7

14. 30 minutes after 12

15. quarter past 10

Problem Solving • Applications

16. THINK SMARTER Lily eats lunch at quarter past 12. Meg eats lunch at 12:30. Katie eats lunch at 12:15. Which girls eat lunch at the same time?

Math on the Spot

_______ and _______

17. Math Processes and Practices 6 **Explain** Soccer practice starts at 4:30. Gabe arrives at soccer practice at 4:15. Does he arrive before or after practice starts? Explain.

____

____

____

18. THINK SMARTER What time is shown on the clock? Fill in the bubble next to all the ways to write or say the time.

○ 3:25
○ quarter past 5
○ 5 minutes after 3
○ 25 minutes after 3

TAKE HOME ACTIVITY • Name a time to 5 minutes. Ask your child to describe where the clock hands point at this time.

Name ______________________________

Practice Telling Time

Learning Objective You will write and tell times to the nearest five minutes in different ways.

Draw the minute hand to show the time. Write the time.

1. quarter past 7

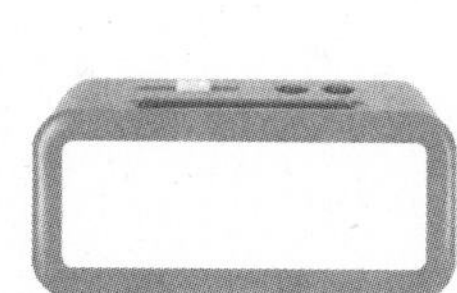

2. half past 3

3. 50 minutes after 1

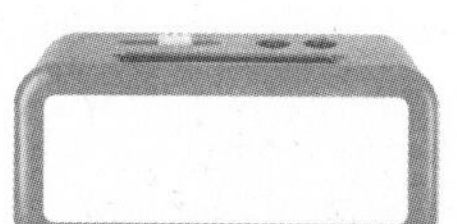

4. quarter past 11

Problem Solving

Draw the minute hand on the clock to solve.

5. Josh got to school at half past 8. Show this time on the clock.

6. WRITE Math Write the time 8:30. Then write this time in two other ways, using words.

____

____

Lesson Check

1. Write the time on this clock using words.

____

Spiral Review

2. What is the value of this group of coins?

____

3. What time is shown on this clock?

____

4. What number can be written as six hundred forty-seven?

____

Name ______________________________

A.M. and P.M.

Essential Question How do you use a.m. and p.m. to describe times?

Learning Objective You will describe times using a.m. and p.m.

Listen and Draw Real World

Draw the clock hands to show each time. Then write each time.

Morning	Evening

Math Processes and Practices 1

Describe some activities that you do in both the morning and in the evening.

FOR THE TEACHER • Have children draw a picture and write a label for the picture for an activity they do in the morning and for an activity they do in the evening. Then have them show the time they do each activity on the clocks.

Model and Draw

Noon is 12:00 in the daytime.
Midnight is 12:00 at night.

Times after midnight and before noon are written with **a.m.**

11:00 a.m. is in the morning.

Times after noon and before midnight are written with **p.m.**

11:00 p.m. is in the evening.

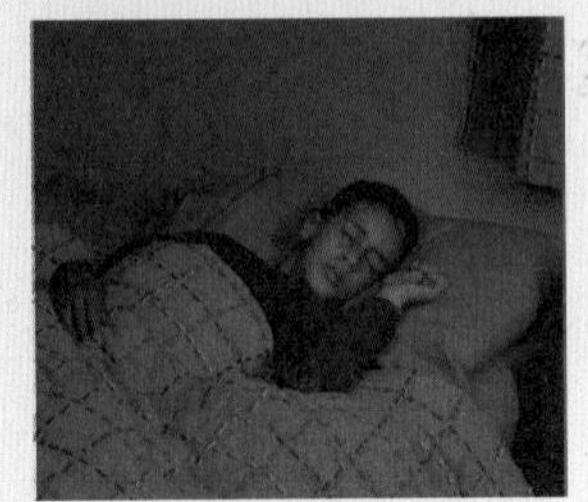

Share and Show

Write the time. Then circle **a.m.** or **p.m.**

1. eat breakfast

a.m.
p.m.

2. go to art class

a.m.
p.m.

3. do homework

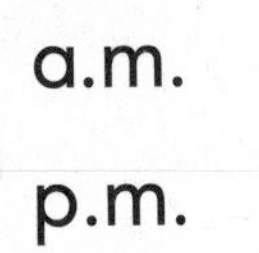

a.m.
p.m.

4. arrive at school

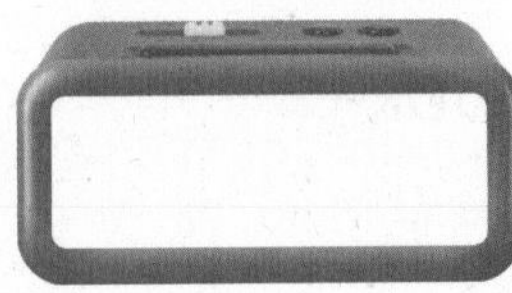

a.m.
p.m.

Name ______________________________

On Your Own

Write the time. Then circle **a.m.** or **p.m.**

5. go to the library

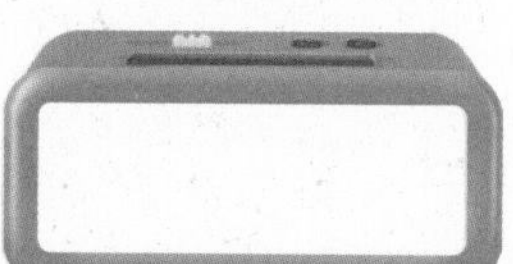

a.m.

p.m.

6. go to science class

a.m.

p.m.

7. eat lunch

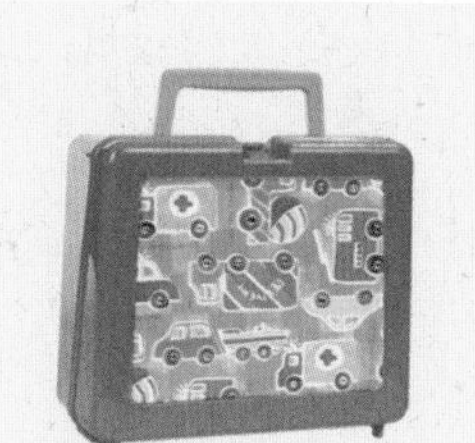

a.m.

p.m.

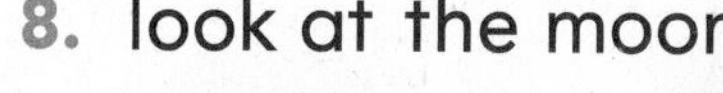

8. look at the moon

a.m.

p.m.

9. THINKSMARTER Use the times in the list to complete the story.

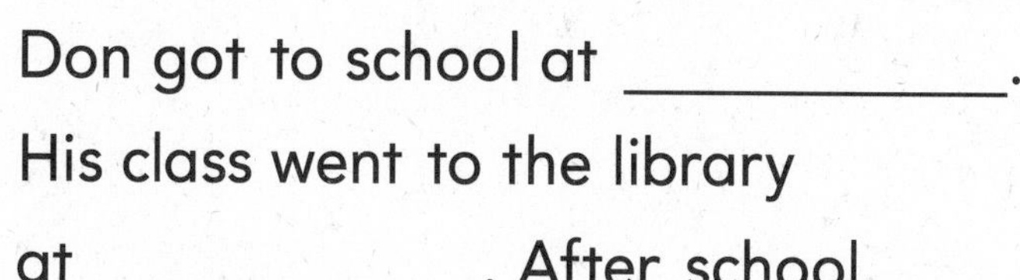

Don got to school at __________.
His class went to the library
at __________. After school,
Don read a book at __________.

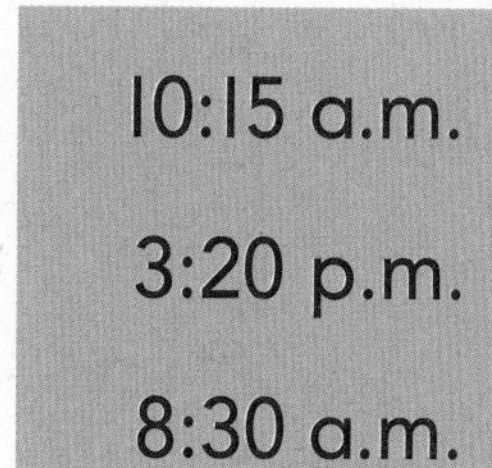

10:15 a.m.

3:20 p.m.

8:30 a.m.

Problem Solving • Applications

10. GO DEEPER Some times are shown on this time line. Write a label for each dot that names something you do at school during that part of the day.

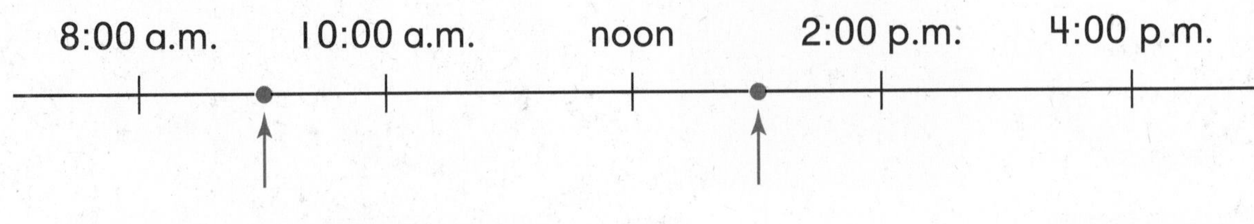

_______________ _______________

At what times would you say the dots are placed on the time line?

_______ and _______

Personal Math Trainer

11. THINK SMARTER + The clock shows the time Jane goes to recess. Write the time. Then circle a.m. or p.m.

_______________ a.m.
p.m.

Recess lasted one hour. Write the time recess was over. Write a.m. or p.m.

____

TAKE HOME ACTIVITY • Name some activities and times. Have your child say a.m. or p.m. for the times.

Name ________________________________

A.M. and P.M.

Learning Objective You will describe times using a.m. and p.m.

Write the time. Then circle a.m. or p.m.

1. walk the dog

a.m.

p.m.

2. finish breakfast

a.m.

p.m.

Problem Solving Real World

Use the list of times. Complete the story.

3. Jess woke up at __________. She got on the bus at __________ and went to school. She left school at __________.

3:15 p.m.
8:30 a.m.
7:00 a.m.

4. WRITE Math List two school activities that you do in the morning and two school activities that you do in the afternoon. Write times for these activities using a.m. and p.m.

____

____

____

____

____

____

____

Lesson Check

1. The clock shows when the soccer game ended. Write the time. Then circle a.m. or p.m.

_______ a.m.
p.m.

2. The clock shows when Jeff gets up for school. Write the time. Then circle a.m. or p.m.

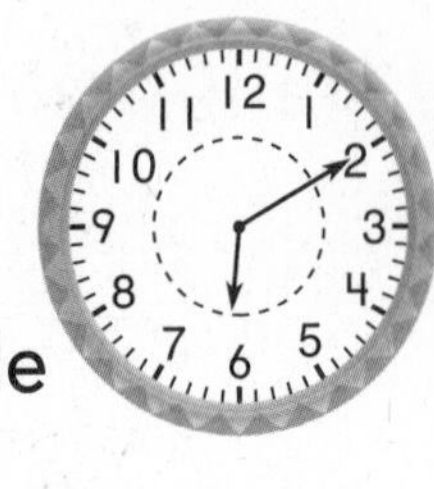

_______ a.m.
p.m.

Spiral Review

3. What coin has the same value as 25 pennies? Draw your answer.

4. Describe 72 as a sum of tens and ones.

___ + ___

5. At the beginning of the school year there were 437 students at Woods Elementary. Over the course of the year, 24 students joined. How many students were there at the end of the year?

$$\begin{array}{r} 437 \\ +\ 24 \\ \hline \end{array}$$

_______ students

6. What time is quarter past 3?

____

Name ___________________________

Chapter 7 Review/Test

1. Andrea pays $2.15 for a jump rope.

   Fill in the bubble next to all the ways that show $2.15.

   ○ two $1 bills, 1 dime, and 1 nickel
   ○ one $1 bill, 4 quarters, and 1 dime
   ○ two $1 bills and 1 quarter
   ○ one $1 bill, 3 quarters, and 4 dimes

---

2. The clock shows the time Michael eats breakfast.

   Write the time. Circle a.m. or p.m.

_______________ a.m.
p.m

Tell how you knew whether to select a.m. or p.m.

____

____

____

3. Does the group of coins have a total value of 60¢? Choose Yes or No.

2 quarters and 1 dime.	○ Yes	○ No
1 quarter, 2 dimes, and 3 nickels.	○ Yes	○ No
5 dimes, 1 nickel, and 6 pennies.	○ Yes	○ No
4 nickels and 20 pennies.	○ Yes	○ No

4. GO DEEPER Tess gave Raul these coins. Tess says she gave Raul $1.00. Is Tess correct? Explain.

____

____

5. Write the time that is shown on this clock.

____:____

6. What time is shown on the clock? Fill in the bubble next to all the ways to write or say the time.

○ 4:35 ○ 35 minutes after 4

○ 7:20 ○ quarter past 4

Name ___________________________________

Personal Math Trainer 

7.  Alicia has this money in her pocket.

Circle the amount to complete the sentence.

Alicia has a total of [$1.40 / $1.60 / $1.70] in her pocket.

8. Kate's father gave her these coins. Write the value of the coins. Explain how you found the the total value.

____

____

____

____

9. Write the times the clocks show.

______ ______ ______

10. Ben has 30¢. Circle coins to show this amount.

11. Mia buys apples that cost 76¢.

Draw and label coins to show a total value of 76¢.

Chapter 8 Length in Customary Units

Curious about Math

The Missouri River is the longest river in the United States.

What is the longest piece of furniture in your classroom? How would you find out?

Name ______________________________

Compare Lengths

1. Order the pencils from shortest to longest.
   Write 1, 2, 3.

____
____
____

Use Nonstandard Units to Measure Length

Use real objects and ■ to measure.

2. about ______ ■

3. Crayon about ______ ■

Measure Length Twice: Nonstandard Units

Use paper clip first. Then use ■.
Measure the length of the pencil.

4. about ______ paper clips

5. about ______ ■

This page checks understanding of important skills needed for success in Chapter 8.

Name ______________________________

Vocabulary Builder

Review Words
length
longer
shorter
longest
shortest

Visualize It

Fill in the graphic organizer to describe the lengths of different objects.

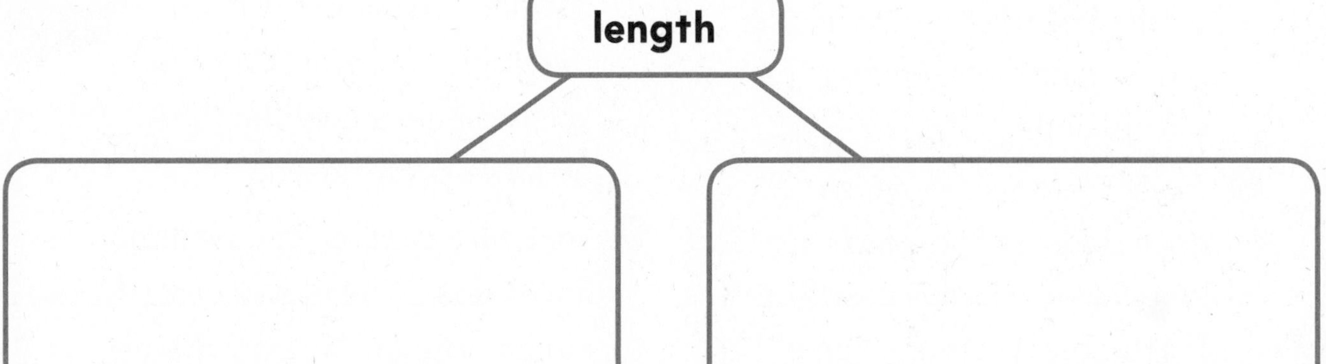

Understand Vocabulary

Use review words. Complete the sentences.

1. The blue pencil is the ______________ pencil.

2. The red pencil is the ______________ pencil.

3. The red pencil is ______________ than the yellow pencil.

4. The blue pencil is ______________ than the yellow pencil.

GO DIGITAL • Interactive Student Edition • Multimedia eGlossary

Chapter 8 **Game**

Longer or Shorter?

Materials

- 9 [cube] • 9 [cube] • [spinner]

Longer | Shorter

Play with a partner.

1. Each player chooses a picture on the board and then finds a real object that matches that picture.
2. Place the objects next to each other to find which is longer and which is shorter. If the objects are the same length, choose another object.
3. Spin the pointer on the spinner. The player with the object that matches the spinner puts a cube on that picture on the board.
4. Take turns until all the pictures have cubes. The player with more cubes on the board wins.

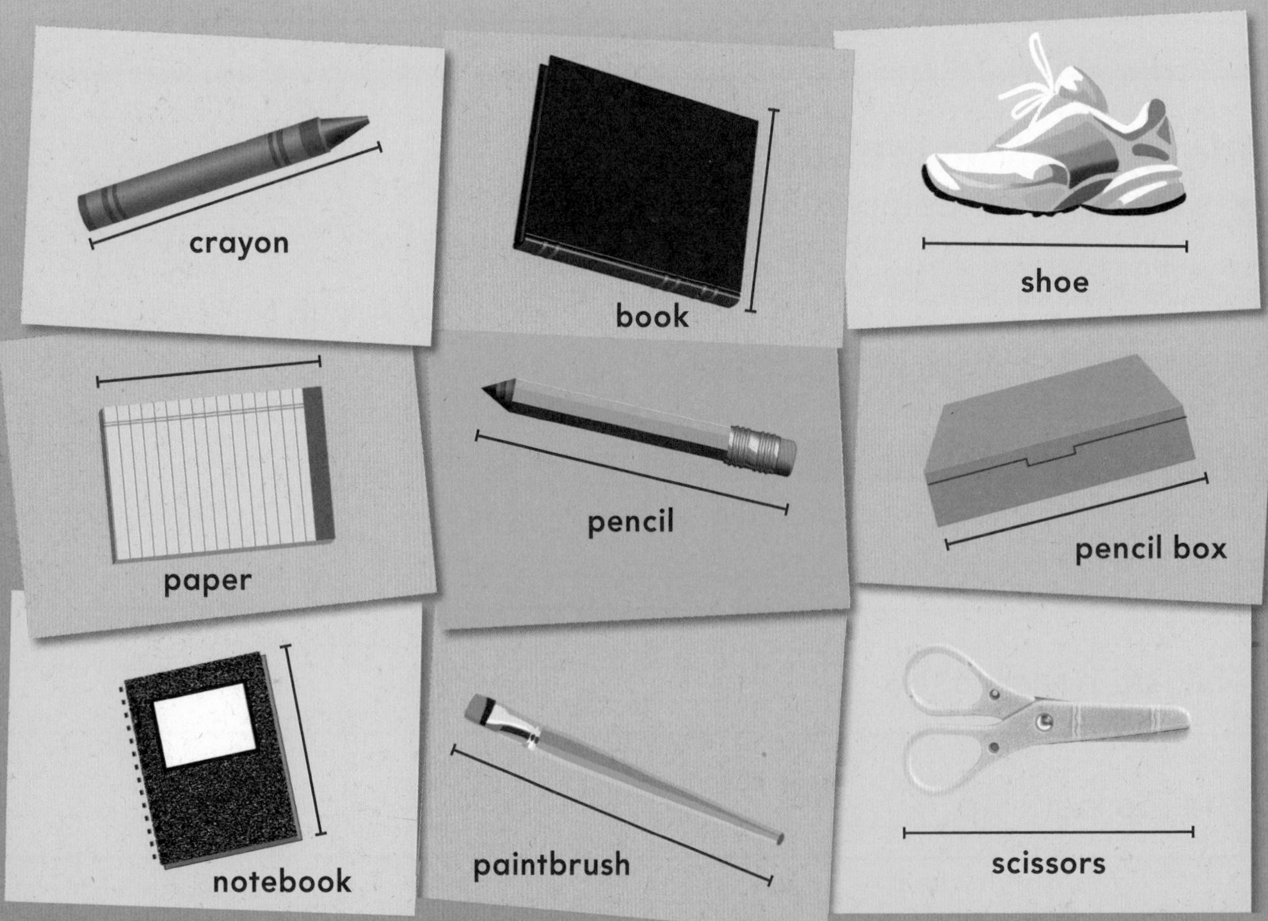

Chapter 8 Vocabulary

English	Spanish	Page
data	datos	12
estimate	estimación	21
foot	pie	24
inch	pulgada	32
line plot	diagrama de puntos	37
measuring tape	cinta métrica	38
sum	suma o total	59
yardstick	regla de 1 yarda	66

An **estimate** is an amount that tells about how many.

Favorite Lunch	
Lunch	**Tally**
pizza	IIII
sandwich	卌 I
salad	III
pasta	卌

The information in this chart is called **data**.

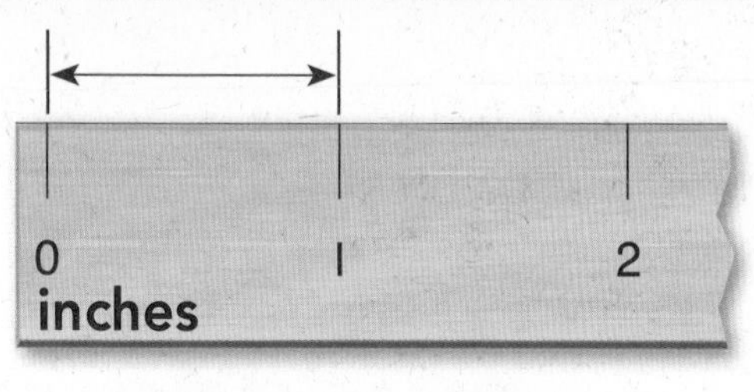

This is 1 **inch**.

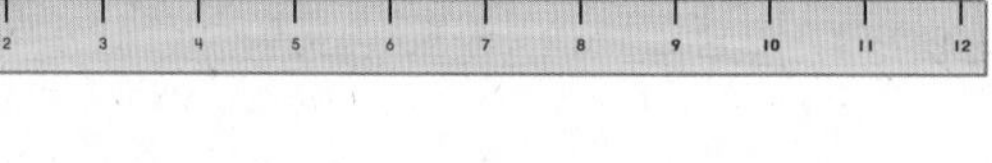

1 **foot** is the same length as 12 inches.

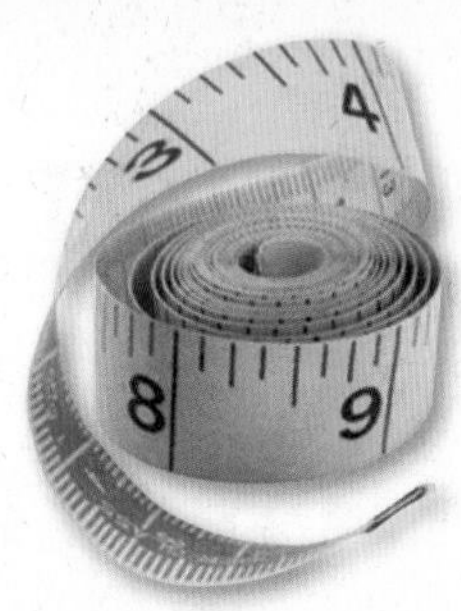

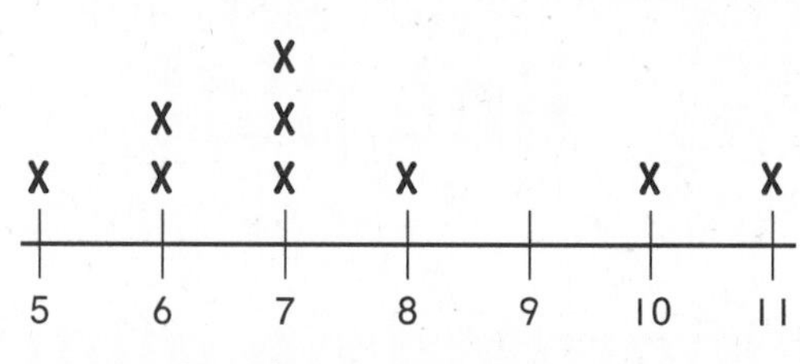

Lengths of Paintbrushes in Inches

A **yardstick** is a measuring tool that shows 3 feet.

4 + 2 = 6

↑ sum

Guess the Word

Word Box
data
estimate
foot
inch
line plot
measuring tape
sum
yardstick

For 3 to 4 players

Materials

- timer

How to Play

1. Take turns to play.
2. Choose a math word, but do not say it aloud.
3. Set the timer for 1 minute.
4. Give a one-word clue about your word. Give each player one chance to guess your word.
5. If nobody guesses correctly, repeat Step 4 with a different clue. Repeat until a player guesses the word or time runs out. Give a different one-word clue each time.
6. The first player to guess the word gets 1 point. If the player can use the word in a sentence, he or she gets 1 more point. Then that player gets the next turn.
7. The first player to score 5 points wins.

The Write Way

Reflect

Choose one idea. Write about it in the space below.

- When would you measure the length of an object? When would you estimate its length? Write 2–3 sentences to explain.
- Explain when you would use each measuring tool.

  measuring tape **yardstick** **inch ruler**

- Tell at least **two** things you know about a line plot.

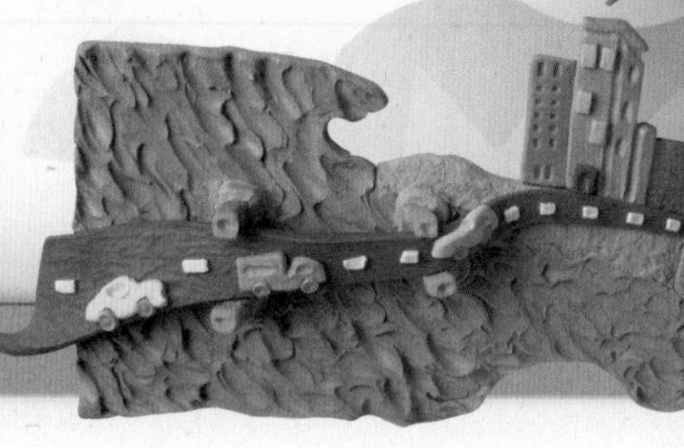

Name ___

Measure with Inch Models

Essential Question How can you use inch models to measure length?

Learning Objective You will use inch models to measure the length of an object.

Listen and Draw

Use color tiles to measure the length.

___ color tiles

___ color tiles

___ color tiles

Math Talk Math Processes and Practices 6

Attend to Precision Describe how to use color tiles to measure the length of an object.

HOME CONNECTION • Your child used color tiles as an introduction to measurement of length before using standard measurement tools.

Model and Draw

A color tile is about 1 **inch** long.

About how many inches long is this string?

Count the color tiles to find how many inches long the string is.

The string is 4 color tiles long.

So, the string is about ___4___ inches long.

Share and Show

MATH BOARD

Use color tiles. Measure the length of the object in inches.

1. about _______ inches

2. about _______ inches

✓ 3. about _______ inches

✓ 4. about _______ inches

Name ______________________________

On Your Own

Use color tiles. Measure the length of the object in inches.

5.

about ________ inches

6.

about ________ inches

7.

about ________ inches

8.

about ________ inches

9.

about ________ inches

10. GO DEEPER Blue paper chains are 4 inches long. Red paper chains are 3 inches long. How many are needed to have 10 inches of paper chains?

________ blue paper chain ________ red paper chains

Problem Solving • Applications

WRITE Math

11. THINKSMARTER Blue paper chains are 8 inches long. Red paper chains are 6 inches long. How many are needed to have 22 inches of paper chains?

_____ blue paper chains

_____ red paper chain

12. Math Processes and Practices 2 **Use Reasoning** Liza has a ribbon that is 12 inches long. She needs to cut it into pieces that are each 4 inches long. How many pieces can she make?

_______ pieces

Personal Math Trainer

13. THINKSMARTER+ Jeremy used color tiles to measure a string. Each tile is 1 inch long. How long is the string? Circle the number in the box to make the sentence true.

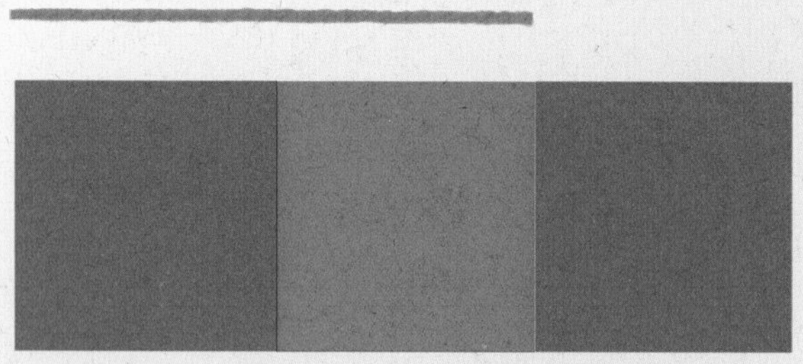

The string is about [2 / 3 / 4] inches long.

TAKE HOME ACTIVITY • Have your child use several of the same small item (such as paper clips) to measure the lengths of some objects at home.

Name ______________________________

Measure with Inch Models

Learning Objective You will use inch models to measure the length of an object.

Use color tiles. Measure the length of the object in inches.

1.

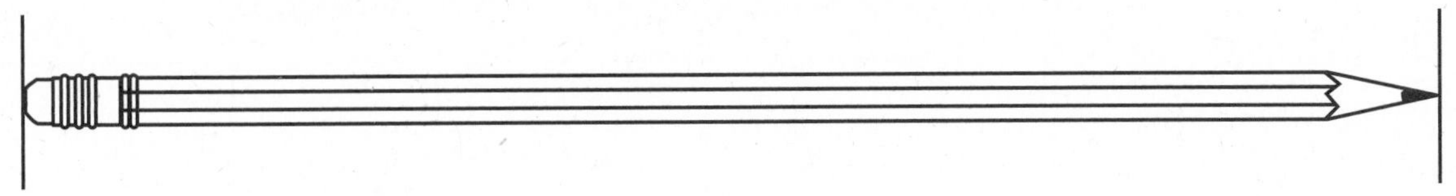

about _____ inches

2.

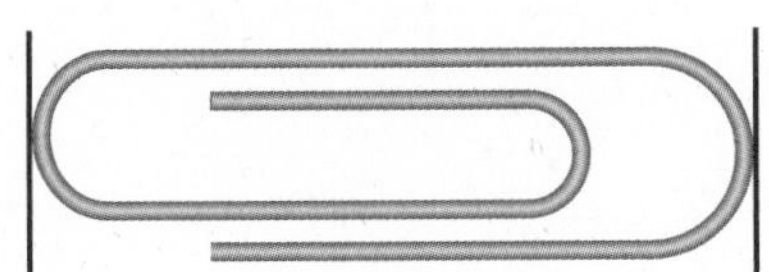

about _____ inches

3.

about _____ inches

Problem Solving

4. Look around your classroom.
Find an object that is about 4 inches long.
Draw and label the object.

5. WRITE Math Describe how you would find an object that is about 8 inches long.

____

Lesson Check

1. Jessie used color tiles to measure the rope. Each color tile measures 1 inch. About how many inches long is the rope?

about _____ inches

Spiral Review

2. Adam has these coins. What is the total value of his coins?

____

3. Look at the clock hands. What time does this clock show?

___ : ___

4. Hank has 84 marbles in a bag. His friend Mario has 71 marbles in his bag. How many marbles do they have altogether?

$$\begin{array}{r} 84 \\ +\ 71 \\ \hline \end{array}$$

FOR MORE PRACTICE GO TO THE Personal Math Trainer

Name ______________________________

Make and Use a Ruler

Essential Question Why is using a ruler similar to using a row of color tiles to measure length?

Learning Objective You will make an inch ruler and use it to measure the length of an object.

Listen and Draw

Use color tiles. Make the given length. Trace along the edge to show the length.

4 inches

2 inches

3 inches

Math Processes and Practices 

Describe how you knew how many color tiles to use for each length.

HOME CONNECTION • Your child used color tiles as 1-inch models to show different lengths. This activity helps to make inch units a more familiar concept.

Model and Draw

Use a color tile to make a ruler on a paper strip.
Color 6 parts that are each about 1 inch long.

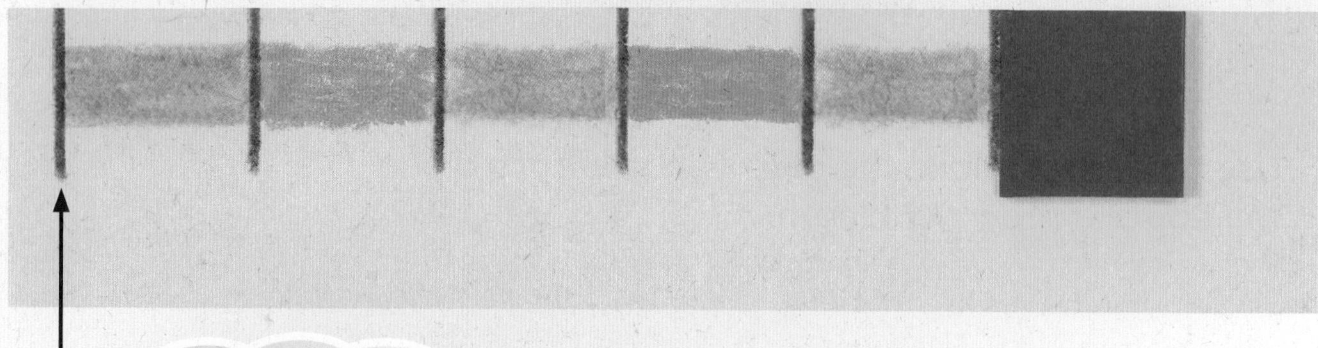

How to use your ruler:
Line up the left edge of an object with the first mark.

Share and Show

Measure the length with your ruler.
Count the inches.

1. about ______ inches

2. about ______ inches

3. about ______ inches

Name ______________________________

On Your Own

Measure the length with your ruler.
Count the inches.

4.

about ________ inches

5.

about ________ inches

6.

about ________ inches

7.

about ________ inches

8.

about ________ inches

Problem Solving • Applications

9. THINK SMARTER Work with a classmate. Use both of your rulers to measure the length of a bulletin board or a window. What is the length?

about ________ inches

10. Math Processes and Practices 6 **Explain** Describe what you did in Exercise 9. How did you measure a length that is longer than your rulers?

____

____

____

11. THINK SMARTER Measure the length of the yarn with your ruler. Does the sentence describe the yarn? Choose Yes or No.

The yarn is about 2 inches long.	○ Yes	○ No
The yarn is about 3 inches long.	○ Yes	○ No
The yarn is shorter than 2 inches.	○ Yes	○ No
The yarn is longer than 2 inches.	○ Yes	○ No

TAKE HOME ACTIVITY • Choose one object in this lesson. Have your child find objects that are longer, about the same length, and shorter.

Name ______________________________

Make and Use a Ruler

Learning Objective You will make an inch ruler and use it to measure the length of an object.

Measure the length with your ruler. Count the inches.

1.

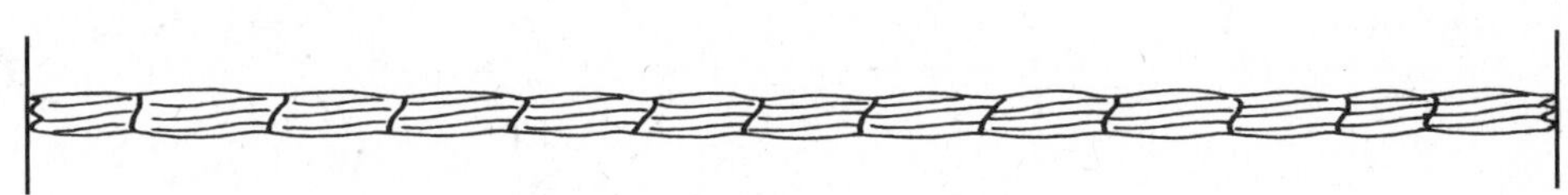

about _____ inches

2.

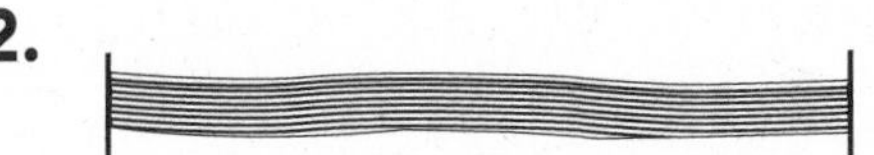

about _____ inches

3.

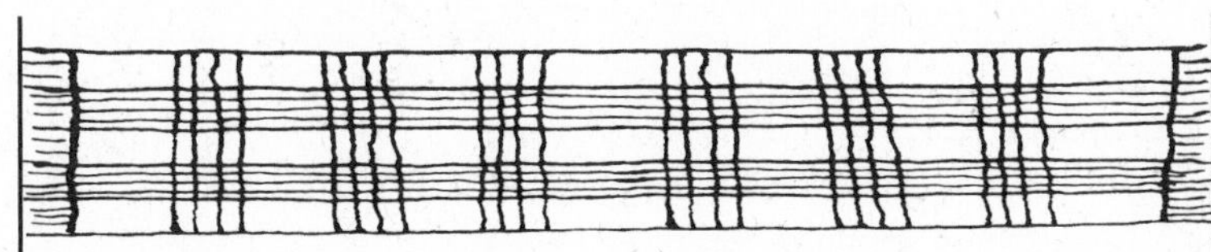

about _____ inches

Problem Solving

4. Use your ruler. Measure the width of this page in inches.

about ____ inches

5. WRITE Math Would you rather use color tiles or your ruler to measure the length of an object? Explain your choice.

____

Lesson Check

1. Use your ruler. What is the length of this ribbon?

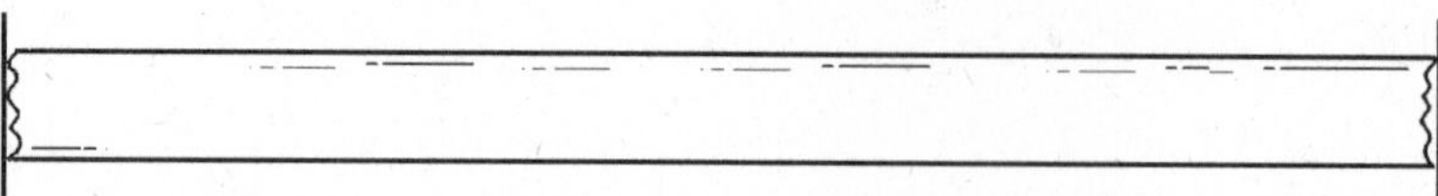

about ____ inches

Spiral Review

2. What time is shown on this clock?

____:____

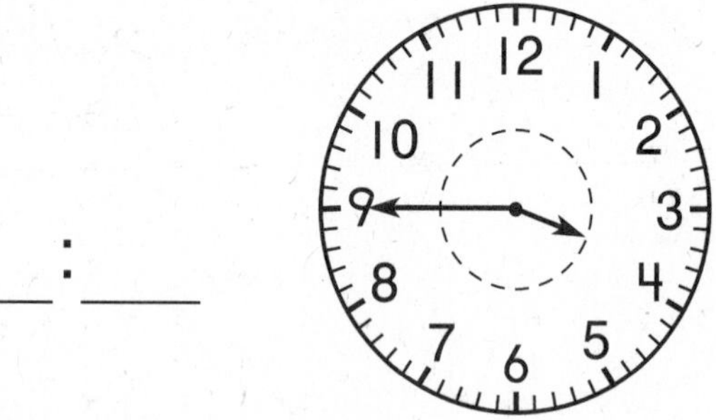

3. What is the total value of these coins?

____ cents

4. The first group collected 238 cans. The second group collected 345 cans. How many cans did the two groups collect?

____

5. There are 2 children in each row. How many children are in 5 rows?

____ children

FOR MORE PRACTICE GO TO THE Personal Math Trainer

Name ____________________

Estimate Lengths in Inches

Essential Question How do you estimate the lengths of objects in inches?

Learning Objective You will estimate the length of an object in inches.

Listen and Draw

Real World

Hands On

Choose three objects. Measure their lengths with your ruler. Draw the objects and write their lengths.

about ______ inches

about ______ inches

about ______ inches

FOR THE TEACHER • Provide a collection of small objects, 2 to 6 inches in length, for children to measure. Have them select one object, measure it, and return it before selecting another object.

Math Talk Math Processes and Practices 6

Describe how the three lengths compare. Which is the longest object?

Model and Draw

The bead is 1 inch long. Use this bead to help find how many beads will fit on the string. Which is the best estimate for the length of the string?

2 inches | 5 inches | 8 inches

2 inches is too short.

5 inches is about right.

8 inches is too long.

Share and Show

Circle the best estimate for the length of the string.

1.

1 inch | 3 inches | 5 inches

2.

2 inches | 4 inches | 6 inches

3.

4 inches | 6 inches | 8 inches

Name ______________________________

On Your Own

Circle the best estimate for the length of the string.

4.

4 inches 7 inches 10 inches

5.

3 inches 6 inches 9 inches

6.

1 inch 3 inches 5 inches

7. THINK SMARTER Use the 1-inch mark. Estimate the length of each ribbon.

Math on the Spot

Estimates:

red ribbon: about _____ inches

blue ribbon: about _____ inches

Problem Solving • Applications

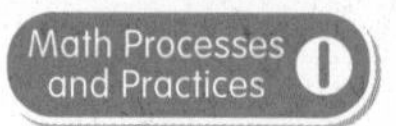

Analyze Relationships

8. Sasha has a string that is the length of 5 beads. Each bead is 2 inches long. What is the length of the string?

_______ inches

9. Maurice has a string that is 15 inches long. He has beads that are each 3 inches long. How many beads will fit on the string?

_______ beads

10.  Tameka has this string. She has many beads that are 1 inch long, like this blue bead. What is the best estimate for the length of the string? Draw more beads on the string to show your estimate.

_______ inches

TAKE HOME ACTIVITY • With your child, estimate the lengths in inches of some small objects, such as books.

Name ___________________________

Estimate Lengths in Inches

Learning Objective You will estimate the length of an object in inches.

The bead is 1 inch long.
Circle the best estimate for the length of the string.

1. 

1 inch   4 inches   7 inches

2. 

3 inches   6 inches   9 inches

3. 

2 inches   3 inches   6 inches

Problem Solving

Solve. Write or draw to explain.

4. Ashley has some beads. Each bead is 2 inches long. How many beads will fit on a string that is 8 inches long?

_____ beads

5. WRITE Math Describe a way that someone could estimate the length of a book.

____

Lesson Check

1. The bead is 1 inch long. Estimate the length of the string.

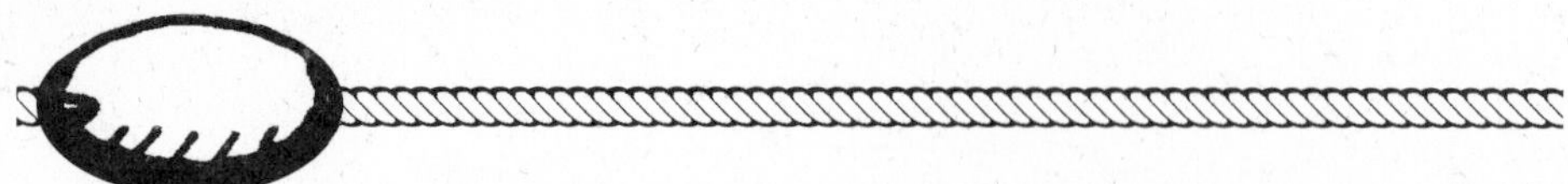

____ inches

Spiral Review

2. Draw hands on the clock to show 5 minutes after 6.

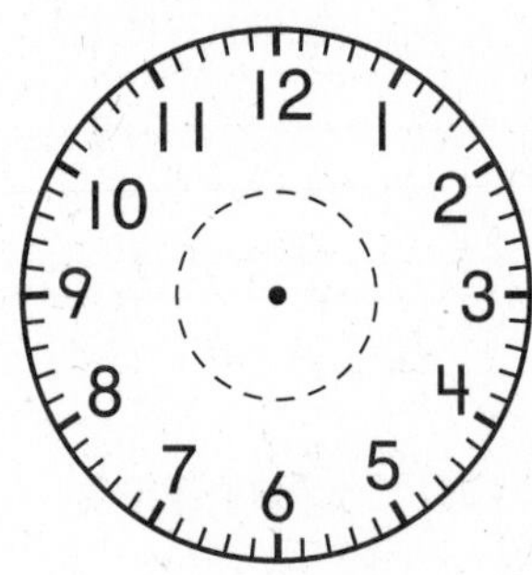

3. Ella read 16 pages of her book on Monday and 26 pages on Tuesday. There are 64 pages in the book. How many more pages are left for Ella to read?

_______ pages

4. What is the sum?

38 + 24 = _______

FOR MORE PRACTICE GO TO THE Personal Math Trainer

Name ____________________

Measure with an Inch Ruler

HANDS ON
Lesson 8.4

Essential Question How do you use an inch ruler to measure lengths?

Learning Objective You will measure the length of an object to the nearest inch using an inch ruler.

Listen and Draw Real World

Draw each worm to match the given length.

Math Talk Math Processes and Practices 2

Use Reasoning Describe how you decided how long to draw the 2-inch and 3-inch worms.

FOR THE TEACHER • Have children use the rulers that they made in Lesson 8.2 to draw a worm that is 1 inch long. Have children use the 1-inch-long worm as a guide to draw a worm that is 2 inches long and a worm that is 3 inches long, without using their rulers.

Model and Draw

What is the length of the string to the nearest inch?

2 inches

Step 1

Line up the end of the string with the zero mark on the ruler.

Step 2

Find the inch mark that is closest to the other end of the string.

Share and Show MATH BOARD

Measure the length to the nearest inch.

1. ______ inches

2. ______ inches

3. ______ inches

4. ______ inches

Name ______________________________

On Your Own

Measure the length to the nearest inch.

5.

________ inches

6.

________ inches

7.

________ inches

8.

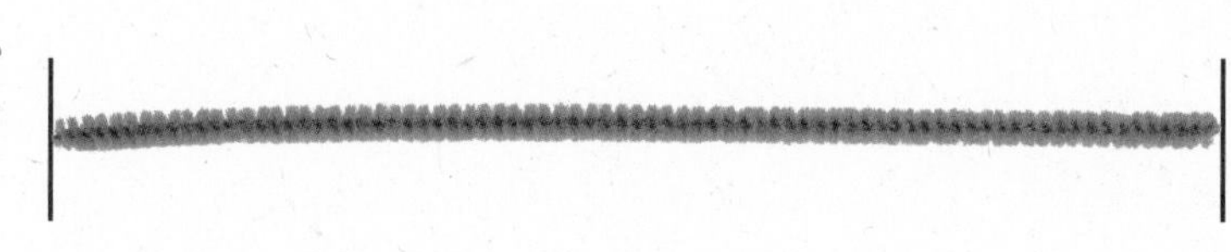

________ inches

9. GO DEEPER Measure the lengths to the nearest inch. How much shorter is the ribbon than the yarn?

______ inch shorter

Problem Solving • Applications

10. THINK SMARTER How much longer is the red string than the blue string?

_____ inches longer

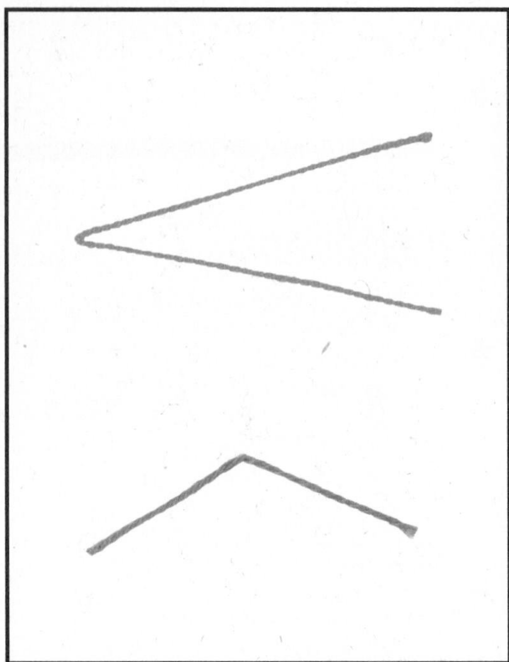

11. THINK SMARTER If the red and blue strings were straight and placed end to end, what would the total length be?

_____ inches

12. THINK SMARTER Mrs. Grant's pencil is 5 inches long. Is this Mrs. Grant's pencil? Use an inch ruler to find out. Use the numbers and words on the tiles to make the sentences true.

3	4	5	is	is not

The pencil is _______ inches long.

This pencil _______ Mrs. Grant's pencil.

TAKE HOME ACTIVITY • Have your child measure the lengths of some objects to the nearest inch using a ruler or a similar measuring tool.

Name ______________________________

Measure with an Inch Ruler

Learning Objective You will measure the length of an object to the nearest inch using an inch ruler.

Measure the length to the nearest inch.

1. 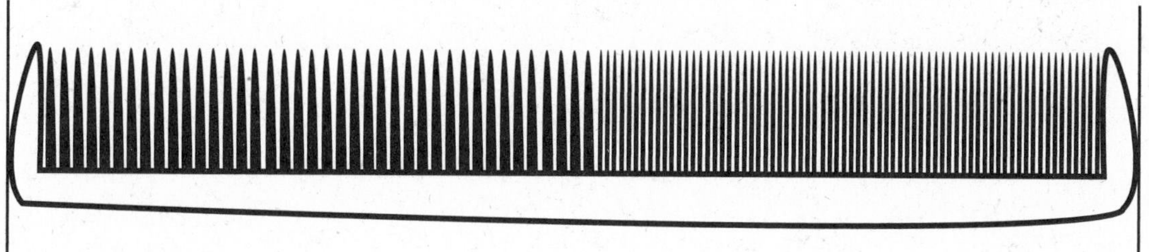

_____ inches

2. 

_____ inches

3. 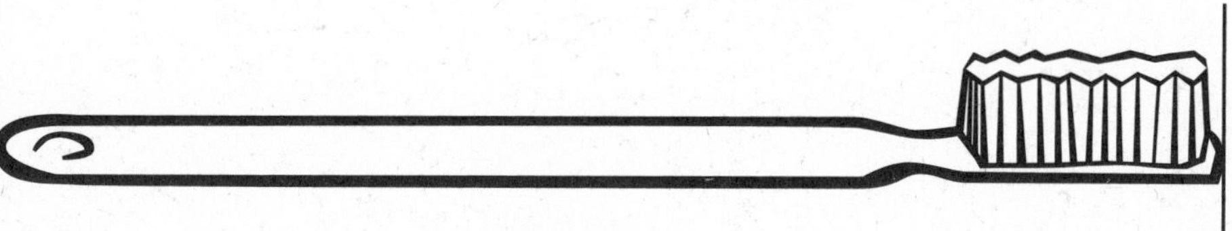

_____ inches

Problem Solving

4. Measure the string. What is its total length?

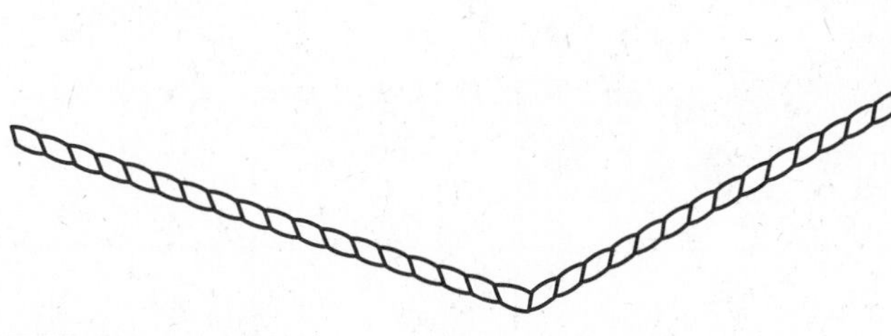

_____ inches

5. WRITE Math Compare the ruler you made to an inch ruler. Describe how they are alike and how they are different.

____

Lesson Check

1. Use an inch ruler. What is the length to the nearest inch?

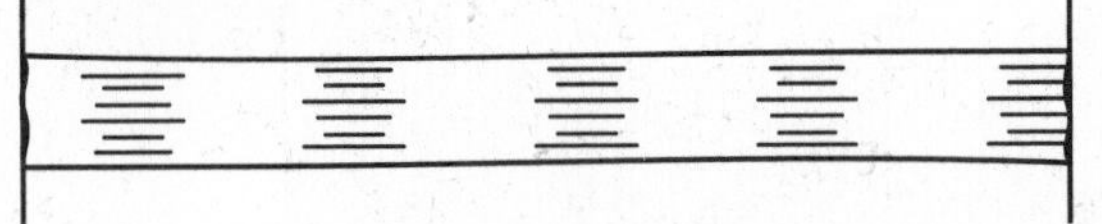

____ inches

2. Use an inch ruler. What is the length to the nearest inch?

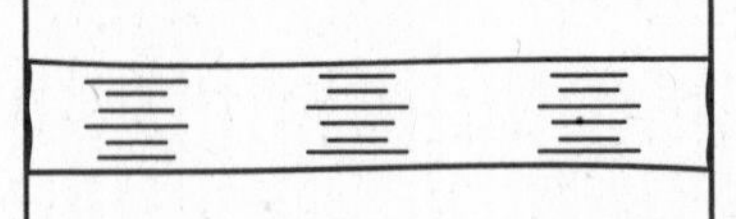

____ inches

Spiral Review

3. The clock shows the time that Jen got to school. Write the time. Then circle a.m. or p.m.

____:____ a.m. p.m.

4. What is the difference?

$13 - 5 =$ ____

5. Each color tile is about 1 inch long. About how long is the ribbon?

about ____ inches

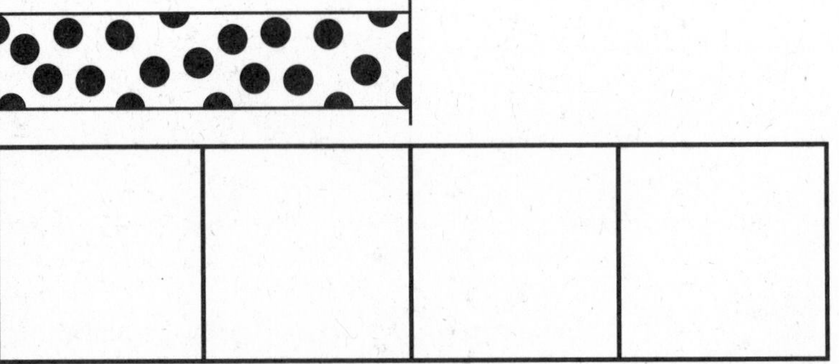

FOR MORE PRACTICE GO TO THE **Personal Math Trainer**

Name ____________________

Problem Solving • Add and Subtract in Inches

PROBLEM SOLVING
Lesson 8.5

Essential Question How can drawing a diagram help when solving problems about length?

Learning Objective You will use a number line and the strategy *draw a diagram* to solve addition and subtraction problems about lengths of objects in inches.

There is a paper clip chain that is 16 inches long. Aliyah removes 9 inches of paper clips from the chain. How long is the paper clip chain now?

Unlock the Problem

What do I need to find?

how long the paper clip chain is now

What information do I need to use?

The chain is ______ inches long.

______ inches of paper clips are removed from the chain.

Show how to solve the problem.

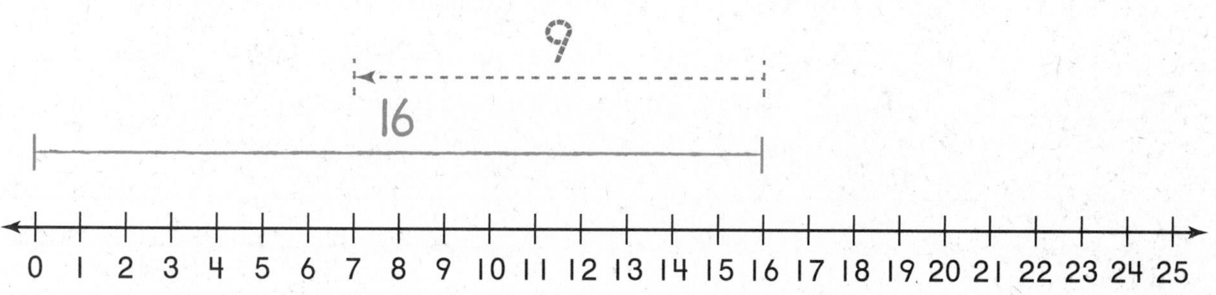

____

The paper clip chain is ______ inches long now.

HOME CONNECTION • Your child drew a diagram to represent a problem about lengths. The diagram can be used to choose the operation for solving the problem.

Try Another Problem

Draw a diagram. Write a number sentence using a ■ for the missing number. Solve.

- What do I need to find?
- What information do I need to use?

1. Carmen has a string that is 13 inches long and a string that is 8 inches long. How many inches of string does she have?

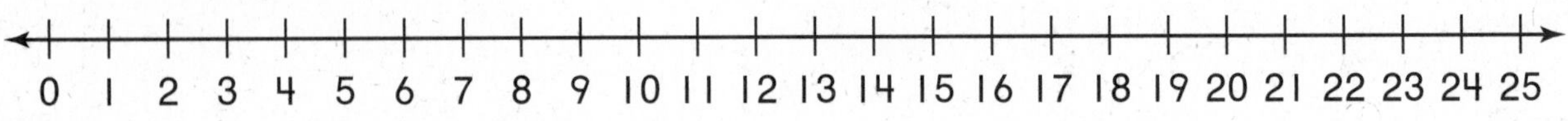

____

Carmen has ________ inches of string.

2. Eli has a cube train that is 24 inches long. He removes 9 inches of cubes from the train. How long is Eli's cube train now?

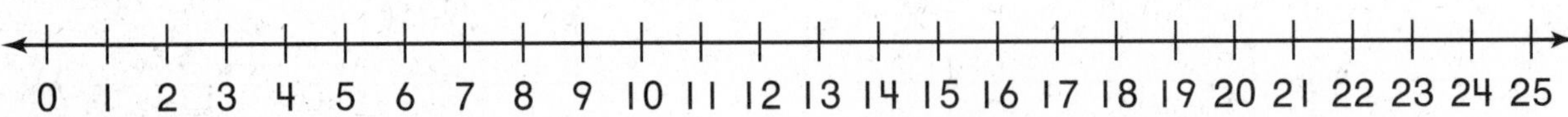

____

Eli's cube train is ________ inches long now.

Math Processes and Practices 6

Describe how your diagram shows what happened in the second problem.

Name ______________________________

Share and Show

Draw a diagram. Write a number sentence using a ■ for the missing number. Solve.

3. Lee has a paper strip chain that is 25 inches long. He unhooks 13 inches from the chain. How long is Lee's paper strip chain now?

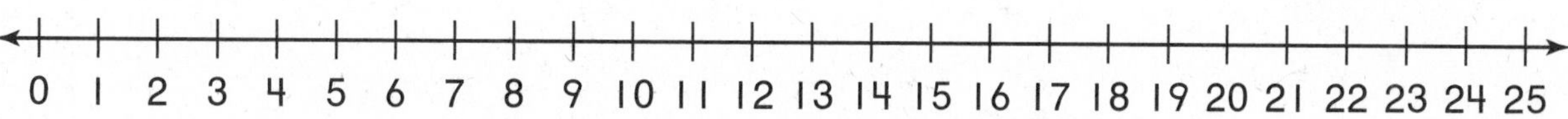

____

Lee's paper strip chain is ________ inches long now.

4. THINK SMARTER Sue has two ribbons that have the same length. She has 18 inches of ribbon in all. How long is each ribbon?

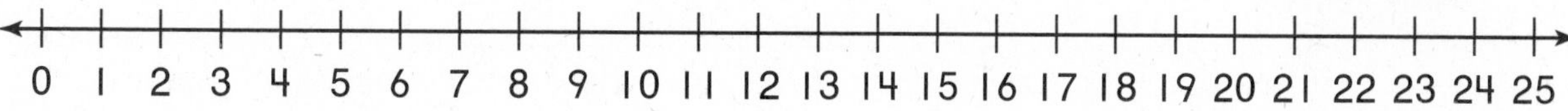

____

Each ribbon is ________ inches long.

TAKE HOME ACTIVITY • Have your child explain how he or she used a diagram to solve a problem in this lesson.

Name ______________________

Mid-Chapter Checkpoint

Personal Math Trainer
Online Assessment and Intervention

Concepts and Skills

Use color tiles. Measure the length of the object in inches.

1.

about _____ inches

The bead is one inch long. Circle the best estimate for the length of the string.

2. 

1 inch   2 inches   5 inches

Draw a diagram. Write a number sentence using a ■ for the missing number. Solve.

3. A mark is 17 inches long. Katy erases 9 inches from the mark. How long is the mark now?

____

The mark is ________ inches long now.

4. THINK SMARTER Use an inch ruler. What is the length of the string to the nearest inch?

________ inches

Name ____________________

Problem Solving • Add and Subtract in Inches

Learning Objective You will use a number line and the strategy *draw a diagram* to solve addition and subtraction problems about lengths of objects in inches.

Draw a diagram. Write a number sentence using a ■ for the missing number. Solve.

1. Molly had a ribbon that was 23 inches long. She cut 7 inches off the ribbon. How long is her ribbon now?

____

Molly's ribbon is ________ inches long now.

2. WRITE Math Describe how you could draw a diagram for a problem about finding the total length for two strings, 15 inches long and 7 inches long.

____

____

____

____

____

____

____

Lesson Check

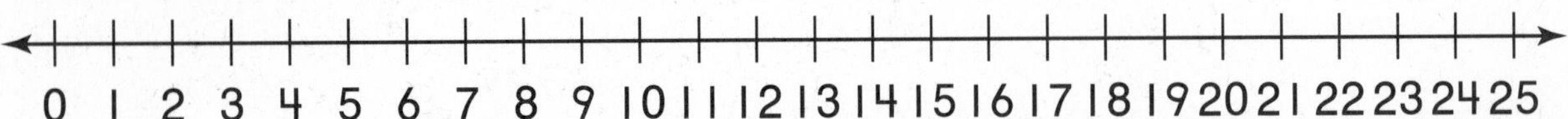

1. Allie has two pieces of string. Each one is 8 inches long. How many inches of string does she have altogether?

____ inches

2. Jeff has a cube train that is 22 inches long. He removes 8 inches of cubes from the train. How long is Jeff's cube train now?

____ inches

Spiral Review

3. Ann buys a pencil for 45 cents. Draw and label coins Ann could use to make 45 cents.

4. Use an inch ruler. About how long is the string?

about ____ inch

5. Jason has these coins in a jar. What is the total value of these coins?

________ or ________ cents

FOR MORE PRACTICE GO TO THE Personal Math Trainer

Name ______________________

Measure in Inches and Feet

Essential Question Why is measuring in feet different from measuring in inches?

Learning Objective You will measure the length of an object to the nearest inch and to the nearest foot.

Listen and Draw

Draw or write to describe how you did each measurement.

First measurement

Second measurement

Math Processes and Practices 

Use Reasoning
Describe how the length of a sheet of paper and the length of a paper clip are different.

FOR THE TEACHER • Have pairs of children stand apart and measure the distance between them with sheets of paper folded in half lengthwise. Then have them measure the same distance using large paper clips.

Model and Draw

12 inches is the same as 1 **foot.**
A 12-inch ruler is 1 foot long.
You can measure lengths in inches and also in feet.

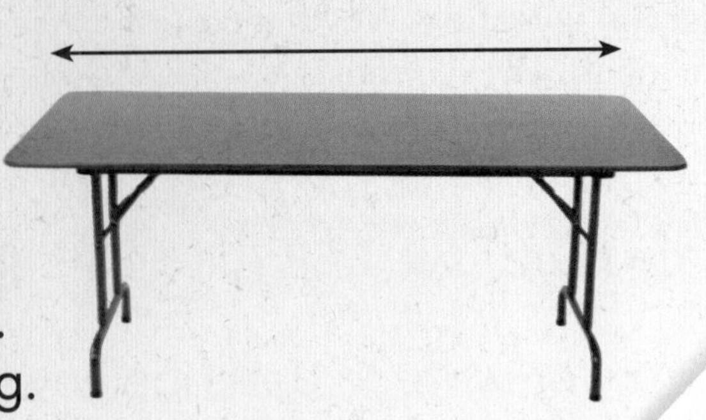

The real table is about 60 inches long.
The real table is also about 5 feet long.

Share and Show

Measure to the nearest inch.
Then measure to the nearest foot.

	Find the real object.	Measure.
1.	desk	______ inches ______ feet
✓ 2.	window	______ inches ______ feet
✓ 3.	door	______ inches ______ feet

Name ___________________________

On Your Own

Measure to the nearest inch.
Then measure to the nearest foot.

	Find the real object.	Measure.
4.	chalkboard	______ inches ______ feet
5.	poster	______ inches ______ feet
6.	teacher's desk	______ inches ______ feet
7.	easel	______ inches ______ feet
8.	bulletin board	______ inches ______ feet

Problem Solving • Applications

9. THINK SMARTER Estimate the length of a real shelf in inches and in feet. Then measure.

Estimates:	Measurements:
_______ inches	_______ inches
_______ feet	_______ feet

10. Math Processes and Practices 6 **Explain**
Look at your measurements for the shelf. Why is the number of inches different from the number of feet?

____

____

____

____

11. THINK SMARTER Use the words on the tiles that make the sentence true.

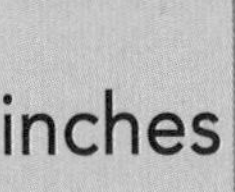

feet

A book shelf is 4 _______ long.

Deb's necklace is 20 _______ long.

A marker is 3 _______ long.

Jim's bicycle is 4 _______ long.

TAKE HOME ACTIVITY • Have your child measure the distance of a few footsteps in inches and then in feet.

Name ______________________

Measure in Inches and Feet

Learning Objective You will measure the length of an object to the nearest inch and to the nearest foot.

Measure to the nearest inch.
Then measure to the nearest foot.

Find the real object.	Measure.
1. bookcase	_____ inches _____ feet
2. window	_____ inches _____ feet

Problem Solving Real World

3. Jake has a piece of yarn that is 4 feet long. Blair has a piece of yarn that is 4 inches long. Who has the longer piece of yarn? Explain.

____

____

4. WRITE Math Would you measure the length of a jump rope in inches or in feet? Explain your choice.

____

Lesson Check

1. Larry is telling his sister about using a ruler to measure length. Write **inch** or **foot** in each blank to make the sentence true.

One ________ is longer than one ________.

Spiral Review

2. Matt put this money in his pocket. What is the total value of this money?

$ ________

3. What time is shown on this clock?

____:____

4. Ali had 38 game cards. Her friend gave her 15 more game cards. How many game cards does Ali have now?

____ cards

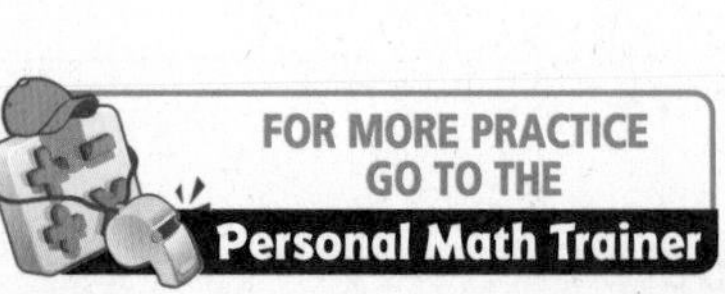

Name ______________________________

Estimate Lengths in Feet

Essential Question How do you estimate the lengths of objects in feet?

Learning Objective You will estimate the length of an object in feet.

Listen and Draw

Look for 3 classroom objects that are about the same length as a 12-inch ruler. Draw and label the objects.

Math Processes and Practices 

Which objects have a greater length than the ruler? **Explain.**

FOR THE TEACHER • Provide a collection of objects for children to choose from. Set a 12-inch ruler on the table with the objects for children to use as a visual comparison.

Model and Draw

Estimate how many 12-inch rulers will be about the same length as this bulletin board.

Think about how many rulers will fit end-to-end.

_____ rulers, or _____ feet

Share and Show

Find each object. Estimate how many 12-inch rulers will be about the same length as the object.

1. bookshelf

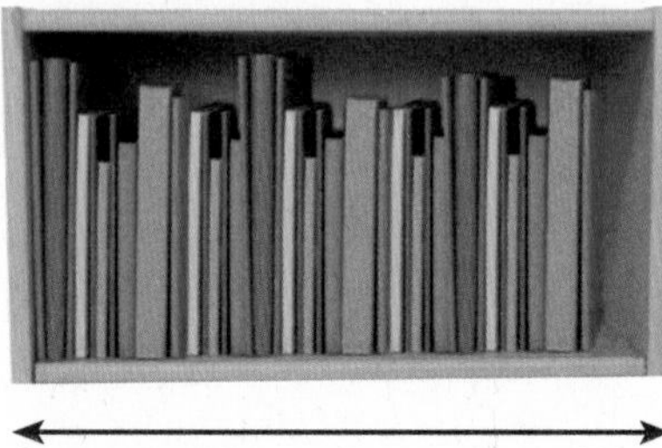

Estimate: _____ rulers, or _____ feet

2. chair

Estimate: _____ rulers, or _____ feet

Name ______________________________

On Your Own

Find each object. Estimate how many 12-inch rulers will be about the same length as the object.

3. desktop

Estimate: _____ rulers, or _____ feet

4. wall map

Estimate: _____ rulers, or _____ feet

5. window

Estimate: _____ rulers, or _____ feet

6. teacher's desk

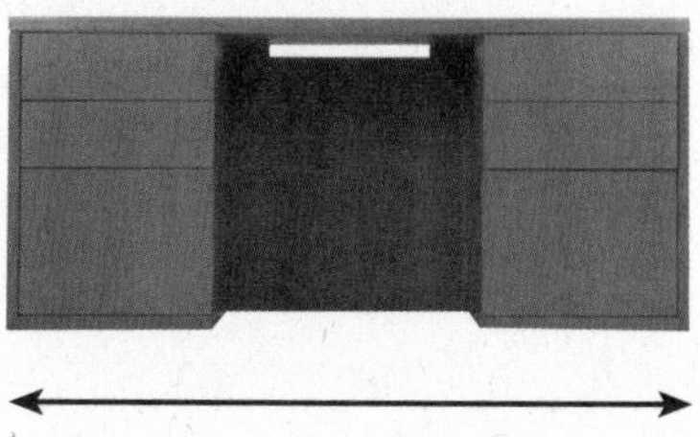

Estimate: _____ rulers, or _____ feet

Problem Solving • Applications

7. THINK SMARTER Estimate the distance from your desk to the door in feet. Then estimate the same distance in inches.

_______ feet

_______ inches

Explain how you made your estimates for the number of feet and for the number of inches.

____

____

____

8. THINK SMARTER Match the object with the estimate of its length in feet.

1 foot	3 feet	7 feet
•	•	•
•	•	•
jump rope	12-inch ruler	baseball bat

TAKE HOME ACTIVITY • With your child, estimate the lengths of some objects in feet.

Name ______________________________

Estimate Lengths in Feet

Learning Objective You will estimate the length of an object in feet.

Find each object.
Estimate how many 12-inch rulers will be about the same length as the object.

1. door

Estimate: _____ rulers, or _____ feet

---

2. flag

Estimate: _____ rulers, or _____ feet

Problem Solving Real World

Solve. Write or draw to explain.

3. Mr. and Mrs. Baker place 12-inch rulers end-to-end along the entire length of a rug. They each use 3 rulers. About how many feet long is the rug?

about _____ feet

4. WRITE Math Choose an object that is about the same length as a real baseball bat. Explain how to estimate its length in feet.

____

____

Lesson Check

1. Estimate how many 12-inch rulers will be about the same length as a bike.

____ rulers, or ____ feet

2. Estimate how many 12-inch rulers will be about the same length as a window.

____ rulers, or ____ feet

Spiral Review

3. What is the total value of 2 quarters, 3 dimes, and 4 nickels?

$ ________

4. What is the total value of 2 dimes, 3 nickels, and 2 pennies?

________ or ________ cents

5. There are 68 children in the school. There are 19 children on the playground. How many more children are in the school than on the playground?

____ children

6. What is the sum?

$$\begin{array}{r} 548 \\ +\ 436 \\ \hline \end{array}$$

FOR MORE PRACTICE GO TO THE Personal Math Trainer

Name ______________________

Choose a Tool

Essential Question How do you choose a measuring tool to use when measuring lengths?

Learning Objective You will choose measuring tools for measuring the length of an object.

Listen and Draw

Draw or write to describe how you measured the distances with the yarn.

Distance 1

Distance 2

Math Processes and Practices 6

Which distance was longer? **Explain** how you know.

FOR THE TEACHER • Have each small group use a 1-yard piece of yarn to measure a distance marked on the floor with masking tape. Have groups repeat the activity to measure another distance that is different from the first one.

Model and Draw

You can use different tools to measure lengths and distances.

inch ruler

An inch ruler can be used to measure shorter lengths.

yardstick

A **yardstick** shows 3 feet. It can be used to measure greater lengths and distances.

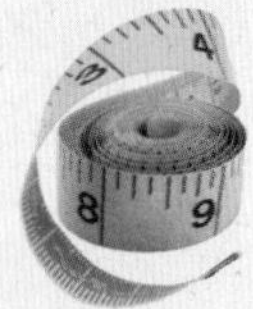

measuring tape

A **measuring tape** can be used to measure lengths and distances that are not flat or straight.

Share and Show

inch ruler
yardstick
measuring tape

Choose the best tool for measuring the real object. Then measure and record the length or distance.

1. the length of a book

Tool: ____________________

Length: ____________________

2. the distance around a cup

Tool: ____________________

Distance: ____________________

Name ____________________

On Your Own

inch ruler
yardstick
measuring tape

Choose the best tool for measuring the real object. Then measure and record the length or distance.

3. the length of a chalkboard

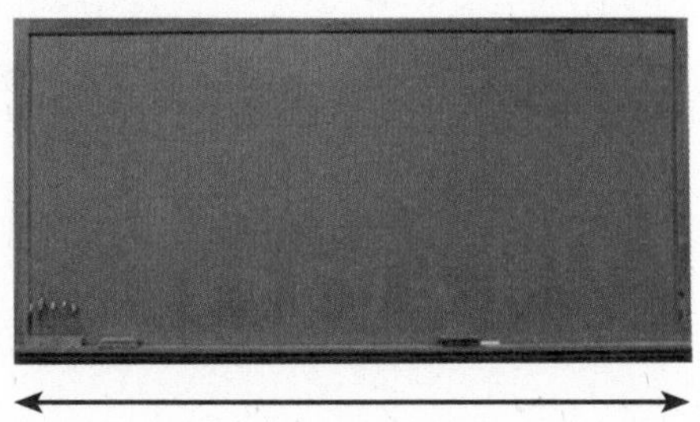

Tool: ____________________

Length: ____________________

4. the length of a marker

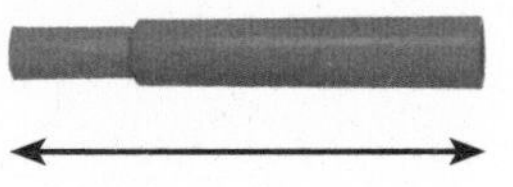

Tool: ____________________

Length: ____________________

5. the distance around a globe

Tool: ____________________

Distance: ____________________

6. the length of a classroom wall

Tool: ____________________

Length: ____________________

Problem Solving • Applications

7. THINK SMARTER Rachel wants to measure the length of a sidewalk. Should she use an inch ruler or a yardstick? Explain.

Rachel should use ____________________ because

____

____

____

8. Math Processes and Practices 3 **Apply**
What is an object that you would measure with a measuring tape? Explain why you would use this tool.

____

____

____

9. THINK SMARTER + Jim measures the length of a picnic table with an inch ruler. Is Jim using the best tool for measuring? Explain.

____

____

____

TAKE HOME ACTIVITY • Have your child name some objects that he or she would measure using a yardstick.

Name ____________________

Choose a Tool

Learning Objective You will choose measuring tools for measuring the length of an object.

Choose the best tool for measuring the real object. Then measure and record the length or distance.

inch ruler yardstick measuring tape

1. the length of your desk

Tool: ____________________

Length: ____________________

2. the distance around a basket

Tool: ____________________

Length: ____________________

Problem Solving

Choose the better tool for measuring.
Explain your choice.

3. Mark wants to measure the length of his room. Should he use an inch ruler or a yardstick?

Mark should use ____________________ because

____

____

4. WRITE Math Describe how you would use a yardstick to measure the length of a rug.

____

Lesson Check

1. Kim wants to measure the distance around her bike tire. Circle the best tool for her to use.

   cup　　yardstick

   color tiles　　measuring tape

2. Ben wants to measure the length of a seesaw. Circle the best tool for him to use.

   cup　　yardstick

   color tiles　　paper clips

Spiral Review

3. Estimate how many 12-inch rulers will be about the same length as a sheet of paper.

   ____ ruler, or ____ foot

4. Andy has a rope that is 24 inches long. He cuts off 7 inches from the rope. How long is the rope now?

   ____ inches

5. Jan is telling her friend about using a ruler to measure length. Write **inches** or **foot** in each blank to make the sentence true.

   12 ________ is the same length as 1 ________.

FOR MORE PRACTICE GO TO THE **Personal Math Trainer**

Name ______________________________

Display Measurement Data

Essential Question How can a line plot be used to show measurement data?

Learning Objective You will measure the lengths of objects and show the data in a line plot.

Listen and Draw

Use an inch ruler. Measure and record each length.

_____ inches

_____ inches

_____ inches

Math Processes and Practices 6

Describe how the lengths of the three strings are different.

HOME CONNECTION • Your child practiced measuring different lengths in inches in preparation for collecting measurement data in this lesson.

Model and Draw

A **line plot** is a way to show data. On this line plot, each ***X*** stands for the length of one pencil in inches.

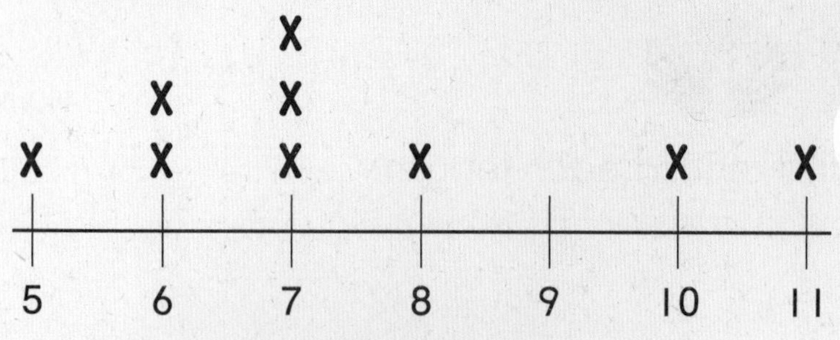

Lengths of Pencils in Inches

How many pencils are just 6 inches long? How many different pencils are shown in this data?

Share and Show

1. Use an inch ruler. Measure and record the lengths of 5 books in inches.

1st book: ________ inches	
2nd book: ________ inches	
3rd book: ________ inches	
4th book: ________ inches	
5th book: ________ inches	

2. Write a title for the line plot. Then write the numbers and draw the ***X***s.

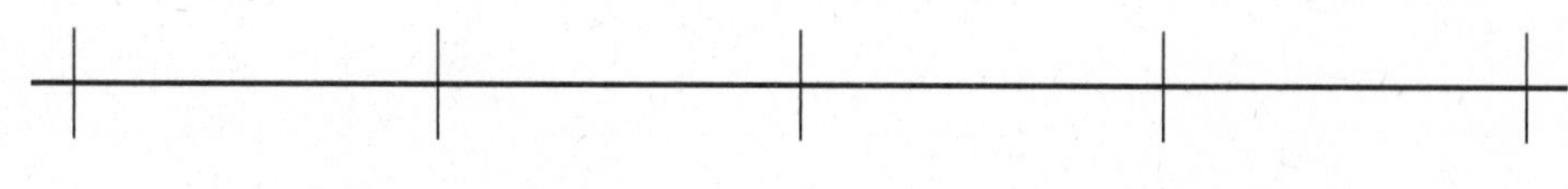

______ ______ ______ ______ ______

____

Name ______________________________

On Your Own

3. Use an inch ruler. Measure and record the lengths of 5 pencils in inches.

1st pencil: ________ inches	
2nd pencil: ________ inches	
3rd pencil: ________ inches	
4th pencil: ________ inches	
5th pencil: ________ inches	

4. Write a title for the line plot. Then write the numbers and draw the ***X***s.

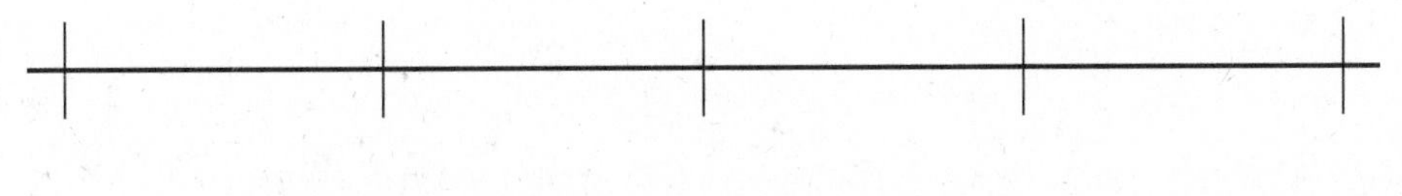

______ ______ ______ ______ ______

____

5. Use an inch ruler. Measure and record the lengths of 4 crayons in inches. Then complete the line plot.

1st crayon: ________ inches	
2nd crayon: ________ inches	
3rd crayon: ________ inches	
4th crayon: ________ inches	

______ ______ ______ ______

____

Problem Solving • Applications

6. 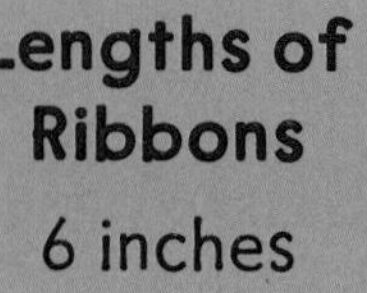 Use the data in the list to complete the line plot.

Lengths of Ribbons
6 inches
5 inches
7 inches
6 inches

______ ______ ______

____

7. THINK SMARTER Sarah made a line plot to show the data about the length of leaves. Is Sarah's line plot correct? Tell why or why not.

The Length of Leaves	
4 inches	6 inches
5 inches	4 inches
3 inches	5 inches
4 inches	

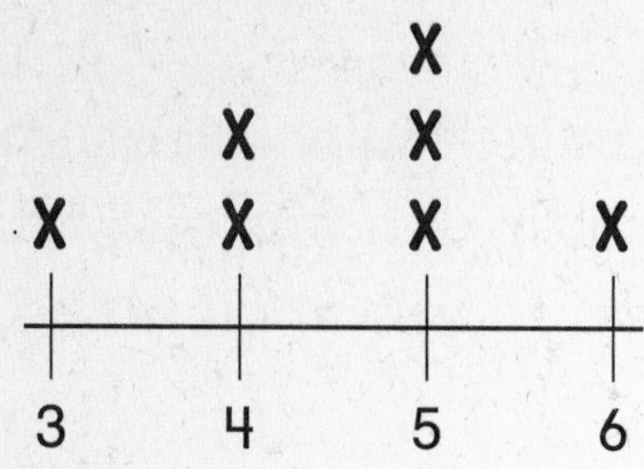

Lengths of Leaves in Inches

____

____

____

TAKE HOME ACTIVITY • Have your child describe how to make a line plot.

Name ______________________

Display Measurement Data

Learning Objective You will measure the lengths of objects and show the data in a line plot.

1. Use an inch ruler. Measure and record the lengths of 4 different books in inches.

1st book: ______ inches
2nd book: ______ inches
3rd book: ______ inches
4th book: ______ inches

2. Write a title for the line plot. Then write the numbers and draw the *X*s.

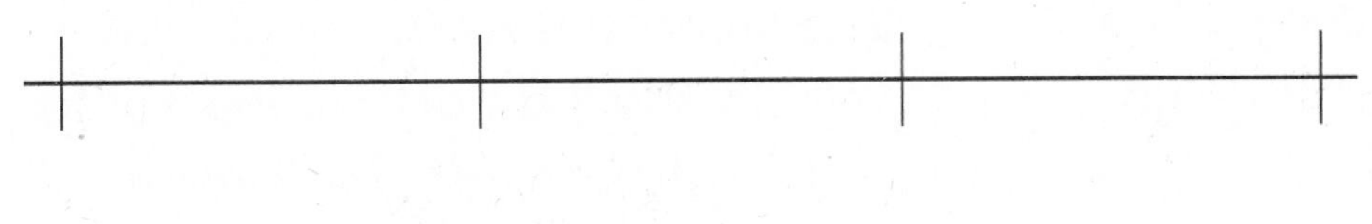

______ ______ ______ ______

____

Problem Solving

3. Jesse measured the lengths of some strings. Use his list to complete the line plot.

Lengths of Strings
5 inches
7 inches
6 inches
8 inches
5 inches

______ ______ ______ ______

____

4. WRITE Math Describe how you made a line plot in this lesson.

____

Lesson Check

1. Use the line plot. How many sticks are 4 inches long?

____ sticks

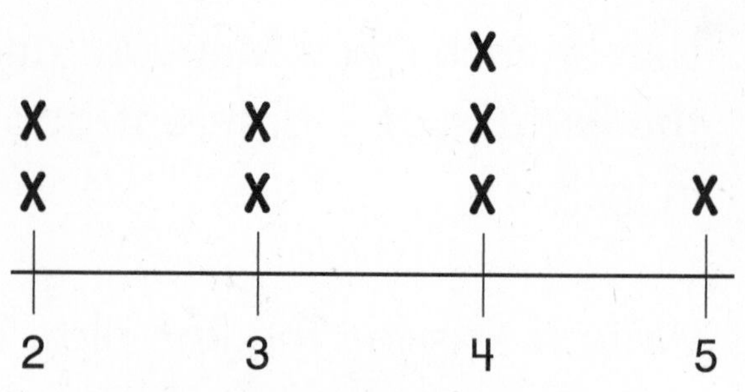

Lengths of Sticks in Inches

Spiral Review

2. Kim wants to measure a ball. Circle the best tool for Kim to use.

counter pencil

paper clip measuring tape

3. Estimate how many 12-inch rulers will be about the same length as a teacher's desk.

____ rulers, or ____ feet

4. Kurt has a string that is 12 inches long and another string that is 5 inches long. How many inches of string does he have altogether?

____ inches

5. One box has 147 books. The other box has 216 books. How many books are there in both boxes?

________ books

FOR MORE PRACTICE GO TO THE **Personal Math Trainer**

Name ________________________________

Chapter 8 Review/Test

Personal Math Trainer
Online Assessment and Intervention

Personal Math Trainer

1. THINK SMARTER+ Josh wants to measure the distance around a soccer ball.

Circle the best choice of tool.

inch ruler   yardstick   measuring tape

Explain your choice of tool.

____

____

2. GO DEEPER Luke has a string that is 6 inches long and a string that is 11 inches long. How many inches of string does Luke have?

Draw a diagram. Write a number sentence using a ▢ for the missing number. Solve.

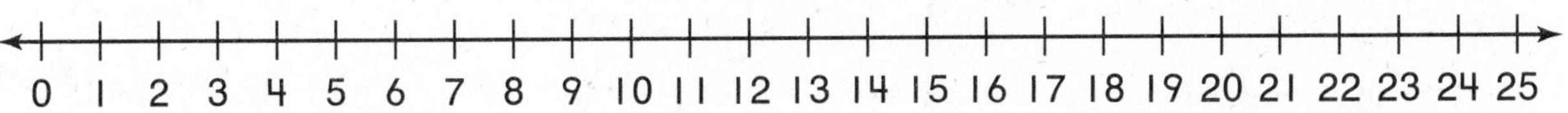

____

Luke has ________ inches of string.

GO DIGITAL Assessment Options Chapter Test

3. Use an inch ruler. What is the length of the lip balm to the nearest inch?

Circle the number in the box to make the sentence true.

	2	
The lip balm is	3	inches long.
	4	

---

4. Tom uses tiles to measure a string. Each tile is 1 inch long. Tom says the string is 3 inches long. Is he correct? Explain.

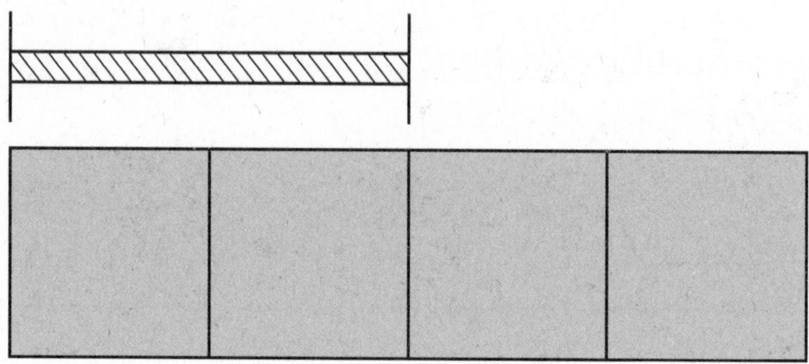

Name ______________________________

5. Dalia made a line plot to show the lengths of her ribbons.

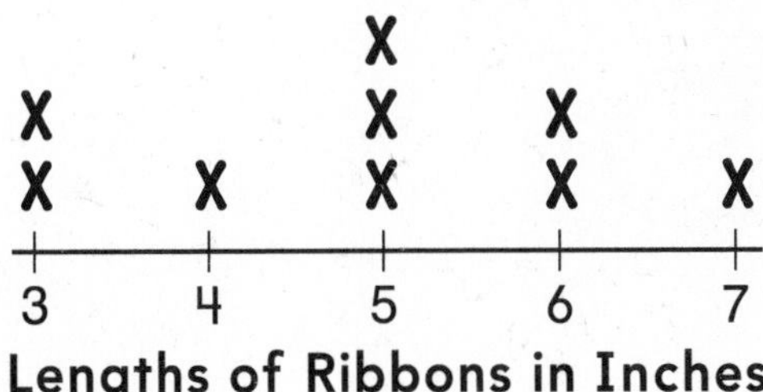

How many ribbons are shown in the line plot?

The line plot shows ______ ribbons.

How many ribbons are 6 inches long?

______ ribbons

---

6. Use the words on the tiles to make the sentence true.

The table is 3 ______ long.

The belt is 30 ______ long.

The hallway is 15 ______ long.

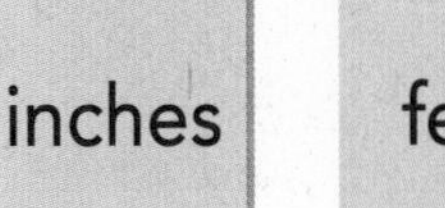

---

7. Use the 1-inch mark. Estimate the length of each object.

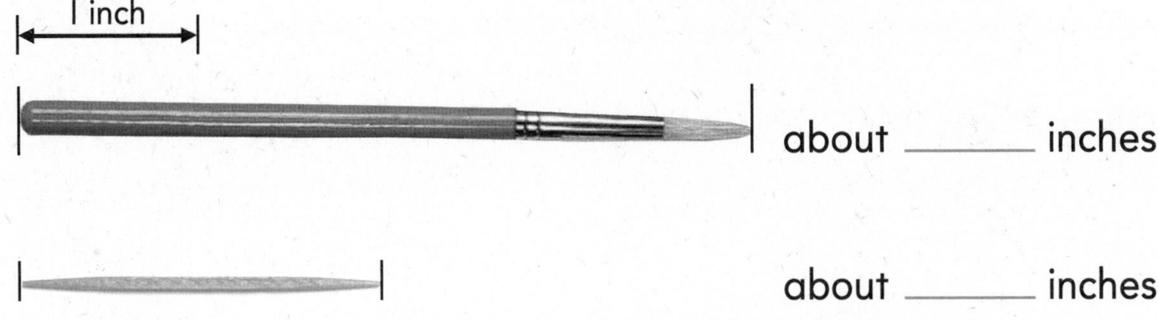

about ______ inches

about ______ inches

8. Use an inch ruler. What is the length of the paper clip to the nearest inch?

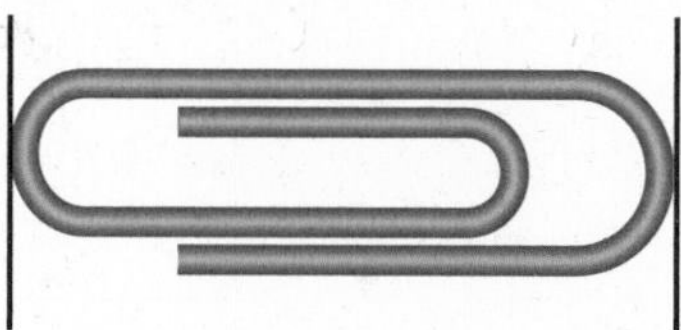

_______ inches

---

9. Estimate how many 12-inch rulers will be about the same height as a classroom door. Does the sentence describe the door? Choose Yes or No.

The door is about 8 feet high.	○ Yes	○ No
The door is less than 3 rulers high.	○ Yes	○ No
The door is more than 20 feet high.	○ Yes	○ No
The door is less than 15 rulers high.	○ Yes	○ No

Chapter 9

Length in Metric Units

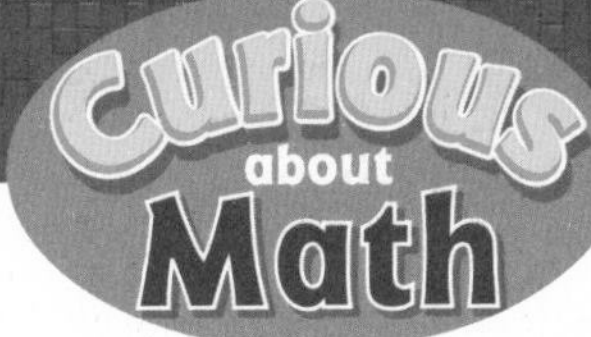

A wind farm is a group of wind turbines used to make electricity. One way to measure the distance between two wind turbines is by counting footsteps. What is another way?

Name ______________________________

Compare Lengths

1. Order the strings from shortest to longest.
Write 1, 2, 3.

____

____

____

Use Nonstandard Units to Measure Length

Use real objects and to measure.

2. 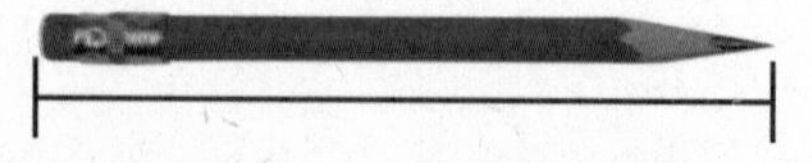

about ______

3. 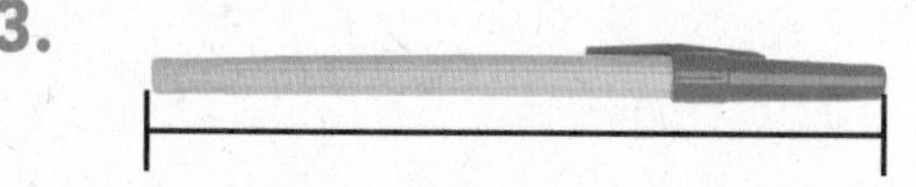

about ______

Measure Length Twice: Nonstandard Units

Use first. Then use .
Measure the length of the ribbon.

4. about ______ 

5. about ______ 

This page checks understanding of important skills needed for success in Chapter 9.

Name ________________________

Vocabulary Builder

Review Words
measure
length
estimate

Visualize It

Fill in the graphic organizer. Think of an object and write about how you can **measure** the **length** of that object.

Understand Vocabulary

Use the color tile to **estimate** the length of each straw.

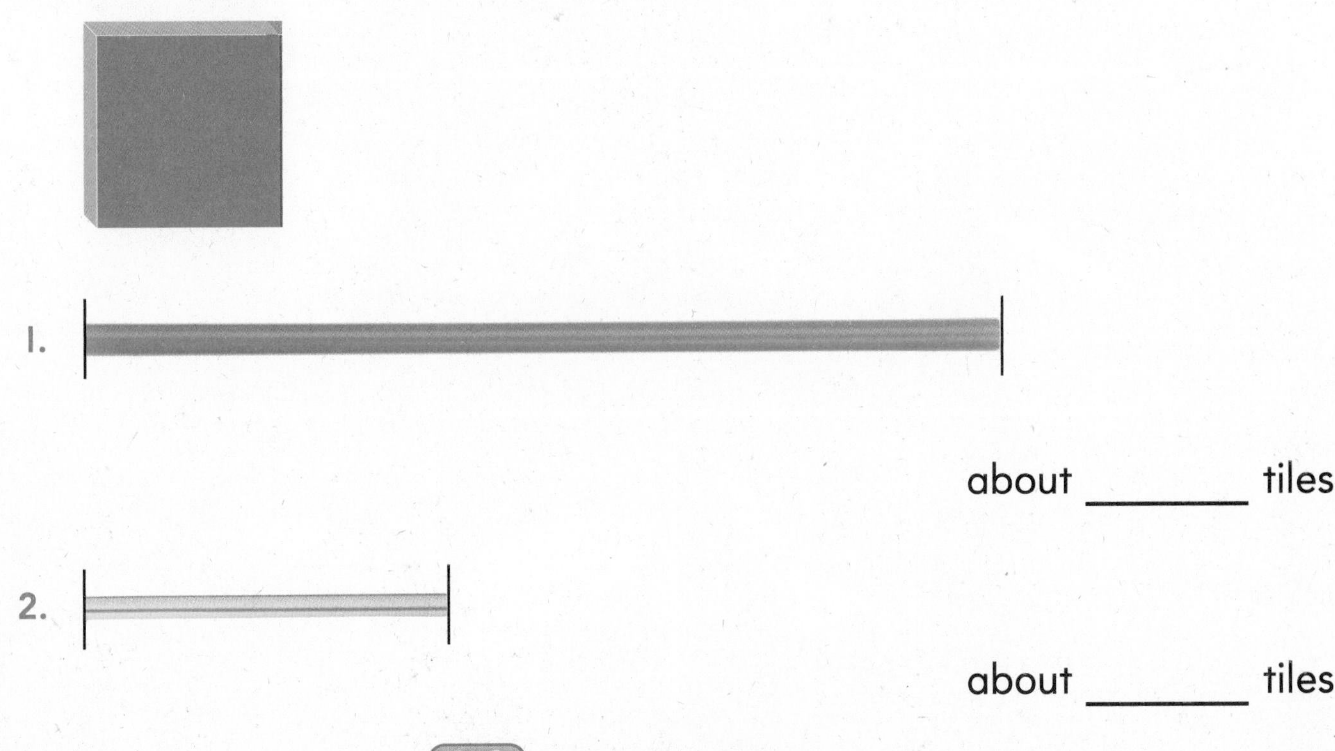

1\. about ______ tiles

2\. about ______ tiles

GO DIGITAL • Interactive Student Edition • Multimedia eGlossary

Game

Estimating Length

Materials

- 12 ● • 12 ○
- 15 ▪ • 15 ▪

Play with a partner.

1. Take turns choosing a picture. Find the real object.
2. Each player estimates the length of the object in cubes and then makes a cube train for his or her estimate.
3. Compare the cube trains to the length of the object. The player with the closer estimate puts a counter on the picture. If there is a tie, both players put a counter on the picture.
4. Repeat until all pictures are covered. The player with more counters on the board wins.

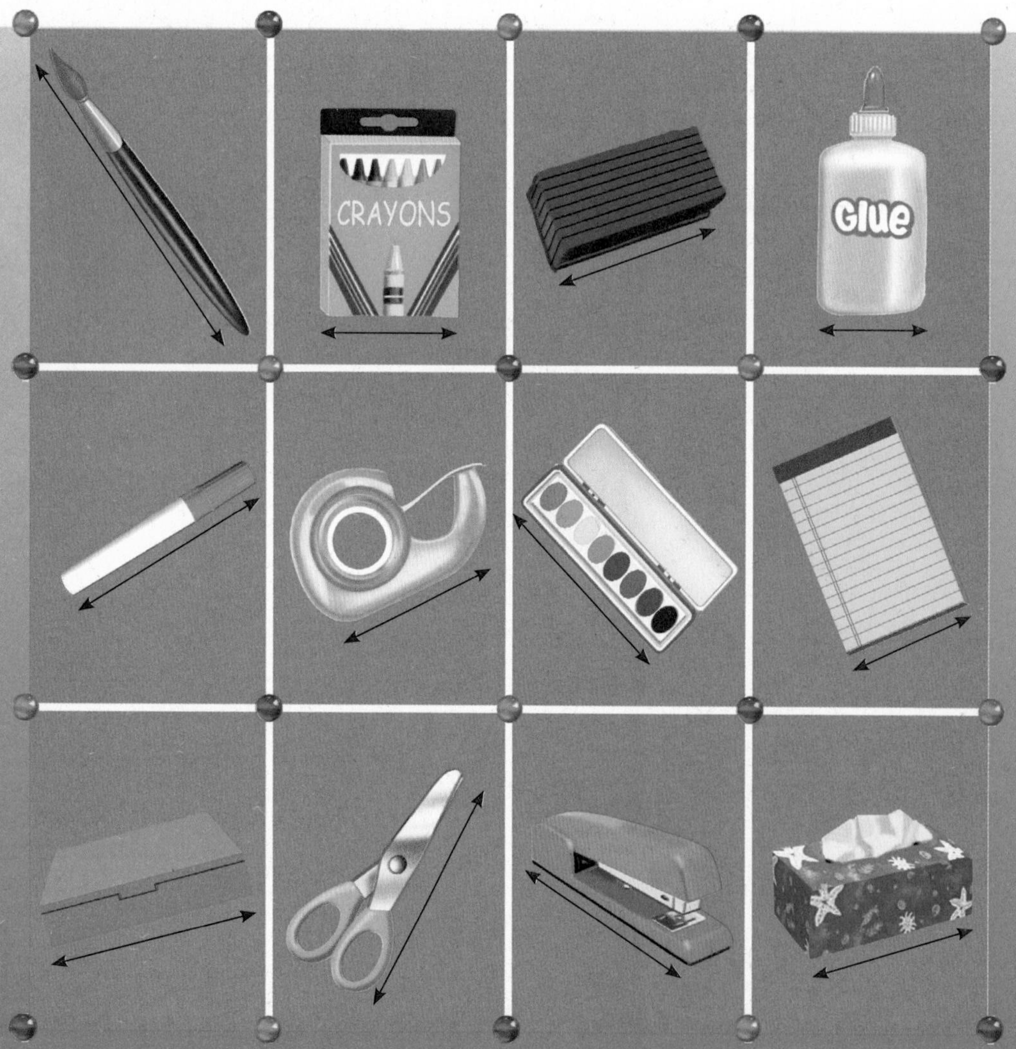

Chapter 9 Vocabulary

English	Spanish	No.
addend	sumando	1
centimeter	centímetro	6
compare	comparar	8
difference	diferencia	14
digit	dígito	15
estimate	estimación	21
meter (m)	metro (m)	39
sum	suma o total	59

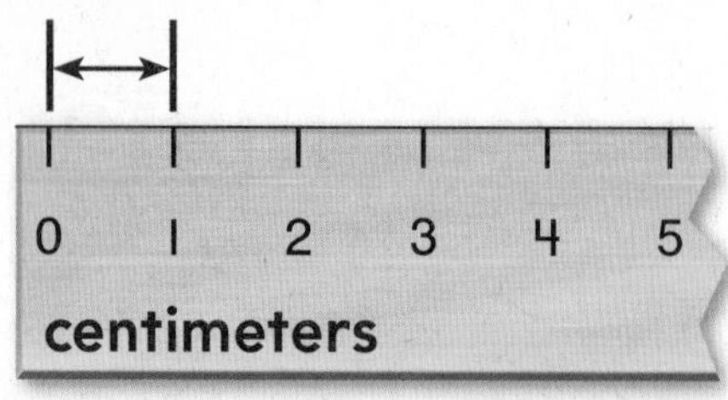

This is 1 **centimeter**.

$5 + 3 = 8$

addends

$5 - 3 = 2$

difference

Compare the lengths of the pencil and the crayon.

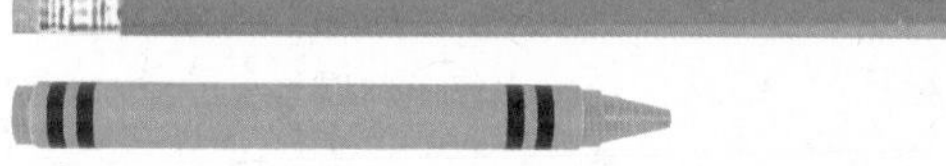

The pencil is longer than the crayon.
The crayon is shorter than the pencil.

An **estimate** is an amount that tells about how many.

0, 1, 2, 3, 4, 5, 6, 7, 8, and 9 are **digits**.

$4 + 2 = 6$

sum

1 **meter** is the same length as 100 centimeters.

Make a Match

Word Box
addend
centimeter
compare
difference
digit
estimate
meter
sum

For 3 players

Materials

- 4 sets of word cards

How to Play

1. Every player is dealt 5 cards. Put the rest face-down in a draw pile.
2. Ask another player for a word card to match a word card you have.
   - If the player has the word card, he or she gives it to you. Put both cards in front of you. Take another turn.
   - If the player does not have the word card, take a card from the pile. If the word you get matches one you are holding, put both cards in front of you. Take another turn. If it does not match, your turn is over.
3. The game is over when one player has no cards left. The player with the most pairs wins.

The Write Way

Reflect

Choose one idea. Write about it in the space below.

- Compare a centimeter to a meter. Explain how they are alike and how they are different.
- Explain how you would find the length of this crayon in centimeters.

- How would you compare the length of a door to the length of a window in meters? Draw pictures and write to explain. Use another piece of paper for your drawing.

Name ____________________

Measure with a Centimeter Model

Essential Question How do you use a centimeter model to measure the lengths of objects?

HANDS ON
Lesson 9.1

Learning Objective You will use unit cubes to measure the length of an object in centimeters.

Listen and Draw

Real World

Hands On

Use [cube] to measure the length.

____ unit cubes

____ unit cubes

____ unit cubes

Math Processes and Practices 

Use Tools Describe how to use unit cubes to measure an object's length.

HOME CONNECTION • Your child used unit cubes as an introduction to measurement of length before using metric measurement tools.

Model and Draw

A unit cube is about 1 **centimeter** long.

About how many centimeters long is this string?

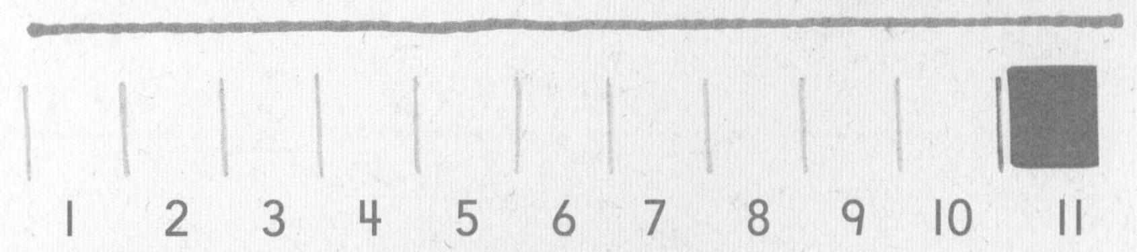

You can make a mark for each centimeter to keep track and to count.

The string is about <u>11</u> centimeters long.

Share and Show

MATH BOARD

Use a unit cube. Measure the length in centimeters.

1\.

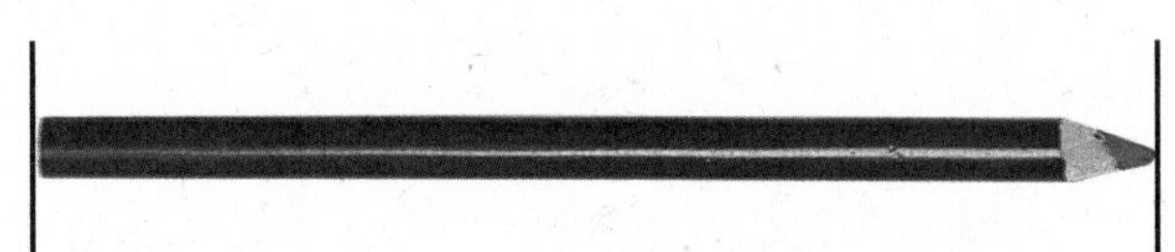

about ______ centimeters

2\.

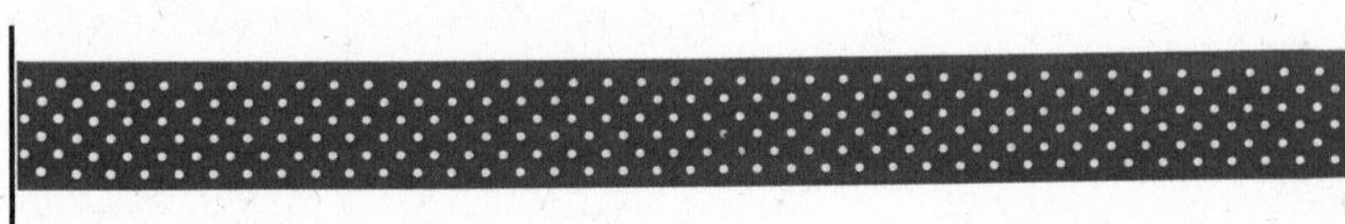

about ______ centimeters

3\.

about ______ centimeters

Name ________________________________

On Your Own

Use a unit cube. Measure the length in centimeters.

4. 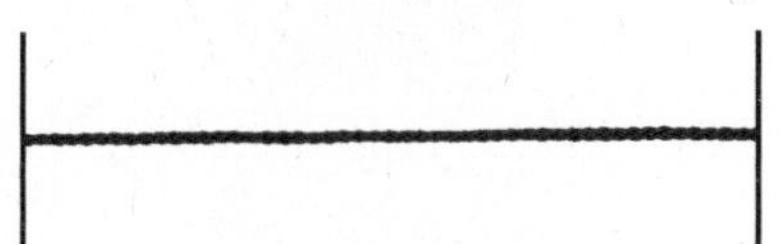

about ________ centimeters

5. 

about ________ centimeters

6. 

about ________ centimeters

7. 

about ________ centimeters

8.

about ________ centimeters

Problem Solving • Applications

Solve. Write or draw to explain.

9. THINKSMARTER Mrs. Duncan measured the lengths of a crayon and a pencil. The pencil is double the length of the crayon. The sum of their lengths is 24 centimeters. What are their lengths?

crayon: ____________________

pencil: ____________________

Personal Math Trainer

10. THINKSMARTER+ Marita uses unit cubes to measure the length of a straw. Circle the number in the box that makes the sentence true.

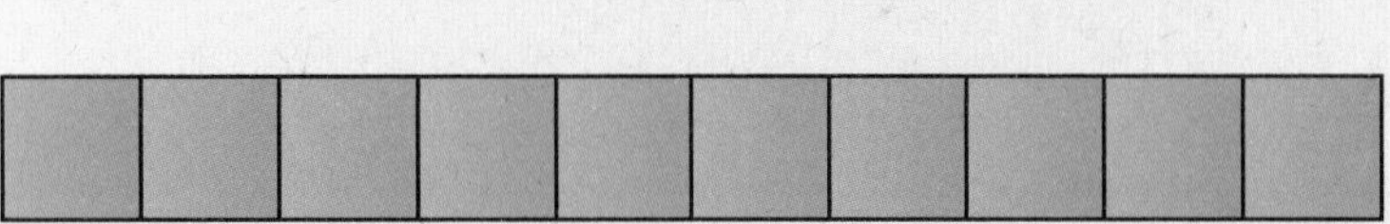

The straw is about [3 / 7 / 10] centimeters long.

TAKE HOME ACTIVITY • Have your child compare the lengths of other objects to those in this lesson.

Name ___________________________

Measure with a Centimeter Model

Learning Objective You will use unit cubes to measure the length of an object in centimeters.

Use a unit cube. Measure the length in centimeters.

1.

about _____ centimeters

2.

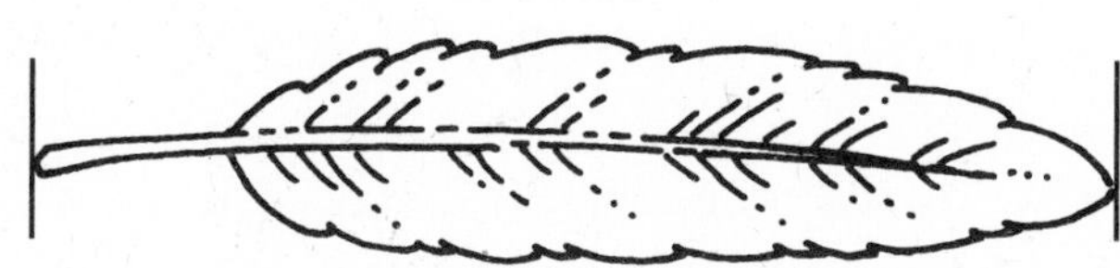

about _____ centimeters

3.

about _____ centimeters

Problem Solving

Solve. Write or draw to explain.

4. Susan has a pencil that is 3 centimeters shorter than this string. How long is the pencil?

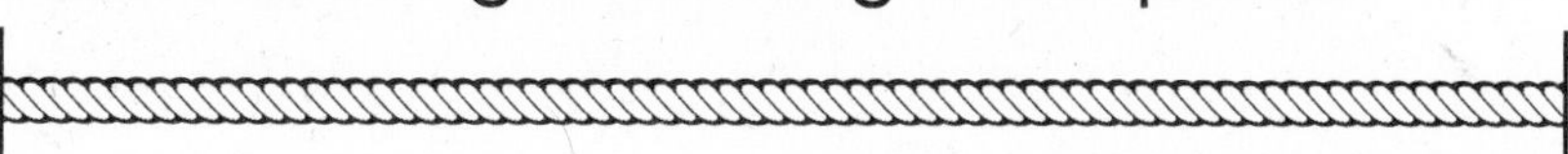

about _____ centimeters

5. WRITE Math Write about using a unit cube to measure lengths in this lesson.

____

____

Lesson Check

1. Sarah used unit cubes to measure the length of a ribbon. Each unit cube is about 1 centimeter long. What is the length of the ribbon?

about ____ centimeters

Spiral Review

2. What is the time on this clock?

____ : ____

3. What is the time on this clock?

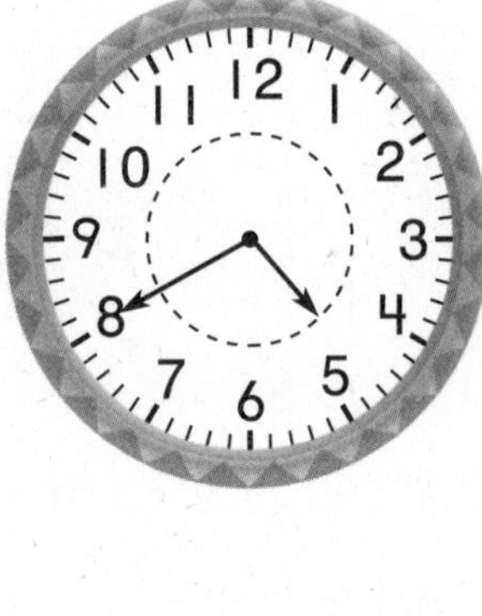

____ : ____

4. Dan has a paper strip that is 28 inches long. He tears 6 inches off the strip. How long is the paper strip now?

$28 - 6 = \blacksquare$

____ inches

5. Rita has 1 quarter, 1 dime, and 2 pennies. What is the total value of Rita's coins?

____ or ____ cents

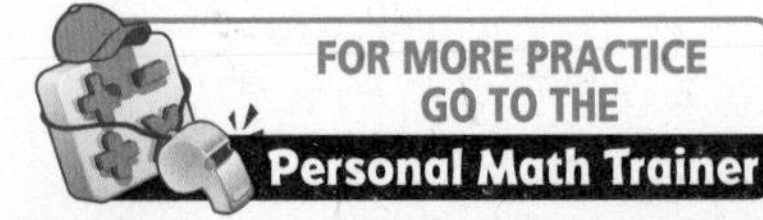

Name ___________________________

Estimate Lengths in Centimeters

Essential Question How do you use known lengths to estimate unknown lengths?

Learning Objective You will estimate the length of an object in centimeters.

Listen and Draw Real World Hands On

Find three classroom objects that are shorter than your 10-centimeter strip. Draw the objects. Write estimates for their lengths.

about _____ centimeters

about _____ centimeters

about _____ centimeters

Math Processes and Practices 

Which object has a length closest to 10 centimeters? **Explain.**

HOME CONNECTION • Your child used a 10-centimeter strip of paper to practice estimating the lengths of some classroom objects.

Model and Draw

This pencil is about 10 centimeters long. Which is the most reasonable estimate for the length of the ribbon?

7 centimeters

13 centimeters

20 centimeters

The ribbon is longer than the pencil. 7 centimeters is not reasonable.

The ribbon is not twice as long as the pencil. 20 centimeters is not reasonable.

The ribbon is a little longer than the pencil. So, 13 centimeters is the most reasonable estimate.

Share and Show

MATH BOARD

1. The yarn is about 5 centimeters long. Circle the best estimate for the length of the crayon.

   10 centimeters

   15 centimeters

   20 centimeters

2. The string is about 12 centimeters long. Circle the best estimate for the length of the straw.

   3 centimeters

   7 centimeters

   11 centimeters

Name ______________________________

On Your Own

3. The rope is about 8 centimeters long. Circle the best estimate for the length of the paper clip.

2 centimeters

4 centimeters

8 centimeters

4. The pencil is about 11 centimeters long. Circle the best estimate for the length of the chain.

6 centimeters

10 centimeters

13 centimeters

5. The hair clip is about 7 centimeters long. Circle the best estimate for the length of the yarn.

10 centimeters

17 centimeters

22 centimeters

6. The ribbon is about 13 centimeters long. Circle the best estimate for the length of the string.

5 centimeters

11 centimeters

17 centimeters

Problem Solving • Applications

7. THINK SMARTER For each question, circle the best estimate.

About how long is a new crayon?

5 centimeters

10 centimeters

20 centimeters

About how long is a new pencil?

20 centimeters

40 centimeters

50 centimeters

8. Math Processes and Practices 1 **Analyze** Mr. Lott has 250 more centimeters of tape than Mrs. Sanchez. Mr. Lott has 775 centimeters of tape. How many centimeters of tape does Mrs. Sanchez have?

_______ centimeters

9. THINK SMARTER This feather is about 7 centimeters long. Rachel says the yarn is about 14 centimeters long. Is Rachel correct? Explain.

____

____

TAKE HOME ACTIVITY • Give your child an object that is about 5 centimeters long. Have him or her use it to estimate the lengths of some other objects.

Name ______________________________

Estimate Lengths in Centimeters

Learning Objective You will estimate the length of an object in centimeters.

1. The toothpick is about 6 centimeters long. Circle the best estimate for the length of the yarn.

6 centimeters

9 centimeters

12 centimeters

2. The pen is about 11 centimeters long. Circle the best estimate for the length of the eraser.

4 centimeters

10 centimeters

14 centimeters

Problem Solving

3. The string is about 6 centimeters long. Draw a pencil that is about 12 centimeters long.

4. WRITE Math Choose one exercise above. Describe how you decided which estimate was the best choice.

____

Lesson Check

1. The pencil is about 12 centimeters long. Circle the best estimate for the length of the yarn.

1 centimeter   5 centimeters   11 centimeters

Spiral Review

2. Jeremy has 58 baseball cards. He gives 23 of them to his sister. How many baseball cards does Jeremy have left?

$$\begin{array}{r} 58 \\ -\ 23 \\ \hline \end{array}$$

____ baseball cards

3. What is the sum?

$14 + 65 =$ ____

4. Adrian has a cube train that is 13 inches long. He adds 6 inches of cubes to the train. How long is the cube train now?

$13 + 6 = \blacksquare$

____ inches

5. What is the total value of this group of coins?

________, or ____ cents

FOR MORE PRACTICE GO TO THE **Personal Math Trainer**

Name ___________________________

Measure with a Centimeter Ruler

HANDS ON
Lesson 9.3

Essential Question How do you use a centimeter ruler to measure lengths?

Learning Objective You will measure the length of an object to the nearest centimeter using a centimeter ruler.

Listen and Draw

Find three small objects in the classroom.
Use unit cubes to measure their lengths.
Draw the objects and write their lengths.

about _______ centimeters

about _______ centimeters

about _______ centimeters

Math Processes and Practices 

Apply Describe how the three lengths compare. Which object is shortest?

HOME CONNECTION • **Your child used unit cubes to measure the lengths of some classroom objects as an introduction to measuring lengths in centimeters.**

Model and Draw

What is the length of the crayon to the nearest centimeter?

Remember: Line up the left edge of the object with the zero mark on the ruler.

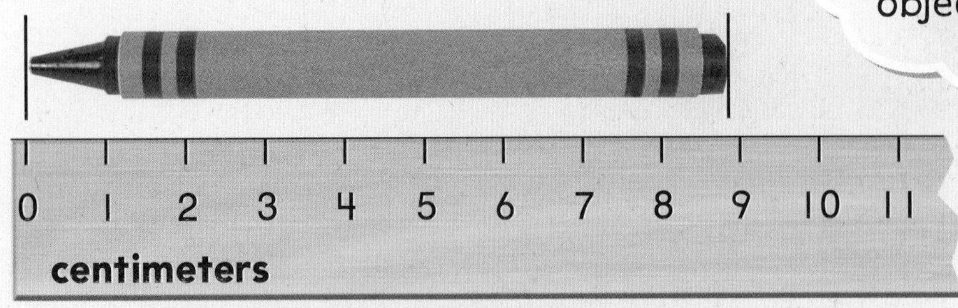

______ centimeters

Share and Show MATH BOARD

Measure the length to the nearest centimeter.

1.

______ centimeters

2.

______ centimeters

3.

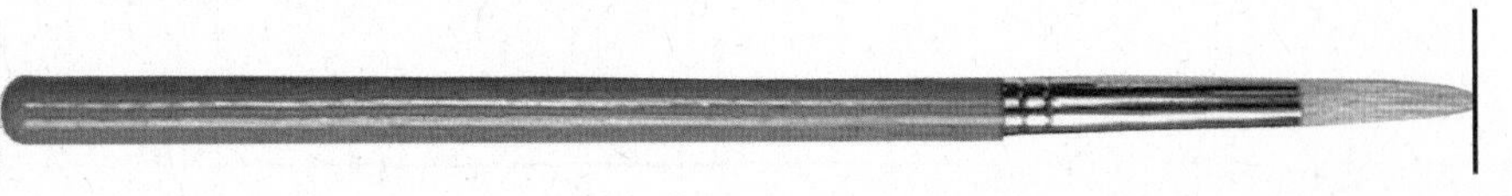

______ centimeters

Name ____________________

On Your Own

Measure the length to the nearest centimeter.

4.

_______ centimeters

5.

_______ centimeters

6.

_______ centimeters

7.

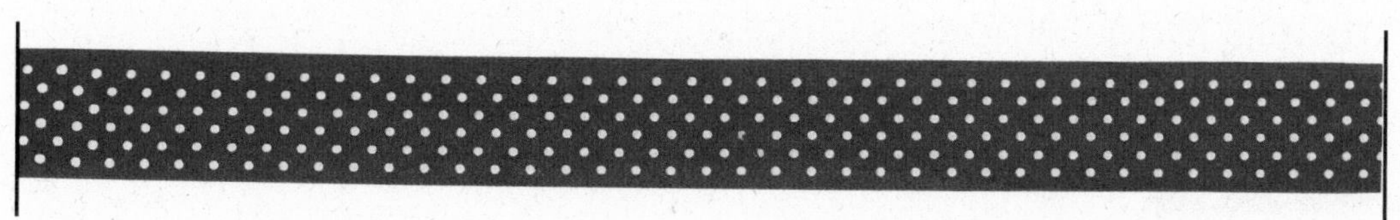

_______ centimeters

8. GO DEEPER A marker is almost 13 centimeters long. This length ends between which two centimeter-marks on a ruler?

____

____

Problem Solving • Applications

9. THINKSMARTER The crayon was on the table next to the centimeter ruler. The left edge of the crayon was not lined up with the zero mark on the ruler.

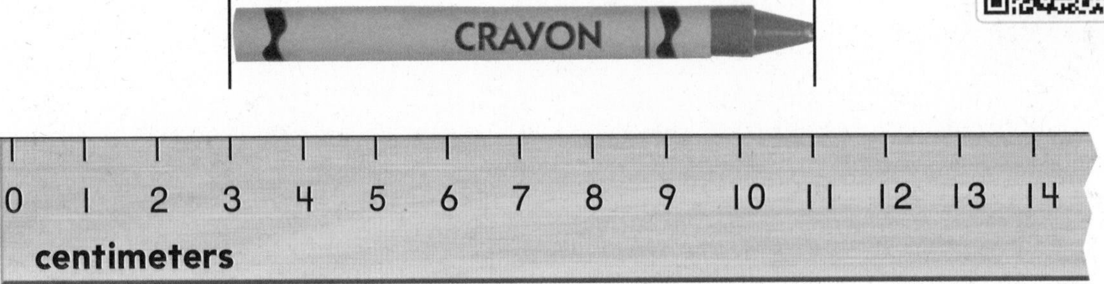

What is the length of the crayon?
Explain how you found your answer.

____

____

____

10. THINKSMARTER This is Lee's string. Hana's string is 7 centimeters long. Whose string is longer? Use a centimeter ruler to find out. Explain.

____

____

TAKE HOME ACTIVITY • Have your child measure the lengths of some objects using a centimeter ruler.

Name ____________________

Measure with a Centimeter Ruler

Learning Objective You will measure the length of an object to the nearest centimeter using a centimeter ruler.

Measure the length to the nearest centimeter.

1\. 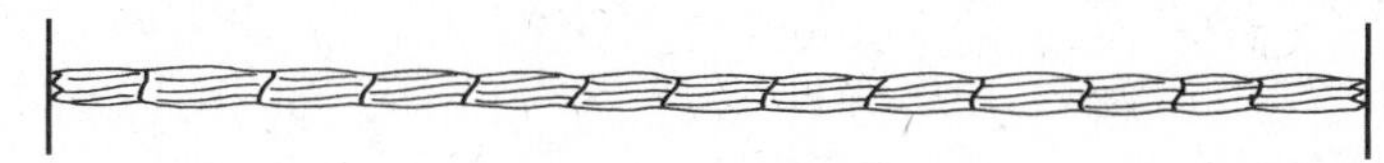

_____ centimeters

2\. 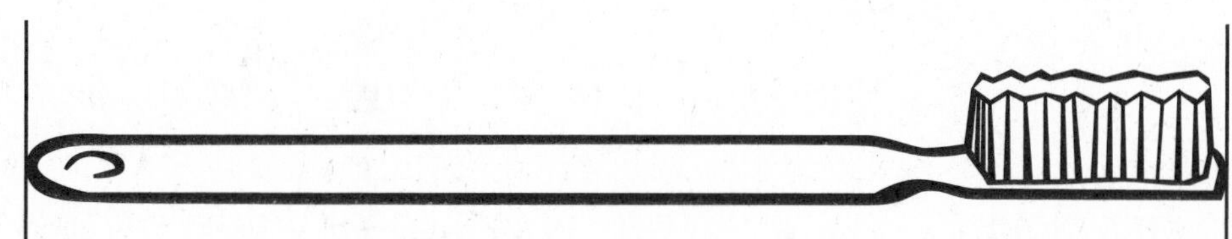

_____ centimeters

Problem Solving 

3\. Draw a string that is about 8 centimeters long. Use the pictures above to help you. Then use a centimeter ruler to check the length.

4\. WRITE Math Measure the length of the top of your desk in centimeters. Describe how you found the length.

____

____

____

____

Lesson Check

1. Use a centimeter ruler. What is the length of this pencil to the nearest centimeter?

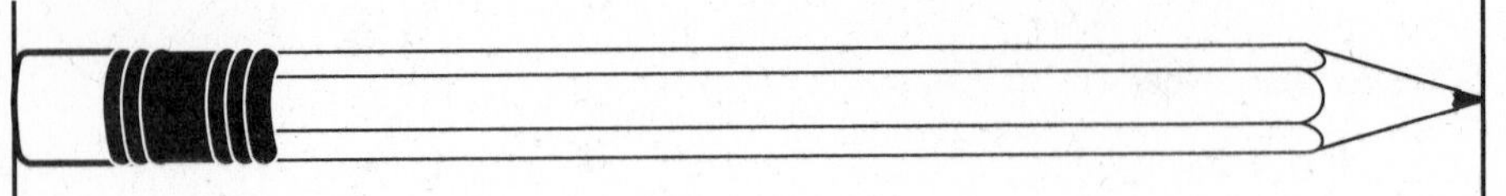

____ centimeters

Spiral Review

2. What is the time on this clock?

____:____

3. What is the total value of this group of coins?

$ ________ or ____ cents

4. Use the line plot. How many pencils are 5 inches long?

____ pencils

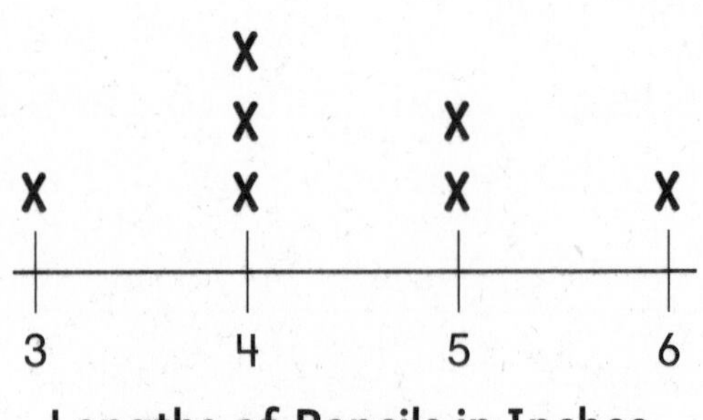

FOR MORE PRACTICE GO TO THE **Personal Math Trainer**

Name ______________________________

Problem Solving • Add and Subtract Lengths

Essential Question How can drawing a diagram help when solving problems about lengths?

Learning Objective You will use the strategy *draw a diagram* to solve problems about lengths of objects in centimeters by adding and subtracting on a number line.

Nate had 23 centimeters of string.
He gave 9 centimeters of string to Myra.
How much string does Nate have now?

Unlock the Problem

What do I need to find?

how much string
Nate has now

What information do I need to use?

Nate had ________ centimeters of string.

He gave ________ centimeters of string to Myra.

Show how to solve the problem.

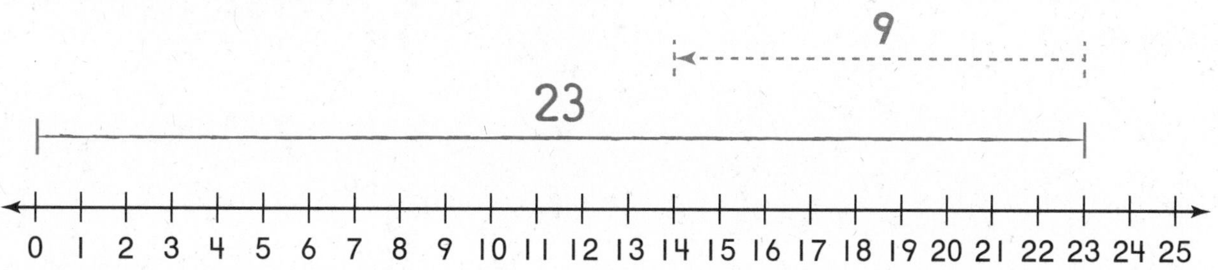

____

Nate has ________ centimeters of string now.

HOME CONNECTION • Your child drew a diagram to represent a problem about lengths. The diagram can be used to choose the operation for solving the problem.

Try Another Problem

Draw a diagram. Write a number sentence using a ■ for the unknown number. Then solve.

- What do I need to find?
- What information do I need to use?

1. Ellie has a ribbon that is 12 centimeters long. Gwen has a ribbon that is 9 centimeters long. How many centimeters of ribbon do they have?

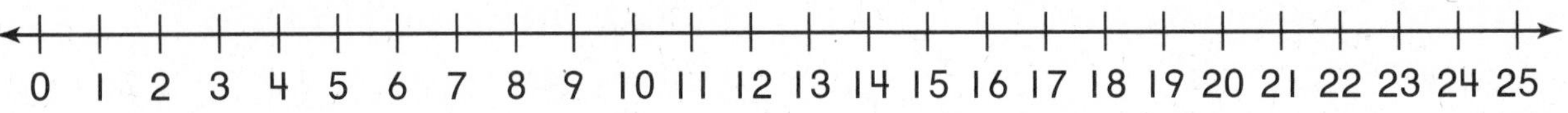

____

They have _____ centimeters of ribbon.

2. A string is 24 centimeters long. Justin cuts 8 centimeters off. How long is the string now?

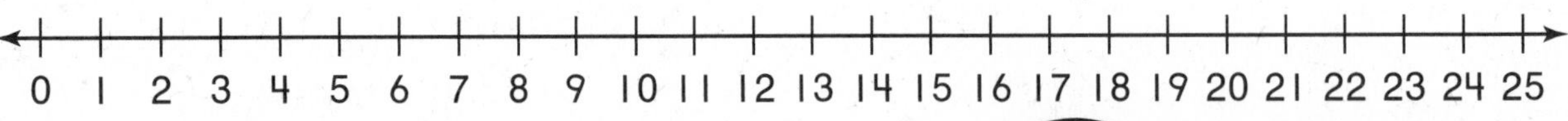

____

Now the string is ________ centimeters long.

Math Talk Math Processes and Practices 4

Explain how your diagram shows what happened in the first problem.

Name ______________________________

Share and Show

Draw a diagram. Write a number sentence using a ■ for the unknown number. Then solve.

✓3. A chain of paper clips is 18 centimeters long. Sondra adds 6 centimeters of paper clips to the chain. How long is the chain now?

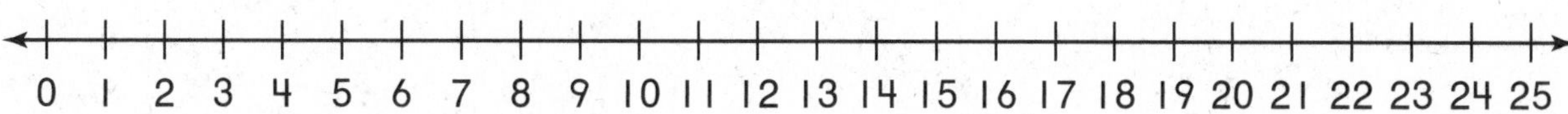

____

The chain is _______ centimeters long now.

4. THINKSMARTER A ribbon was 22 centimeters long. Then Martha cut a piece off to give to Tao. Now the ribbon is 5 centimeters long. How many centimeters of ribbon did Martha give to Tao?

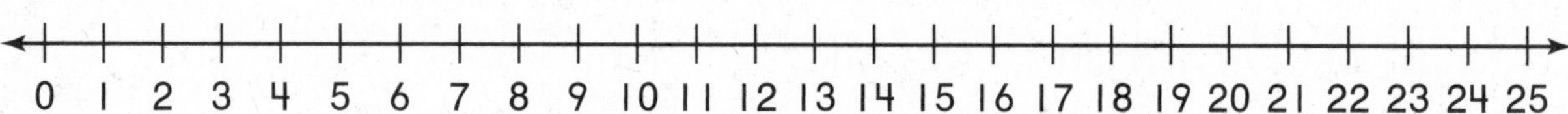

Martha gave _______ centimeters of ribbon to Tao.

TAKE HOME ACTIVITY • Have your child explain how he or she used a diagram to solve one problem in this lesson.

Name ____________________

Mid-Chapter Checkpoint

Concepts and Skills

Use a unit cube. Measure the length in centimeters.

1.

about ____ centimeters

2.

about ____ centimeters

3. The pencil is about 11 centimeters long. Circle the best estimate for the length of the string.

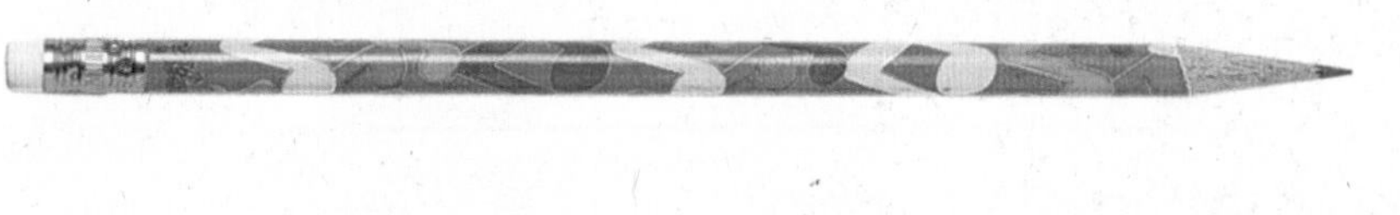

7 centimeters

10 centimeters

16 centimeters

4. THINKSMARTER Use a centimeter ruler. What is the length of this ribbon to the nearest centimeter?

____ centimeters

Name ______________________________

Problem Solving • Add and Subtract Lengths

Learning Objective You will use the strategy *draw a diagram* to solve problems about lengths of objects in centimeters by adding and subtracting on a number line.

Draw a diagram. Write a number sentence using a ■ for the unknown number. Then solve.

1. A straw is 20 centimeters long. Mr. Jones cuts 8 centimeters off the straw. How long is the straw now?

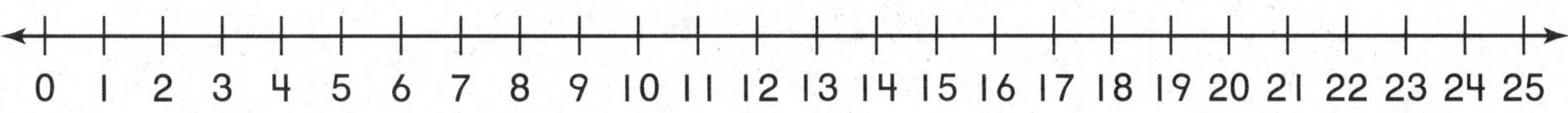

____

The straw is ______ centimeters long now.

2. WRITE Math Draw and describe a diagram for a problem about the total length of two ribbons, 13 centimeters long and 5 centimeters long.

Lesson Check

1. Tina has a paper clip chain that is 25 centimeters long. She takes off 8 centimeters of the chain. How long is the chain now?

_______________ ____ centimeters

Spiral Review

2. What is the sum?

$$\begin{array}{r} 327 \\ +145 \\ \hline \end{array}$$

3. What is another way to write the time half past 7?

____ : ____

4. Molly has these coins in her pocket. How much money does she have in her pocket?

_______ or ____ cents

FOR MORE PRACTICE GO TO THE Personal Math Trainer

Name ______________________________

HANDS ON
Lesson 9.5

Centimeters and Meters

Essential Question How is measuring in meters different from measuring in centimeters?

Learning Objective You will measure the length of an object to the nearest centimeter and to the nearest meter.

Listen and Draw

Draw or write to describe how you did each measurement.

1st measurement

2nd measurement

Math Processes and Practices 1

Describe how the lengths of the yarn and the sheet of paper are different.

FOR THE TEACHER • Have each small group use a 1-meter piece of yarn to measure a distance marked on the floor with masking tape. Then have them measure the same distance using a sheet of paper folded in half lengthwise.

Model and Draw

1 **meter** is the same as 100 centimeters.

The real door is about 200 centimeters tall.
The real door is also about 2 meters tall.

Share and Show

Measure to the nearest centimeter.
Then measure to the nearest meter.

	Find the real object.	Measure.
1.	chair	_____ centimeters _____ meters
✓2.	teacher's desk	_____ centimeters _____ meters
✓3.	wall	_____ centimeters _____ meters

Name ___________________________

On Your Own

Measure to the nearest centimeter.
Then measure to the nearest meter.

	Find the real object.	Measure.
4.	chalkboard	_____ centimeters _____ meters
5.	bookshelf	_____ centimeters _____ meters
6.	table	_____ centimeters _____ meters

7. GO DEEPER Write these lengths in order from shortest to longest.

200 centimeters
10 meters
1 meter

____

Problem Solving • Applications

8. THINKSMARTER Mr. Ryan walked next to a barn. He wants to measure the length of the barn. Would the length be a greater number of centimeters or a greater number of meters? Explain your answer.

____

____

____

9. THINKSMARTER Write the word on the tile that makes the sentence true.

centimeters	meters

A bench is 2 ____________ long.

A pencil is 15 ____________ long.

A paper clip is 3 ____________ long.

A bed is 3 ____________ long.

TAKE HOME ACTIVITY • Have your child describe how centimeters and meters are different.

Name ______________________________

Centimeters and Meters

Learning Objective You will measure the length of an object to the nearest centimeter and to the nearest meter.

Measure to the nearest centimeter. Then measure to the nearest meter.

Find the real object.	Measure.
1. bookcase	______ centimeters ______ meters
2. window	______ centimeters ______ meters

Problem Solving Real World

3. Sally will measure the length of a wall in both centimeters and meters. Will there be fewer centimeters or fewer meters? Explain.

____

____

____

4. WRITE Math Would you measure the length of a bench in centimeters or in meters? Explain your choice.

____

Lesson Check

1. Use a centimeter ruler. What is the length of the toothbrush to the nearest centimeter?

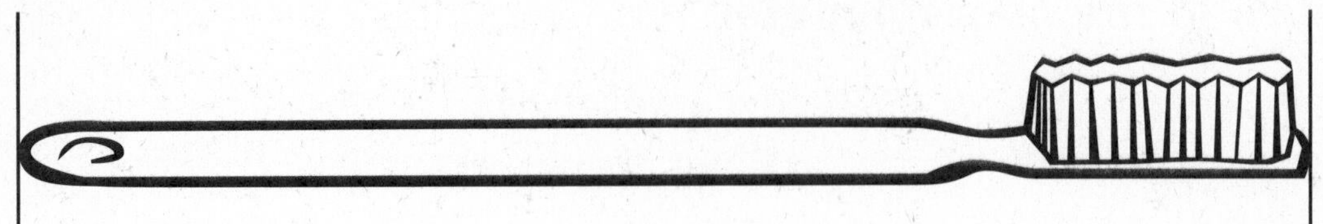

____ centimeters

Spiral Review

2. Draw and label a group of coins that has a total value of 65 cents.

3. Janet has a poster that is about 3 feet long. Write **inches** or **feet** in each blank to make the statement true.

   3 ____________ is longer than

   12 ____________.

4. Last week, 483 children checked books out from the library. This week, only 162 children checked books out from the library. How many children checked out library books in the last two weeks?

$$\begin{array}{r} 483 \\ +\ 162 \\ \hline \end{array}$$

5. Draw and label a group of coins that has a total value of $1.00.

FOR MORE PRACTICE GO TO THE **Personal Math Trainer**

Name ___________________________________

Estimate Lengths in Meters

Essential Question How do you estimate the lengths of objects in meters?

Learning Objective You will estimate the length of an object in meters.

Find an object that is about 10 centimeters long. Draw and label it.

Is there a classroom object that is about 50 centimeters long? Draw and label it.

Math Processes and Practices 6

Describe how the lengths of the two real objects compare.

FOR THE TEACHER • Provide a collection of objects for children to choose from. Above the table of displayed objects, draw and label a 10-centimeter line segment and a 50-centimeter line segment.

Model and Draw

Estimate. About how many meter sticks will match the width of a door?

A 1-meter measuring stick is about 100 centimeters long.

about ____ meters

Share and Show 

Find the real object.
Estimate its length in meters.

1. bookshelf

about ____ meters

2. bulletin board

about ____ meters

Name ____________________

On Your Own

Find the real object.
Estimate its length in meters.

3. teacher's desk

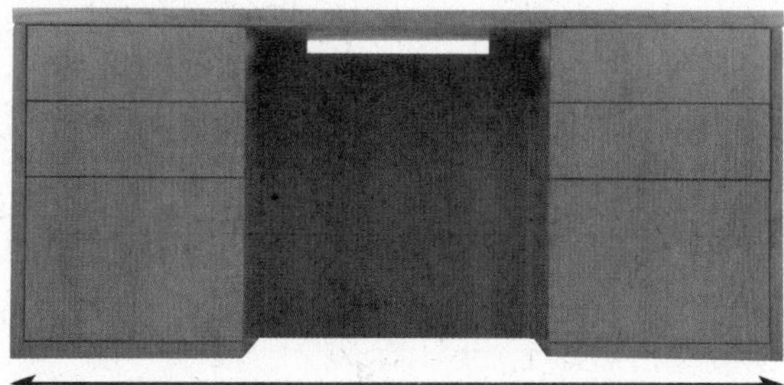

about _____ meters

4. wall

about _____ meters

5. window

about _____ meters

6. chalkboard

about _____ meters

Problem Solving • Applications

7. THINK SMARTER In meters, estimate the distance from your teacher's desk to the door of your classroom.

about _____ meters

Explain how you made your estimate.

____

____

____

____

8. THINK SMARTER Estimate the length of an adult's bicycle. Fill in the bubble next to all the sentences that are true.

- ○ The bicycle is about 2 meters long.
- ○ The bicycle is about 200 centimeters long.
- ○ The bicycle is less than 1 meter long.
- ○ The bicycle is about 2 centimeters long.
- ○ The bicycle is more than 200 meters long.

TAKE HOME ACTIVITY • With your child, estimate the lengths of some objects in meters.

Name ___________________________

Estimate Lengths in Meters

Learning Objective You will estimate the length of an object in meters.

**Find the real object.
Estimate its length in meters.**

1. poster

about _____ meters

2. chalkboard

about _____ meters

Problem Solving Real World

3. Barbara and Luke each placed 2 meter sticks end-to-end along the length of a large table. About how long is the table?

about _____ meters

4. WRITE Math Choose one object from above. Describe how you estimated its length.

____

____

Lesson Check

1. What is the best estimate for the length of a real baseball bat?

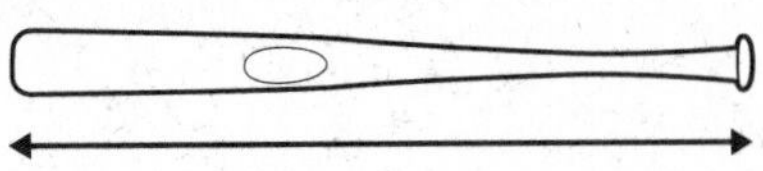

____ meter

2. What is the best estimate for the length of a real couch?

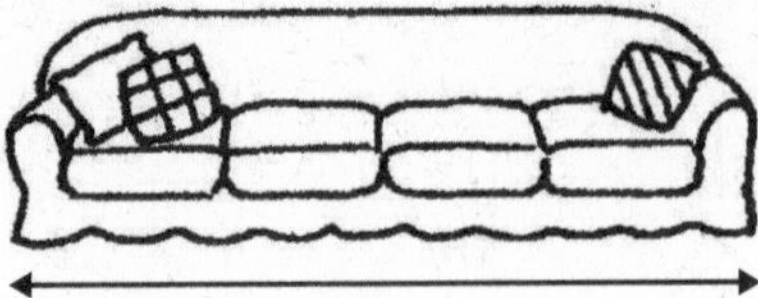

____ meters

Spiral Review

3. Sara has two $1 bills, 3 quarters, and 1 dime. How much money does she have?

$ ________

4. Use an inch ruler. What is the length of this straw to the nearest inch?

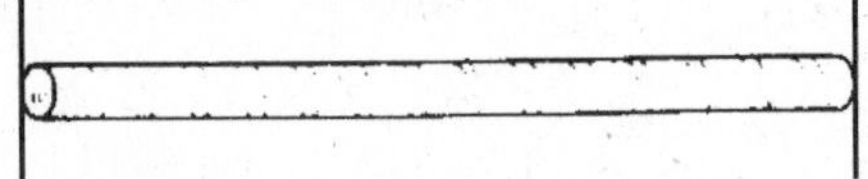

____ inches

5. Scott has this money in his pocket. What is the total value of this money?

$ ________

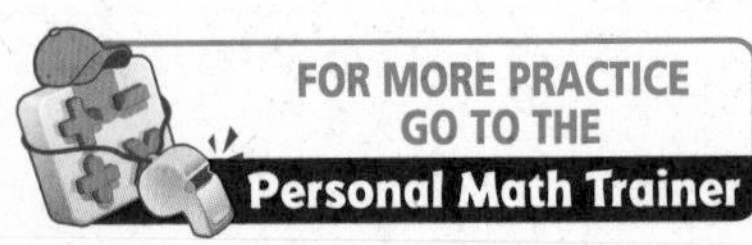

Name ______________________________

Measure and Compare Lengths

Essential Question How do you find the difference between the lengths of two objects?

Learning Objective You will find the difference between the lengths of two objects.

Listen and Draw

Measure and record each length.

________ centimeters

________ centimeters

Math Talk Math Processes and Practices 

Name a classroom object that is longer than the paintbrush. **Explain** how you know.

HOME CONNECTION • Your child measured these lengths as an introduction to measuring and then comparing lengths.

Model and Draw

How much longer is the pencil than the crayon?

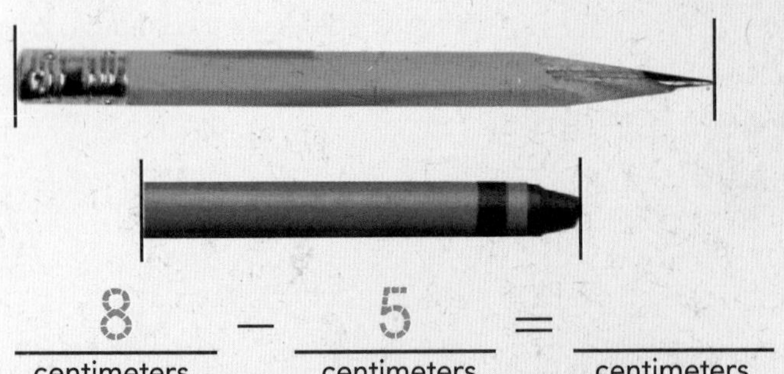

8 centimeters

5 centimeters

8 centimeters − 5 centimeters = ____ centimeters

The pencil is ____ centimeters longer than the crayon.

Share and Show

Measure the length of each object. Complete the number sentence to find the difference between the lengths.

1. 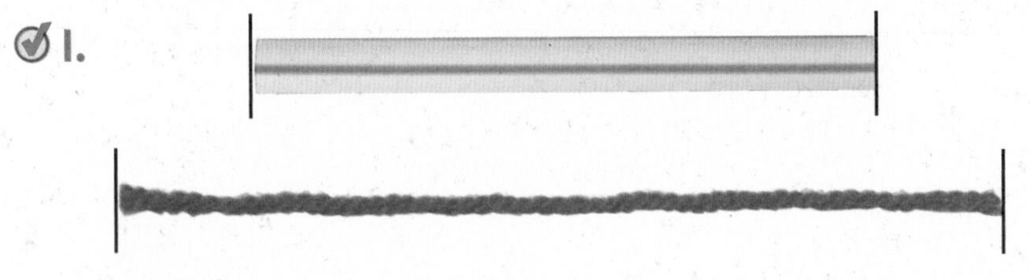

____ centimeters

____ centimeters

____ centimeters − ____ centimeters = ____ centimeters

The string is ____ centimeters longer than the straw.

2. 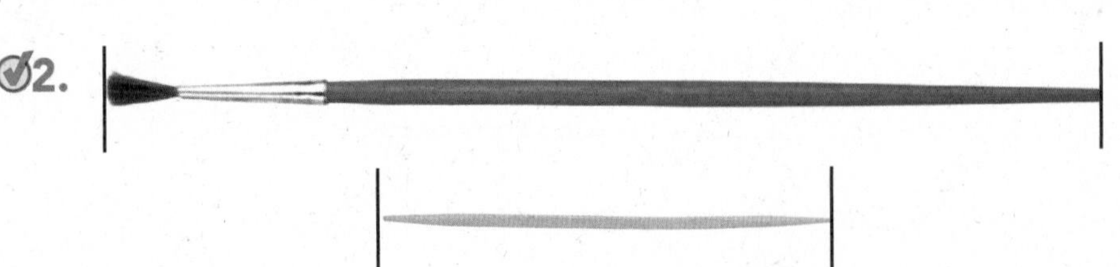

____ centimeters

____ centimeters

____ centimeters − ____ centimeters = ____ centimeters

The paintbrush is ________ centimeters longer than the toothpick.

Name ______________________________

On Your Own

Measure the length of each object. Complete the number sentence to find the difference between the lengths.

3. 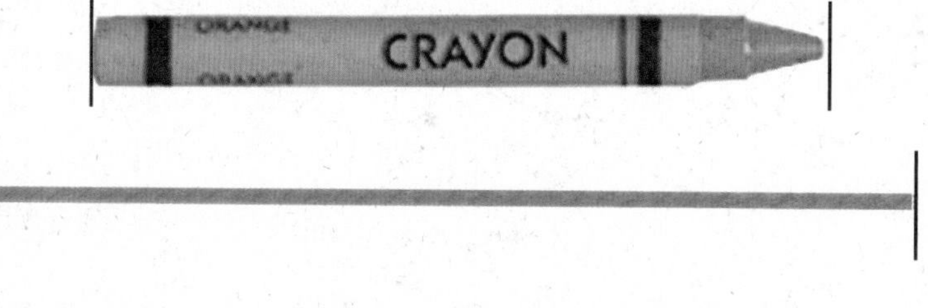

______ centimeters

______ centimeters

______ − ______ = ______
centimeters centimeters centimeters

The yarn is ______ centimeters longer than the crayon.

4. ______ centimeters

______ centimeters

______ − ______ = ______
centimeters centimeters centimeters

The string is ____ centimeters longer than the paper clip.

5. THINK SMARTER Use a centimeter ruler. Measure the length of your desk and the length of a book.

desk: ______ centimeters

book: ______ centimeters

Which is shorter? ______________________

How much shorter is it? ______________________

Problem Solving • Applications

Math Processes and Practices 1 **Analyze Relationships**

6. Mark has a rope that is 23 centimeters long. He cuts 15 centimeters off. What is the length of the rope now?

_______ centimeters

7. The yellow ribbon is 15 centimeters longer than the green ribbon. The green ribbon is 29 centimeters long. What is the length of the yellow ribbon?

_______ centimeters

Personal Math Trainer

8. THINKSMARTER+ Measure the length of each object. Which object is longer? How much longer? Explain.

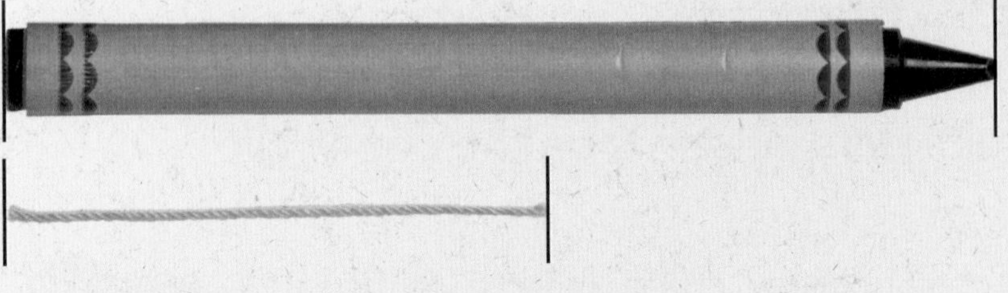

____

____

____

____

TAKE HOME ACTIVITY • Have your child tell you how he or she solved one of the problems in this lesson.

Name ______________________

Measure and Compare Lengths

Learning Objective You will find the difference between the lengths of two objects.

Measure the length of each object. Write a number sentence to find the difference between the lengths.

1. 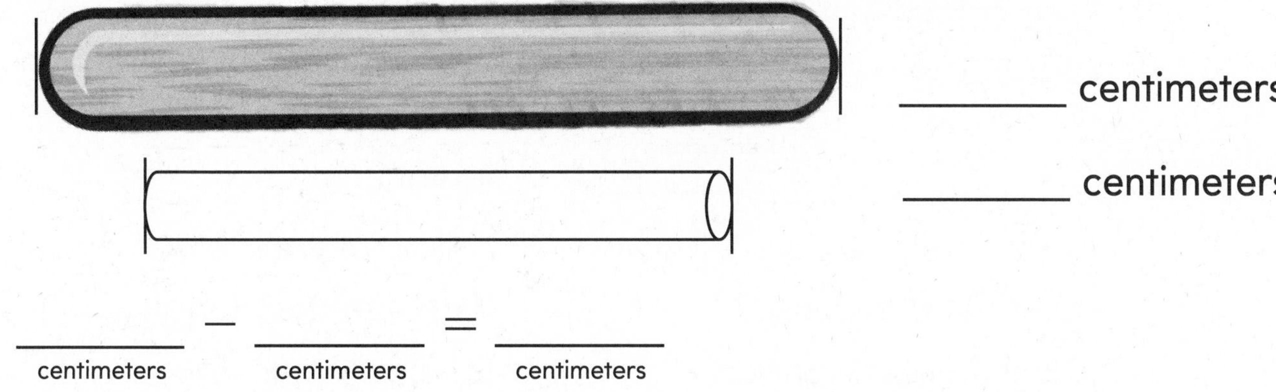

_______ centimeters

_______ centimeters

_______ − _______ = _______
centimeters centimeters centimeters

The craft stick is _______ centimeters longer than the chalk.

Problem Solving Real World

Solve. Write or draw to explain.

2. A string is 11 centimeters long, a ribbon is 24 centimeters long, and a large paper clip is 5 centimeters long. How much longer is the ribbon than the string?

_____ centimeters longer

3. 

Suppose the lengths of two strings are 10 centimeters and 17 centimeters. Describe how the lengths of these two strings compare.

____

____

Lesson Check

1. How much longer is the marker than the paper clip? Circle the correct answer.

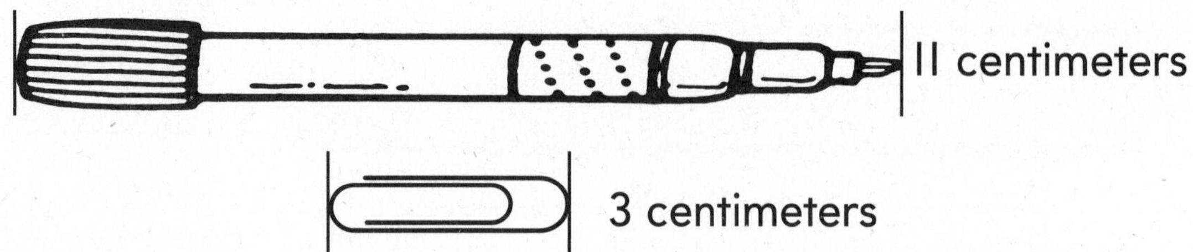

11 centimeters longer

10 centimeters longer

8 centimeters longer

5 centimeters longer

Spiral Review

2. What is the total value of these coins?

_______ or ____ cents

3. What is a reasonable estimate for the length of a real chalkboard?

____ feet

4. Cindy leaves at half past 2. At what time does Cindy leave?

____:____

FOR MORE PRACTICE GO TO THE **Personal Math Trainer**

Name ____________________

Chapter 9 Review/Test

1. Michael uses unit cubes to measure the length of the yarn. Circle the number in the box that makes the sentence true.

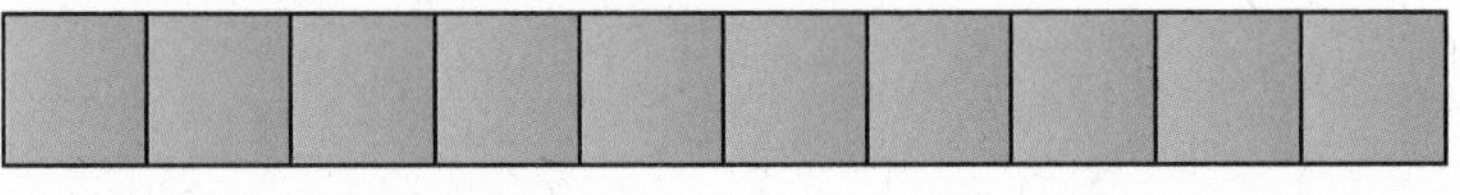

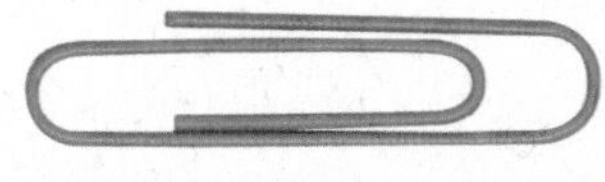

The yarn is about [2 / 4 / 6] centimeters long.

2. The paper clip is about 4 centimeters long. Robin says the string is about 7 centimeters long. Gale says the string is about 20 centimeters long.

Which girl has the better estimate? Explain.

____

____

GO DIGITAL Assessment Options Chapter Test

3. GO DEEPER Sandy's paper chain is 14 centimeters long. Tim's paper chain is 6 centimeters long. How many centimeters of paper chain do they have? Draw a diagram. Write a number sentence using a ■ for the missing number. Then solve.

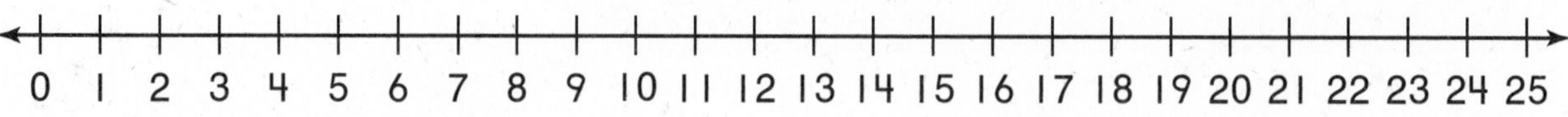

____

The paper chain is _______ centimeters long now.

4. Write the word on the tile that makes the sentence true.

centimeters	meters

A hallway is 4 __________ long.

A marker is 15 __________ long.

A toothpick is 5 __________ long.

A sofa is 2 __________ long.

Name ___________________________

5. Estimate the length of a real car. Fill in the bubble next to all the sentences that are true.

○ The car is more than 100 centimeters long.

○ The car is less than 1 meter long.

○ The car is less than 10 meters long.

○ The car is about 20 centimeters long.

○ The car is more than 150 meters long.

Personal Math Trainer

6. THINKSMARTER+ Measure the length of each object. Does the sentence describe the objects? Choose Yes or No.

______ centimeters

GREEN

______ centimeters

The marker is 11 centimeters longer than the crayon.	○ Yes	○ No
The crayon is 4 centimeters shorter than the marker.	○ Yes	○ No
The total length of the marker and the crayon is 18 centimeters.	○ Yes	○ No

7. Ethan's rope is 25 centimeters long. Ethan cuts the rope and gives a piece to Hank. Ethan's rope is now 16 centimeters long. How many centimeters of rope did Hank get from Ethan?

Draw a diagram. Write a number sentence using a ■ for the unknown number. Then solve.

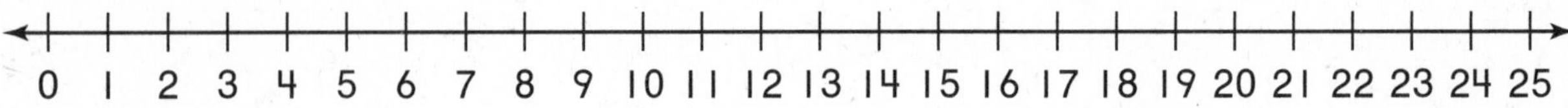

____

Hank got ________ centimeters of rope.

---

8. Measure the length of the paintbrush to the nearest centimeter. Circle the number in the box that makes the sentence true.

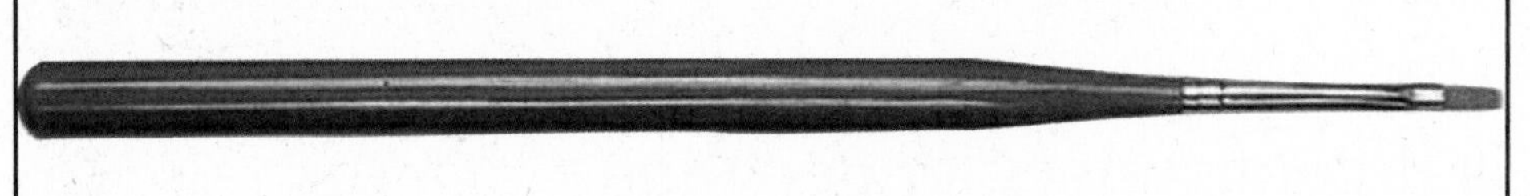

The paintbrush is about [12 / 13 / 14] centimeters long.

12
13
14

Chapter 10

Data

Curious about Math

Look at the different kinds of balloons.

What are some ways you can sort these balloons?

Name ___________________________

✓ Show What You Know

Personal Math Trainer
Online Assessment and Intervention

Read a Picture Graph

Use the picture graph.

Fruit We Like				
orange	●	●	●	●
pear	●	●		

1. How many children chose pear? ________ children

2. Circle the fruit that more children chose.

Read a Tally Chart

Complete the tally chart.

Color We Like		Total
green	|||	
red	𝍸 |	
blue	𝍸 |||	

3. How many children chose red?

________ children

4. Which color did the fewest children choose?

____

Addition and Subtraction Facts

Write the sum or difference.

5. $10 - 4 =$ ____

6. $4 + 5 =$ ____

7. $6 + 5 =$ ____

8. $9 - 3 =$ ____

9. $5 + 7 =$ ____

10. $11 - 3 =$ ____

This page checks understanding of important skills needed for success in Chapter 10.

Name ___________________________

Vocabulary Builder

Review Words

tally marks
more than
fewer than

Visualize It

Draw **tally marks** to show each number.

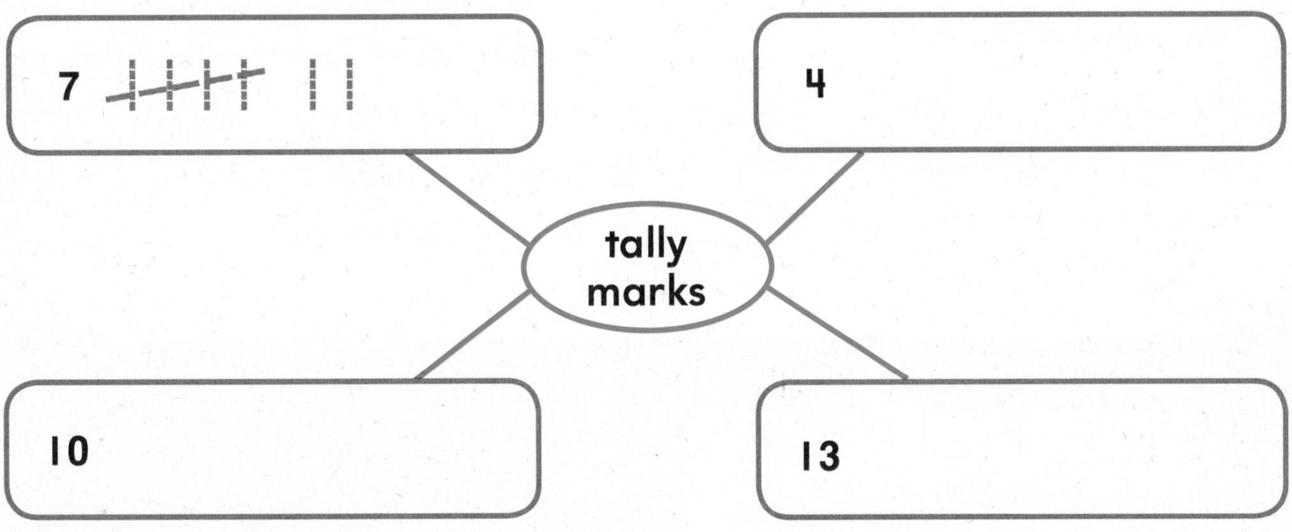

Understand Vocabulary

Write a number to complete the sentence.

1. 10 apples is **more than** ______ apples.

2. 6 bananas is **fewer than** ______ bananas.

3. ______ grapes is **more than** 6 grapes.

4. ______ oranges is **fewer than** 5 oranges.

GO DIGITAL • Interactive Student Edition • Multimedia eGlossary

Chapter 10

Game

Making Tens

Materials •  • 25 cubes
• small bag

Play with a partner.

1. Put 25 cubes in a bag.
2. Toss the number cube. Take that many cubes and put them on your ten frame. Take turns.
3. When you have 10 cubes on your ten frame, make a tally mark on the tally chart. Then put the 10 cubes back in the bag.
4. The first player to make 10 tally marks wins.

Player 1

Player 2

Making Tens

Player	Tally
Player 1	
Player 2	

Chapter 10 Vocabulary

bar graph gráfica de barras 4	**compare** comparar 8
data datos 12	**digit** dígito 15
key clave 36	**picture graph** gráfica con dibujos 48
sum suma o total 59	**survey** encuesta 60

Use these symbols when you **compare**: >, <, =.

$241 > 234$

$123 < 128$

$247 = 247$

© Houghton Mifflin Harcourt Publishing Company

Children Playing Games

Outdoor Game	
kickball	
four square	
tag	
jump rope	

0 1 2 3 4 5 6 7 8 9

Number of Children

© Houghton Mifflin Harcourt Publishing Company

0, 1, 2, 3, 4, 5, 6, 7, 8, and 9 are **digits**.

© Houghton Mifflin Harcourt Publishing Company

Favorite Lunch

Lunch	Tally
pizza	IIII
sandwich	~~IIII~~ I
salad	III
pasta	~~IIII~~

The information in this chart is called **data**.

© Houghton Mifflin Harcourt Publishing Company

Playground Toys

soccer ball	★ ★ ★
jump ropes	★
soft ball	★ ★

Key: Each ★ stands for 5 toys.

A **picture graph** uses pictures to show data.

© Houghton Mifflin Harcourt Publishing Company

Number of Soccer Games

March	⚽	⚽	⚽	⚽			
April	⚽	⚽	⚽				
May	⚽	⚽	⚽	⚽	⚽	⚽	
June	⚽	⚽	⚽	⚽	⚽	⚽	⚽

Key: Each ⚽ stands for 1 game.

The **key** tells how many each picture stands for.

© Houghton Mifflin Harcourt Publishing Company

Favorite Lunch

Lunch	Tally
pizza	IIII
sandwich	~~IIII~~ I
salad	III
pasta	~~IIII~~

A **survey** is a collection of data from answers to a question.

© Houghton Mifflin Harcourt Publishing Company

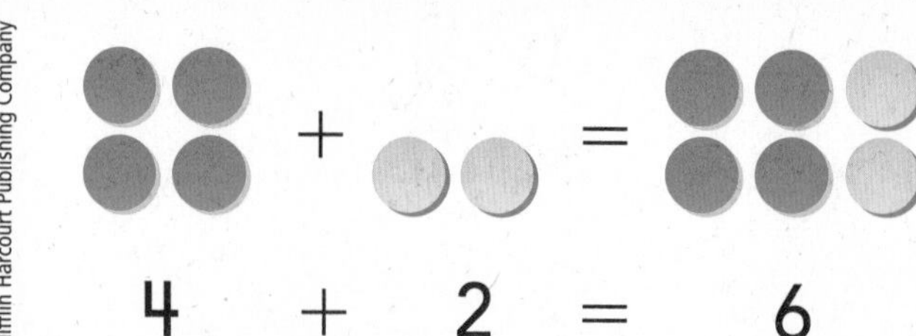

$4 + 2 = 6$

↑ sum

Picture It

Word Box
bar graph
compare
data
digit
key
picture graph
sum
survey

For 3 to 4 players

Materials

- timer
- sketch pad

How to Play

1. Choose a math word from the Word Box. Do not tell the other players.
2. Set the timer for 1 minute.
3. Draw pictures to give clues about the word. Draw only pictures and numbers.
4. The first player to guess the word gets 1 point. If that player can use the word in a sentence, he or she gets 1 more point. Then that player takes a turn.
5. The first player to score 5 points wins.

The Write Way

Reflect

Choose one idea. Write about it in the space below.

- Explain how you would take a survey and record the data.
- Tell when you would use a picture graph and a bar graph.
- Write two questions you have about the chapter we are working on.

Name ______________________________

Collect Data

Essential Question How do you use a tally chart to record data from a survey?

Learning Objective You will take a survey to collect data and then represent the data in a tally chart.

Listen and Draw

Take turns choosing a cube from the bag.
Draw a tally mark in the chart for each cube.

Cube Colors	
Color	**Tally**
blue	
red	
green	

Math Talk Math Processes and Practices 4

Use Diagrams Explain how tally marks help you keep track of what has been chosen.

HOME CONNECTION • Your child made tally marks to record the color of cubes chosen from a bag. This activity prepares children for using and recording data in this chapter.

Model and Draw

You can take a **survey** to collect **data**.
You can record the data with tally marks.

Greg asked his classmates which lunch was their favorite.

Favorite Lunch	
Lunch	**Tally**
pizza	||||
sandwich	卌 |
salad	|||
pasta	卌

The tally marks in the tally chart show the children's answers. Each tally mark stands for one child's choice.

Share and Show

1. Take a survey. Ask 10 classmates which pet is their favorite. Use tally marks to show their choices.

Favorite Pet	
Pet	**Tally**
cat	
dog	
fish	
bird	

2. How many classmates chose dog?

_______ classmates

3. Which pet did the fewest classmates choose?

____

4. Did more classmates choose cat or dog? _______________

How many more? _______ more classmates

Name ______________________________

On Your Own

5. Take a survey. Ask 10 classmates which indoor game is their favorite. Use tally marks to show their choices.

Favorite Indoor Game	
Game	**Tally**
board	
card	
computer	
puzzle	

6. How many classmates chose board game?

_______ classmates

7. Which game did the most classmates choose?

____

8. GO DEEPER Did more classmates choose a card game or a computer game?

____

How many more? _______ more classmates

9. Which game did the fewest classmates choose?

____

10. Math Processes and Practices 3 **Apply** How many classmates did not choose a board game or a puzzle? **Explain** how you know.

____

____

____

____

Problem Solving • Applications

11. THINKSMARTER Maeko asked her classmates to choose their favorite subject. She made this tally chart.

Favorite Subject	
Subject	**Tally**
reading	卌 I
math	卌 IIII
science	卌 卌

How many more classmates chose math than reading?

_________ more classmates

Write a question about the data in the chart. Then write the answer to your question.

____

____

____

12. THINKSMARTER Fill in the bubble next to all the sentences that describe data in the tally chart.

Favorite Meal	
Meal	**Tally**
breakfast	卌 III
lunch	卌 卌
dinner	卌 卌 II

○ 10 children voted for lunch.

○ 13 children voted for breakfast.

○ More children voted for dinner than for lunch.

○ A total of 35 children voted for their favorite meal.

TAKE HOME ACTIVITY • With your child, take a survey about favorite games and make a tally chart to show the data.

Name ______________________

Collect Data

Learning Objective You will take a survey to collect data and then represent the data in a tally chart.

1. Take a survey. Ask 10 classmates how they got to school. Use tally marks to show their choices.

How We Got to School	
Way	**Tally**
walk	
bus	
car	
bike	

2. How many classmates rode in a bus to school?

_____ classmates

3. How many classmates rode in a car to school?

_____ classmates

4. In which way did the fewest classmates get to school?

____

5. In which way did the most classmates get to school?

____

6. WRITE Math Explain how you would take a survey to find your classmates' favorite shirt color.

____

Lesson Check

1. Use the tally chart. Which color did the fewest children choose?

______

Favorite Color	
Color	**Tally**
blue	III
green	~~IIII~~ IIII
red	~~IIII~~ II
yellow	~~IIII~~ I

Spiral Review

2. How many dimes have the same value as $1.00?

____ dimes

3. Jared has two ropes. Each rope is 9 inches long. How many inches of rope does he have in all?

____ inches

4. The clock shows the time Lee got to school. At what time did she get to school?

____ : ____

5. Liza finished studying at half past 3. What time did Liza finish studying?

____ : ____

FOR MORE PRACTICE GO TO THE Personal Math Trainer

Name ____________________

Read Picture Graphs

Essential Question How do you use a picture graph to show data?

Learning Objective You will read data in picture graphs and use that information to solve problems.

Listen and Draw Real World

Use the tally chart to solve the problem.
Draw or write to show what you did.

Favorite Hobby	
Hobby	**Tally**
crafts	𝍸 I
reading	IIII
music	𝍸
sports	𝍸 II

_______ more children

Math Processes and Practices 

Use Reasoning Can the chart be used to find how many girls chose music? Explain.

FOR THE TEACHER • Read the following problem. Mr. Martin's class made this tally chart. How many more children in his class chose sports than chose reading as their favorite hobby?

Model and Draw

A **picture graph** uses pictures to show data.

Number of Soccer Games							
March	⚽	⚽	⚽	⚽			
April	⚽	⚽	⚽				
May	⚽	⚽	⚽	⚽	⚽	⚽	
June	⚽	⚽	⚽	⚽	⚽	⚽	⚽

Key: Each ⚽ stands for 1 game.

A **key** tells how many each picture stands for.

Share and Show

Use the picture graph to answer the questions.

Favorite Snack									
pretzels	☺	☺	☺	☺	☺	☺	☺	☺	
grapes	☺	☺	☺	☺	☺	☺	☺		
popcorn	☺	☺	☺						
apples	☺	☺	☺	☺	☺	☺			

Key: Each ☺ stands for 1 child.

✓ 1. Which snack was chosen by the fewest children? ______________

✓ 2. How many more children chose pretzels than apples? ________ more children

Name ______________________

On Your Own

Use the picture graph to answer the questions.

Number of Pencils									
Alana	✏	✏	✏						
Kiana	✏	✏	✏	✏	✏				
Dante	✏	✏	✏	✏					
Brad	✏	✏	✏	✏	✏	✏	✏	✏	

Key: Each ✏ stands for 1 pencil.

3. How many pencils do Alana and Brad have? ________ pencils

4. How many more pencils does Kiana have than Alana has? ________ more pencils

5. THINK SMARTER Mrs. Green has the same number of pencils as the four children. How many pencils does she have?

________ pencils

6. Math Processes and Practices 4 **Use Graphs** Christy has 7 pencils. Write two sentences to describe how her number of pencils compares to the data in the picture graph.

____

____

____

____

Problem Solving • Applications

Favorite Balloon Color								
green	🎈	🎈	🎈	🎈				
blue	🎈	🎈	🎈	🎈	🎈			
red	🎈	🎈	🎈	🎈	🎈	🎈	🎈	
purple	🎈	🎈	🎈	🎈				

Key: Each 🎈 stands for 1 child.

7. GO DEEPER Which three colors were chosen by a total of 13 children? ____________________

8. THINK SMARTER Use the numbers on the tiles to complete the sentence about the picture graph.

1	2	3
4	5	6

Number of Pets				
Scott	◆	◆	◆	
Andre	◆			
Maddie	◆	◆		

Key: Each ◆ stands for 1 pet.

Scott has ____ pets.

Andre has ____ fewer pets than Scott.

Maddie and Scott have ____ more pets than Andre.

TAKE HOME ACTIVITY • Have your child explain how he or she solved one of the problems in this lesson.

Name ______________________

Read Picture Graphs

Use the picture graph to answer the questions.

Learning Objective You will read data in picture graphs and use that information to solve problems.

Number of Books Read						
Ryan	📘	📘	📘	📘		
Gwen	📘	📘				
Anna	📘	📘	📘	📘	📘	📘
Henry	📘	📘	📘			

Key: Each  📘 stands for 1 book.

1. How many books in all did Henry and Anna read? ________ books

2. How many more books did Ryan read than Gwen? ______ more books

3. How many fewer books did Gwen read than Anna? ____ fewer books

Problem Solving Real World

Use the picture graph above. Write or draw to explain.

4. Carlos read 4 books. How many children read fewer books than Carlos?

____ children

5. WRITE Math Write a few sentences to describe the different parts of a picture graph.

____

____

____

Lesson Check

1. Use the picture graph. Who has the most fish?

____

Our Fish					
Jane	🐟				
Will	🐟	🐟	🐟		
Gina	🐟	🐟	🐟	🐟	
Evan	🐟	🐟			

Key: Each 🐟 stands for 1 fish.

Spiral Review

2. What time is shown on this clock?

____ : ____

3. Each unit cube is about 1 centimeter long. What is the length of the paper clip?

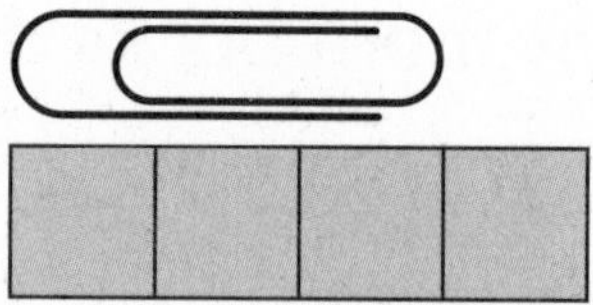

about ____ centimeters

4. What is the total value of this group of coins?

____ ¢ or ____ cents

FOR MORE PRACTICE GO TO THE **Personal Math Trainer**

Name ______________________

Make Picture Graphs

Essential Question How do you make a picture graph to show data in a tally chart?

Learning Objective You will draw a picture graph to represent a data set with up to four choices from a tally chart.

Listen and Draw

Take turns choosing a cube from the bag.
Draw a smiley face in the graph for each cube.

Cube Colors					
blue					
red					
green					
orange					

Key: Each ☺ stands for 1 cube.

Math Processes and Practices 6

Explain how you know that the number of smiley faces for blue matches the number of blue cubes.

HOME CONNECTION • Your child made a graph by recording smiley faces for the colors of cubes taken from a bag. This activity prepares children for working with picture graphs in this lesson.

Model and Draw

Each picture in the graph stands for 1 flower.
Draw pictures to show the data in the tally chart.

Number of Flowers Picked	
Name	**Tally**
Jessie	|||
Inez	卌
Paulo	||||

Number of Flowers Picked					
Jessie	(oval)	(oval)	(oval)		
Inez					
Paulo					

Key: Each (oval) stands for 1 flower.

Share and Show

1. Use the tally chart to complete the picture graph.
   Draw a ☺ for each child.

Favorite Sandwich	
Sandwich	**Tally**
cheese	卌
ham	||
tuna	||||
turkey	|||

Favorite Sandwich					
cheese					
ham					
tuna					
turkey					

Key: Each ☺ stands for 1 child.

✓2. How many children chose tuna? ________ children

✓3. How many more children chose cheese than ham? ________ more children

Name ________________________________

On Your Own

4. Use the tally chart to complete the picture graph. Draw a ☺ for each child.

Favorite Fruit	
Fruit	**Tally**
apple	IIII
plum	II
banana	~~IIII~~
orange	III

Favorite Fruit					
apple					
plum					
banana					
orange					

Key: Each ☺ stands for 1 child.

5. How many children chose banana? ________ children

6. How many fewer children chose plum than banana? ________ fewer children

7. THINK SMARTER How many children chose a fruit that was not a plum?

________ children

8. GO DEEPER Which three fruits were chosen by a total of 10 children?

____

TAKE HOME ACTIVITY • Ask your child to explain how to read the picture graph on this page.

Name ______________________________

Mid-Chapter Checkpoint

Concepts and Skills

Use the picture graph to answer the questions.

Favorite Season									
spring	☺	☺	☺	☺	☺	☺			
summer	☺	☺	☺	☺	☺	☺	☺	☺	
fall	☺	☺	☺	☺					
winter	☺	☺	☺	☺	☺	☺	☺		

Key: Each ☺ stands for 1 child.

1. Which season did the fewest children choose? ______________

2. How many more children chose spring than fall? ______ more children

3. How many children chose a season that was not winter? ______ children

4. THINK SMARTER How many children chose a favorite season?

   ______ children

   Draw tally marks to show this number.

   ____

Name ______________________________

Make Picture Graphs

Learning Objective You will draw a picture graph to represent a data set with up to four choices from a tally chart.

1. Use the tally chart to complete the picture graph. Draw a ☺ for each child.

Favorite Cookie	
Cookie	**Tally**
chocolate	III
oatmeal	I
peanut butter	~~IIII~~
shortbread	IIII

Favorite Cookie					
chocolate					
oatmeal					
peanut butter					
shortbread					

Key: Each ☺ stands for 1 child.

2. How many children chose chocolate? ____ children

3. How many fewer children chose oatmeal than peanut butter? ____ fewer children

4. Which cookie did the most children choose?

____

5. How many children in all chose a favorite cookie? ____ children

6. Look at the picture graph above. Write about the information shown in this graph.

____

____

Lesson Check

I. Use the picture graph. How many more rainy days were there in April than in May?

____ more rainy days

Number of Rainy Days					
March	☂	☂	☂	☂	☂
April	☂	☂	☂	☂	
May	☂	☂			

Key: Each ☂ stands for I day.

Spiral Review

2. Rita has one $I bill, 2 quarters, and 3 dimes. What is the total value of Rita's money?

$________

3. Lucas put 4 quarters and 3 nickels into his coin bank. How much money did Lucas put into his coin bank?

$________

4. Use a centimeter ruler. What is the length of this string to the nearest centimeter?

____ centimeters

5. What is the total value of this group of coins?

____ ¢ or ____ cents

FOR MORE PRACTICE GO TO THE Personal Math Trainer

Name ____________________

Read Bar Graphs

Essential Question How is a bar graph used to show data?

Learning Objective You will read data in bar graphs and use that information to solve problems.

Listen and Draw Real World

Use the picture graph to solve the problem. Draw or write to show what you did.

Red Trucks Seen Last Week								
Morgan	■	■	■					
Terrell	■	■	■	■	■	■		
Jazmin	■	■	■	■	■	■	■	■
Carlos	■	■	■	■				

Key: Each ■ stands for 1 red truck.

_______ red trucks

Math Processes and Practices 

Describe Relationships Describe how the data in the graph for Terrell and for Jazmin are different.

FOR THE TEACHER • Read this problem to children. Morgan made a picture graph to show the number of red trucks that she and her friends saw last week. How many red trucks did the four children see last week?

Model and Draw

A **bar graph** uses bars to show data.
Look at where the bars end.
This tells how many.

There are 8 children playing soccer.

Share and Show

Use the bar graph.

1. How many green marbles are in the bag?

   _______ green marbles

2. How many more blue marbles than purple marbles are in the bag?

   _______ more blue marbles

3. How many marbles are in the bag?

   _______ marbles

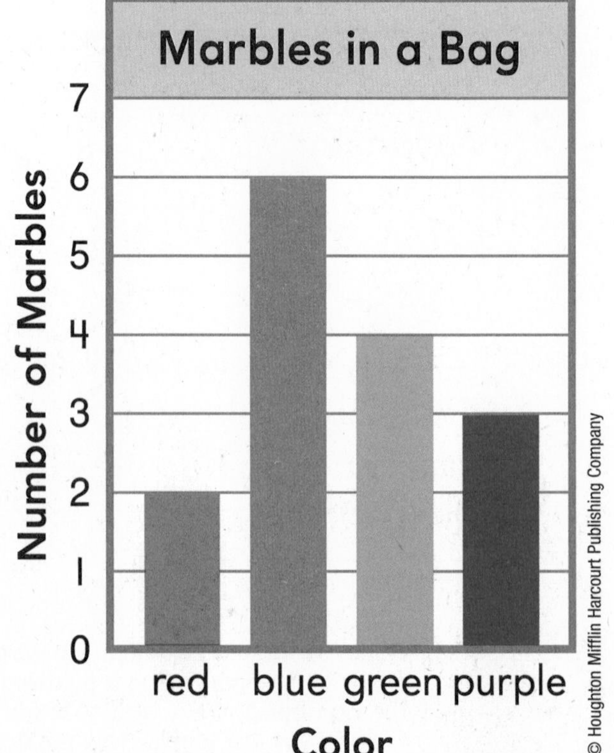

Name ________________________________

On Your Own

Use the bar graph.

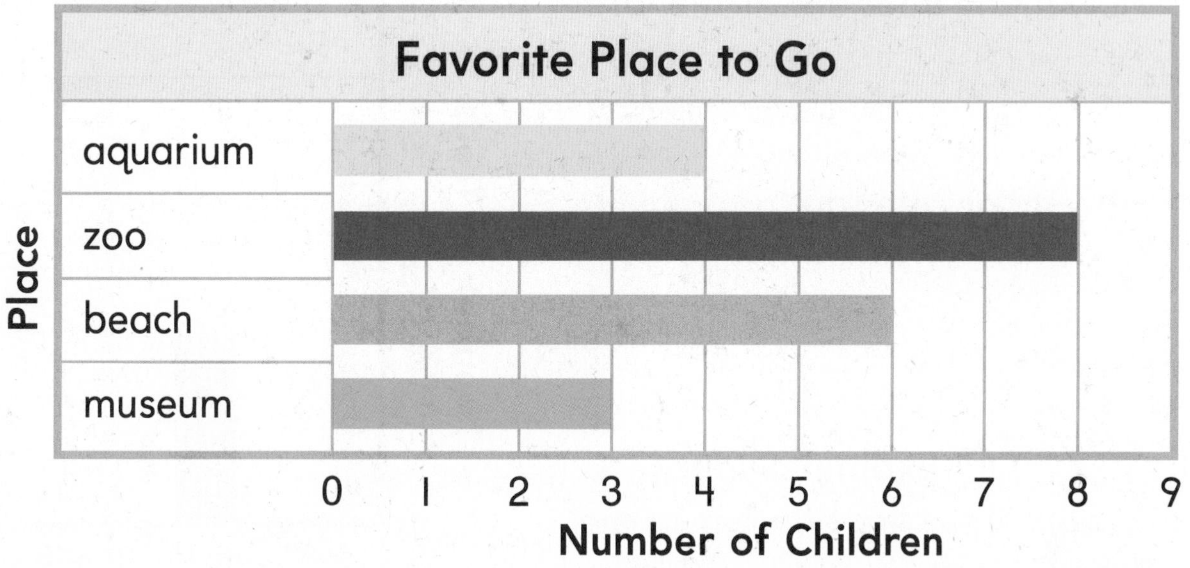

4. How many children chose the beach?

_______ children

5. Which place did the fewest children choose?

____

6. How many more children chose the zoo than the aquarium?

_______ more children

7. GO DEEPER How many children chose a place that was not the zoo?

_______ children

8. THINK SMARTER Greg chose a place that has more votes than the aquarium and the museum together. Which place did Greg choose?

____

Problem Solving • Applications

Use the bar graph.

9. How many trees are at the farm?

_______ trees

10. How many trees are not apple trees?

_______ trees

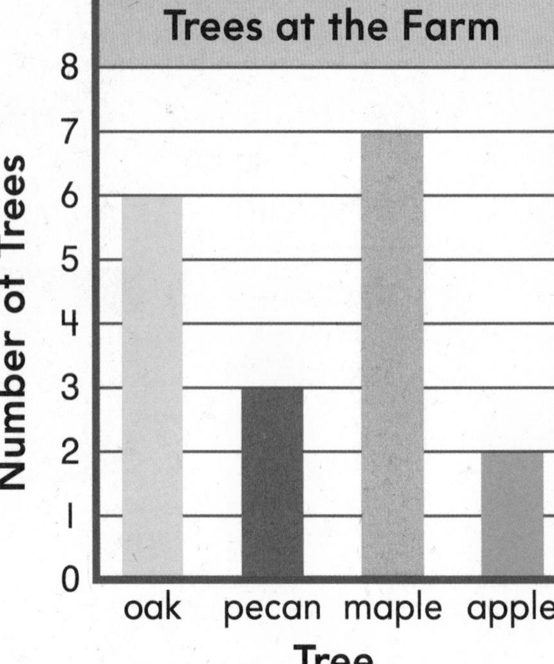

11. Math Processes and Practices 6 **Explain** Suppose 7 more trees are brought to the farm. How many trees would be at the farm then? Explain.

____

____

____

____

12. THINK SMARTER Use the data in the bar graph about trees to finish the sentences.

There are _____ fewer apple trees than oak trees. Explain.

____

TAKE HOME ACTIVITY • Ask your child to explain how to read a bar graph.

Name ______________________

Read Bar Graphs

Learning Objective You will read data in bar graphs and use that information to solve problems.

Use the bar graph.

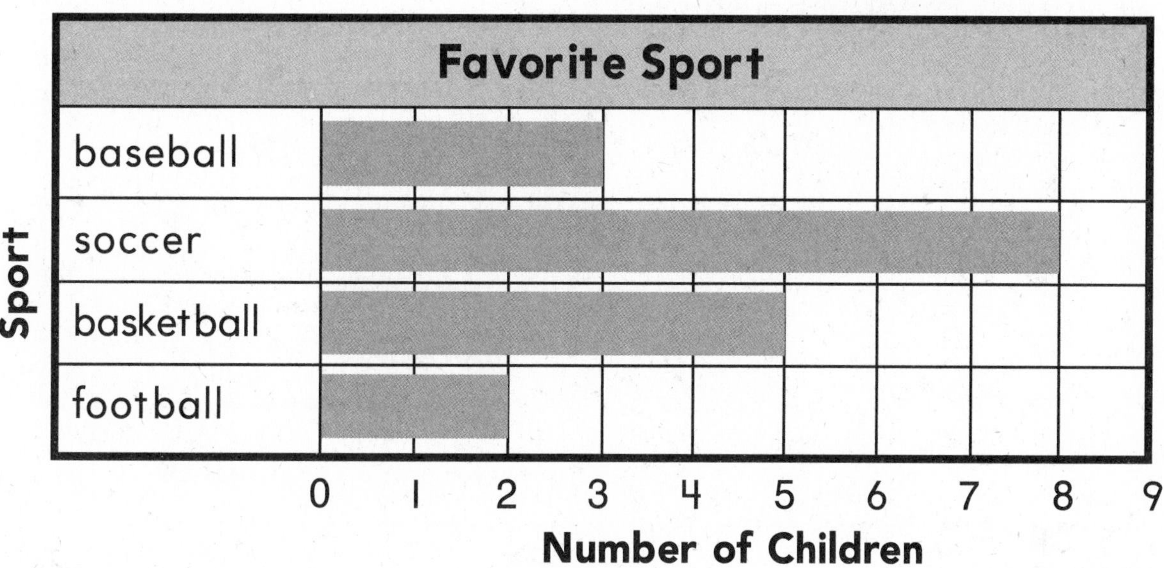

1. How many children chose basketball? _____ children

2. Which sport did the most children choose? _____________

3. How many more children chose basketball than baseball? _____ more children

4. Which sport did the fewest children choose? _____________

Problem Solving Real World

5. How many children chose baseball or basketball?

_____ children

6. WRITE Math Look at the bar graph above. Write about the information shown in the graph.

____
____
____

Lesson Check

1. Use the bar graph. How many shells do the children have in all?

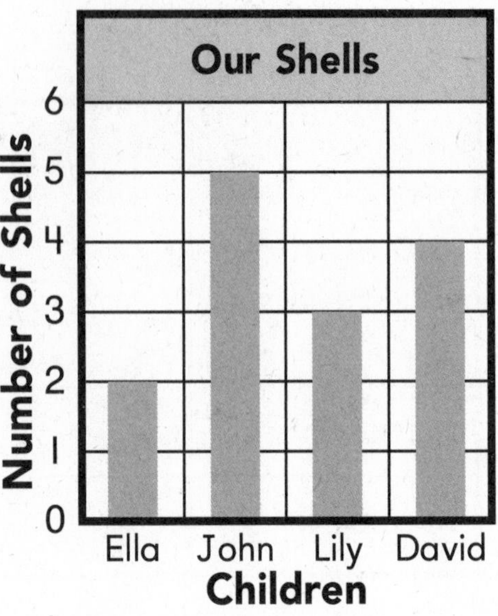

____ shells

Spiral Review

2. Use the line plot. How many twigs are 3 inches long?

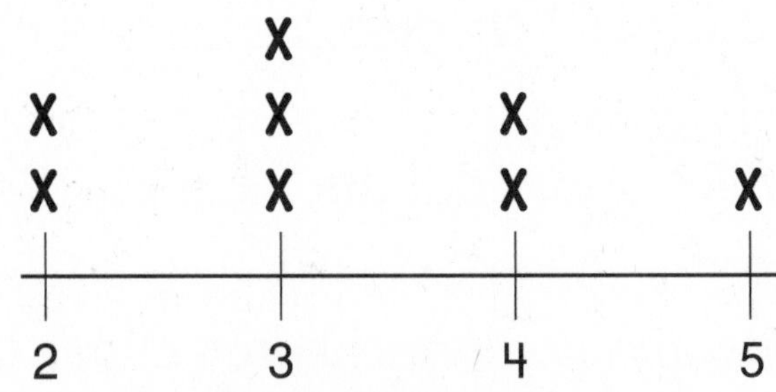

____ twigs

3. Use a centimeter ruler. What is the length of the yarn to the nearest centimeter?

____ centimeters

4. Noah uses 1 quarter and 2 nickels to pay for a pencil. How much money does he pay for the pencil?

____ ¢ or ____ cents

FOR MORE PRACTICE GO TO THE Personal Math Trainer

Name ______________________________

Make Bar Graphs

Essential Question How do you make a bar graph to show data?

Learning Objective You will draw a bar graph to represent a data set with up to four choices.

Listen and Draw (Real World)

Use the bar graph to solve the problem. Draw or write to show what you did.

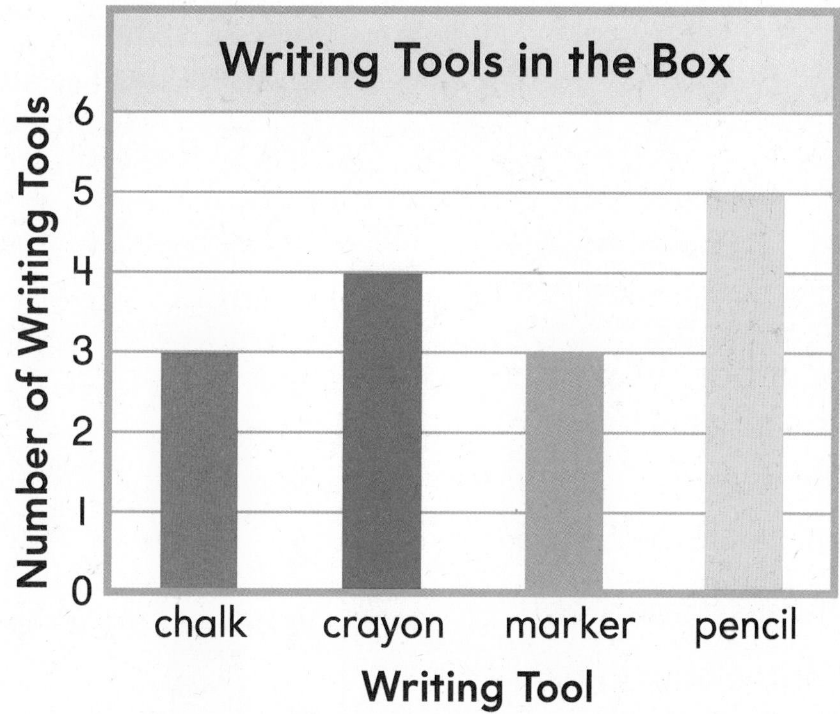

_______ writing tools

Math Processes and Practices 

Compare Representations
Describe how the information in the graph for crayon and for marker is different.

FOR THE TEACHER • Read the following problem. Barry made this bar graph. How many writing tools are in the box?

Model and Draw

Abel read 2 books, Jiang read 4 books, Cara read 1 book, and Jamila read 3 books.

Complete the bar graph to show this data.

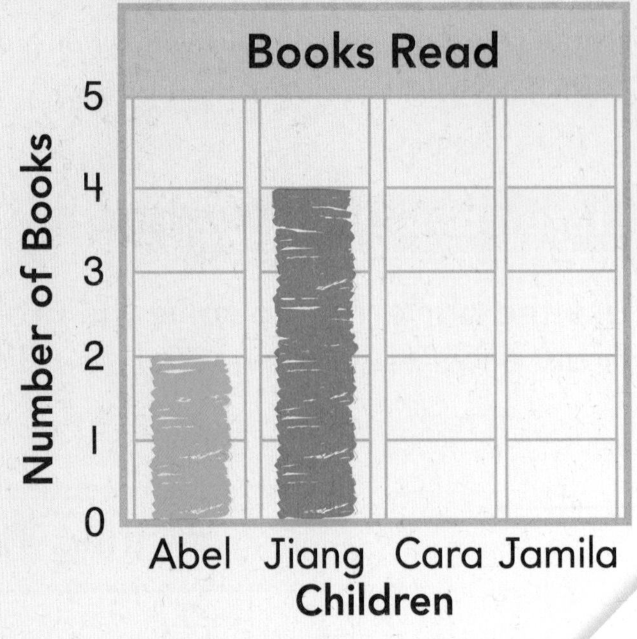

Share and Show

Ella is making a bar graph to show the kinds of pets her classmates have.

- 5 classmates have a dog.
- 7 classmates have a cat.
- 2 classmates have a bird.
- 3 classmates have fish.

1. Write labels and draw bars to complete the graph.

2. How will the graph change if one more child gets a bird?

____

____

____

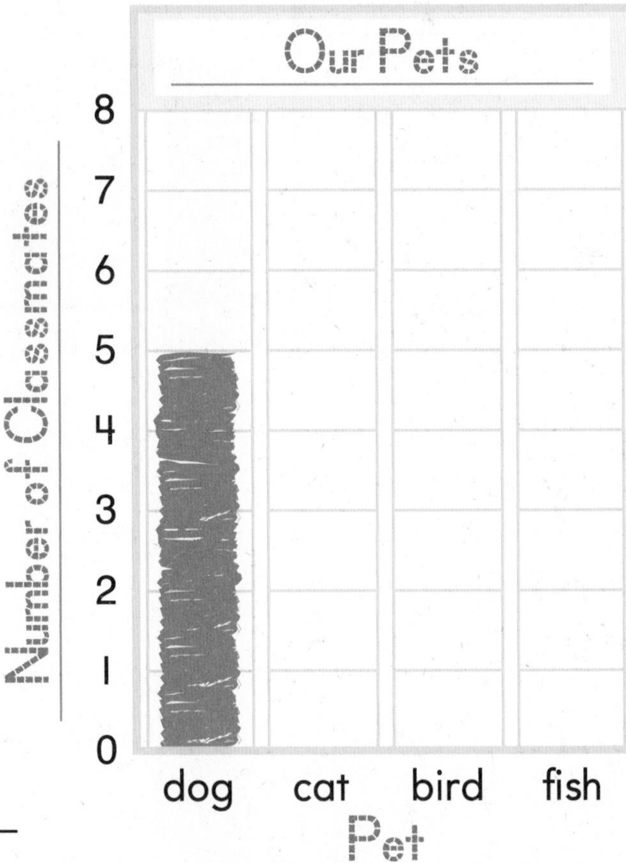

Name ________________________

On Your Own

Dexter asked his classmates which pizza topping is their favorite.

- 4 classmates chose peppers.
- 7 classmates chose meat.
- 5 classmates chose mushrooms.
- 2 classmates chose olives.

3. Write a title and labels for the bar graph.

4. Draw bars in the graph to show the data.

________________										
peppers										
meat										
mushrooms										
olives										
	0	1	2	3	4	5	6	7	8	9	10

____

5. Which topping did the most classmates choose? ____________

6. THINK SMARTER Did more classmates choose peppers and olives than meat? Explain.

____

____

____

Problem Solving • Applications

Cody asked his classmates which zoo animal is their favorite.

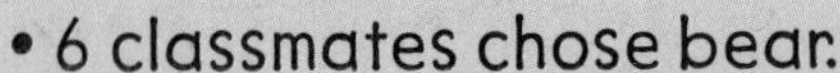

- 6 classmates chose bear.
- 4 classmates chose lion.
- 7 classmates chose tiger.
- 3 classmates chose zebra.

7. Use the data to complete the bar graph. Write a title and labels. Draw bars.

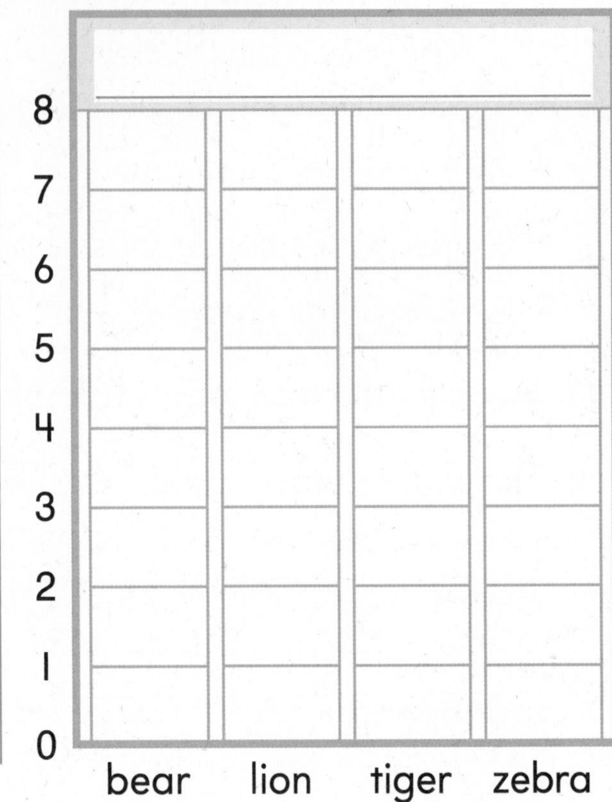

8. GO DEEPER How many fewer classmates chose lion than classmates that chose the other zoo animals?

_______ fewer classmates

Personal Math Trainer

9. THINK SMARTER + Look at the bar graph above. Suppose 2 of Cody's classmates chose zebra instead of bear. Explain how the bar graph would change.

____

____

____

TAKE HOME ACTIVITY • Ask your child to describe how to make a bar graph to show data.

Name ______________________

Make Bar Graphs

Learning Objective You will draw a bar graph to represent a data set with up to four choices.

Maria asked her friends how many hours they practice soccer each week.

- Jessie practices for 3 hours.
- Victor practices for 2 hours.
- Samantha practices for 5 hours.
- David practices for 6 hours.

1. Write a title and labels for the bar graph.

2. Draw bars in the graph to show the data.

______________________										
Jessie										
Victor										
Samantha										
David										

0 1 2 3 4 5 6 7 8 9 10

____

3. Which friend practices soccer for the most hours each week? ______________

Problem Solving Real World

4. Which friends practice soccer for fewer than 4 hours each week? ______________

5. WRITE Math Look at the bar graph above. Describe how you shaded bars to show the data. ______________

____

Lesson Check

1. Use the bar graph. How many more children chose summer than spring?

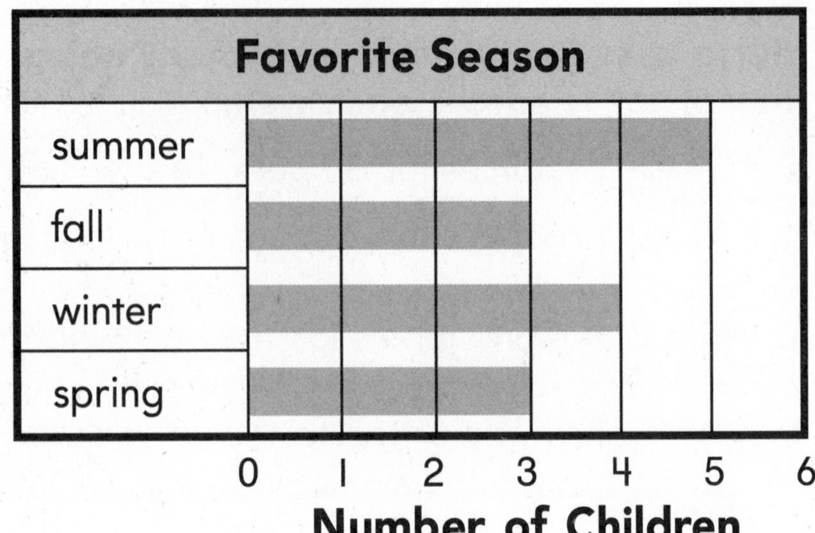

____ more children

Spiral Review

2. Rachel's chain is 22 centimeters long. She takes 9 centimeters off the chain. How long is Rachel's chain now?

____ centimeters

3. Use an inch ruler. What is the length of the yarn to the nearest inch?

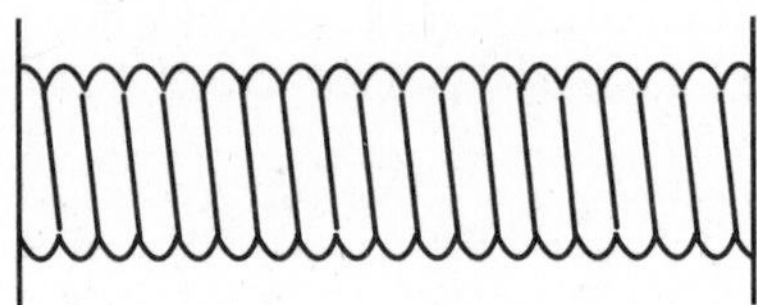

____ inches

4. Gail finished studying at quarter past 1. What time did Gail finish studying?

____ : ____

5. Jill has two $1 bills, 1 quarter, and 1 nickel. How much money does Jill have?

$________

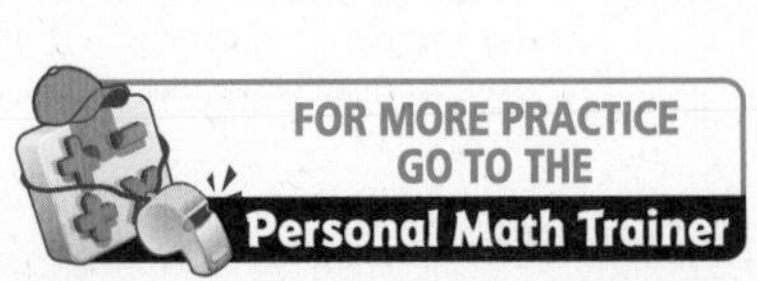

Name ______________________________

Problem Solving • Display Data

Essential Question How does making a bar graph help when solving problems about data?

Learning Objective You will use the strategy *make a graph* to solve problems about data.

Maria recorded the rainfall in her town for four months. How did the amount of rainfall change from September to December?

September	4 inches
October	3 inches
November	2 inches
December	1 inch

Unlock the Problem

What do I need to find?

how the amount of rainfall changed from September to December

What information do I need to use?

the amount of rainfall in each of the four months

Show how to solve the problem.

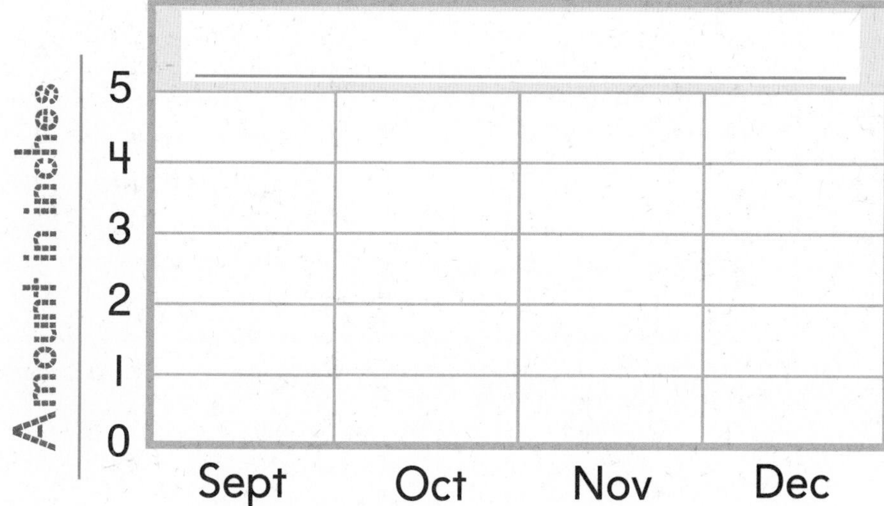

____

The amount of rainfall ______________________________

____

HOME CONNECTION • Your child made a bar graph to show the data. Making a graph helps your child organize data to solve problems.

Try Another Problem

Make a bar graph to solve the problem.

- What do I need to find?
- What information do I need to use?

I. Matthew measured the height of his plant once a week for four weeks. Describe how the height of the plant changed from May 1 to May 22.

May 1	2 inches
May 8	3 inches
May 15	5 inches
May 22	7 inches

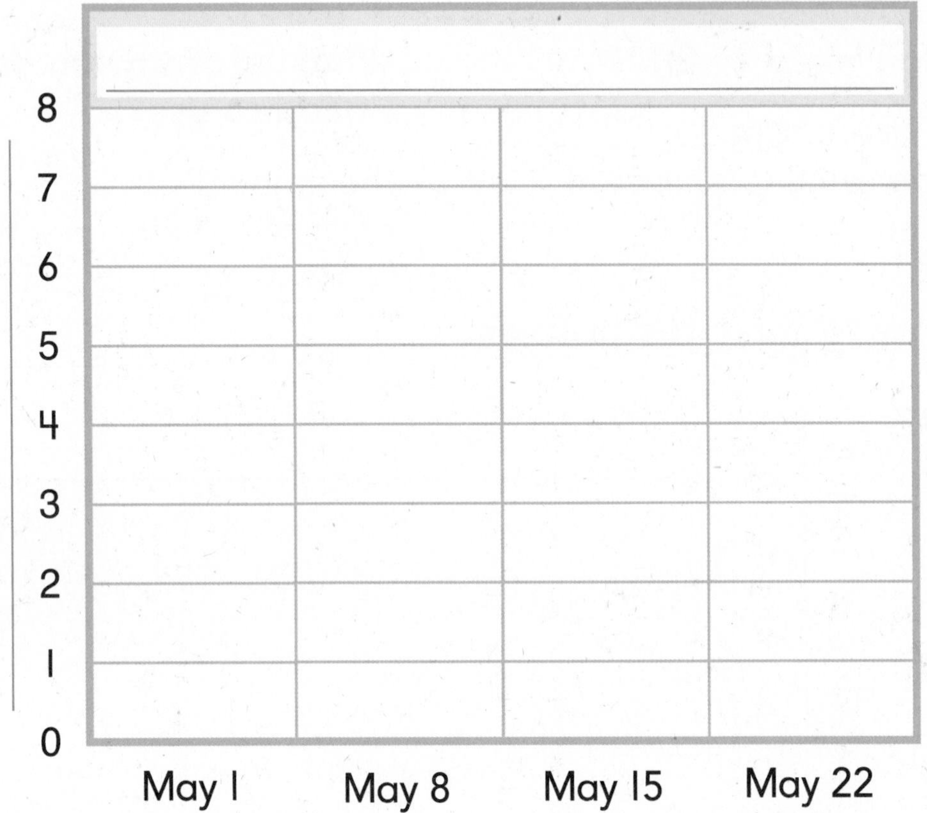

The height of the plant ______________________

____

Math Processes and Practices 

How many inches did the plant grow from May 1 to May 22? **Explain.**

Name ___________________________

Share and Show

MATH BOARD

Make a bar graph to solve the problem.

Week 1	1 hour
Week 2	2 hours
Week 3	4 hours
Week 4	5 hours

2. Bianca wrote the number of hours that she practiced playing guitar in June. Describe how the amount of practice time changed from Week 1 to Week 4.

The amount of practice time ___________________________

____

3. THINKSMARTER If Bianca's practice time is 4 hours in Week 5, how does her practice time change from Week 1 to Week 5?

____

____

____

Problem Solving • Applications

4. How many strings are 9 inches long?

_______ strings

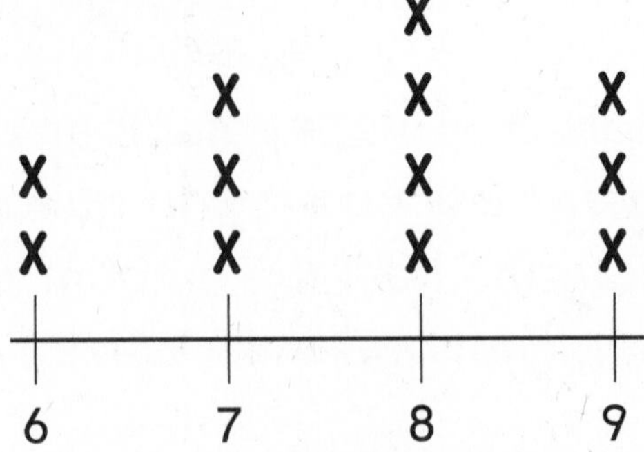

5. GO DEEPER How many strings are more than 6 inches long?

_______ strings

Personal Math Trainer

6. THINK SMARTER+ David measured the snowfall for four weeks. Fill in the bubble next to all the sentences that describe the data. Make a bar graph to solve the problem.

Week 1	1 inch
Week 2	2 inches
Week 3	3 inches
Week 4	4 inches

- ○ There were 2 inches of snow in Week 2.
- ○ The amount of snowfall increased each week.
- ○ Snowfall decreased from Week 3 to Week 4.
- ○ There were a total of 4 inches of snow in Week 2 and Week 3.
- ○ There were 3 more inches of snow in Week 4 than in Week 1.

TAKE HOME ACTIVITY • Have your child explain how he or she solved one of the problems in this lesson.

Name ______________________________

Problem Solving • Display Data

Learning Objective You will use the strategy *make a graph* to solve problems about data.

Make a bar graph to solve the problem.

1. The list shows the number of books that Abby read each month. Describe how the number of books she read changed from February to May.

February	8 books
March	7 books
April	6 books
May	4 books

______________________										
February										
March										
April										
May										

0 1 2 3 4 5 6 7 8 9 10

____

The number of books read ______________________________

____

2. How many books in all did Abby read in February and March? ____ books

3. In which months did Abby read fewer than 7 books? ______________

4. WRITE Math Explain how you decided where the bar for March should end. ______________

____

Lesson Check

1. Use the bar graph. Describe how the amount of practice time changed from Week 1 to Week 4.

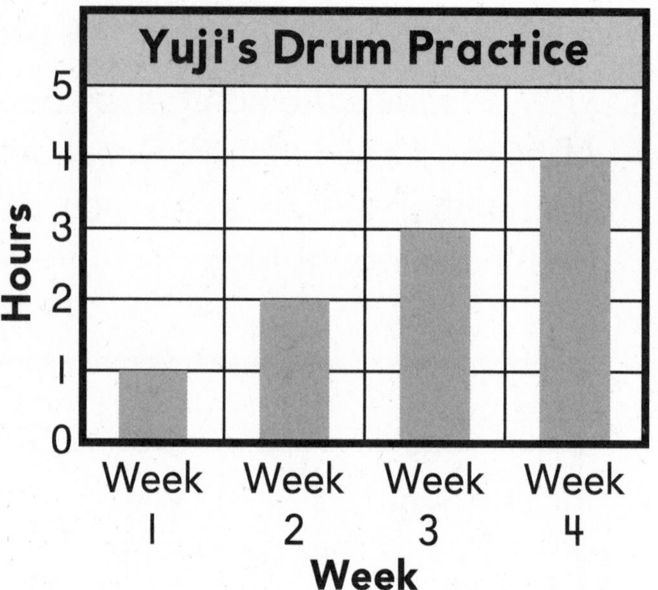

The amount of practice time

____

____

____

Spiral Review

2. The string is about 10 centimeters long.
Circle the best estimate for the length of the feather.

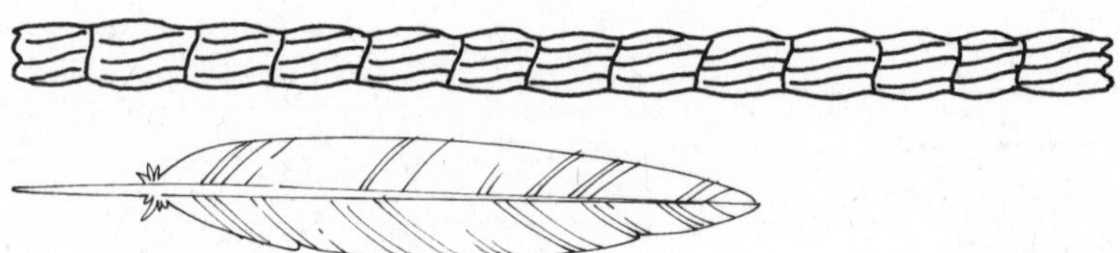

2 centimeters   3 centimeters   7 centimeters

3. What is the total value of this group of coins?

____ ¢ or ____ cents

4. Rick has one $1 bill, 2 dimes, and 3 pennies. How much money does Rick have?

$________

FOR MORE PRACTICE GO TO THE Personal Math Trainer

Name ______________________________

Chapter 10 Review/Test

1. Hara asked her friends to choose their favorite yogurt flavor. Use the data to make a tally chart.

peach - 3 friends
berry - 5 friends
lime - 2 friends
vanilla - 7 friends

Favorite Yogurt Flavor	
Yogurt	**Tally**
peach	
berry	
lime	
vanilla	

2. Does the sentence describe the data in the tally chart above? Choose Yes or No.

7 friends chose berry and peach together	○ Yes	○ No
More friends chose peach than lime	○ Yes	○ No
More friends chose vanilla than any other flavor.	○ Yes	○ No

3. Hara asked 5 more friends to choose their favorite flavor. 3 friends chose berry and 2 friends chose lime. Do more friends like berry or vanilla now? Explain.

____

____

____

GO DIGITAL Assessment Options Chapter Test

4. Teresa counted the leaves on her plant once a month for four months. Describe how the number of leaves on the plant changed from May 1 to August 1. Make a bar graph to solve the problem.

May 1	2 leaves
June 1	4 leaves
July 1	6 leaves
August 1	8 leaves

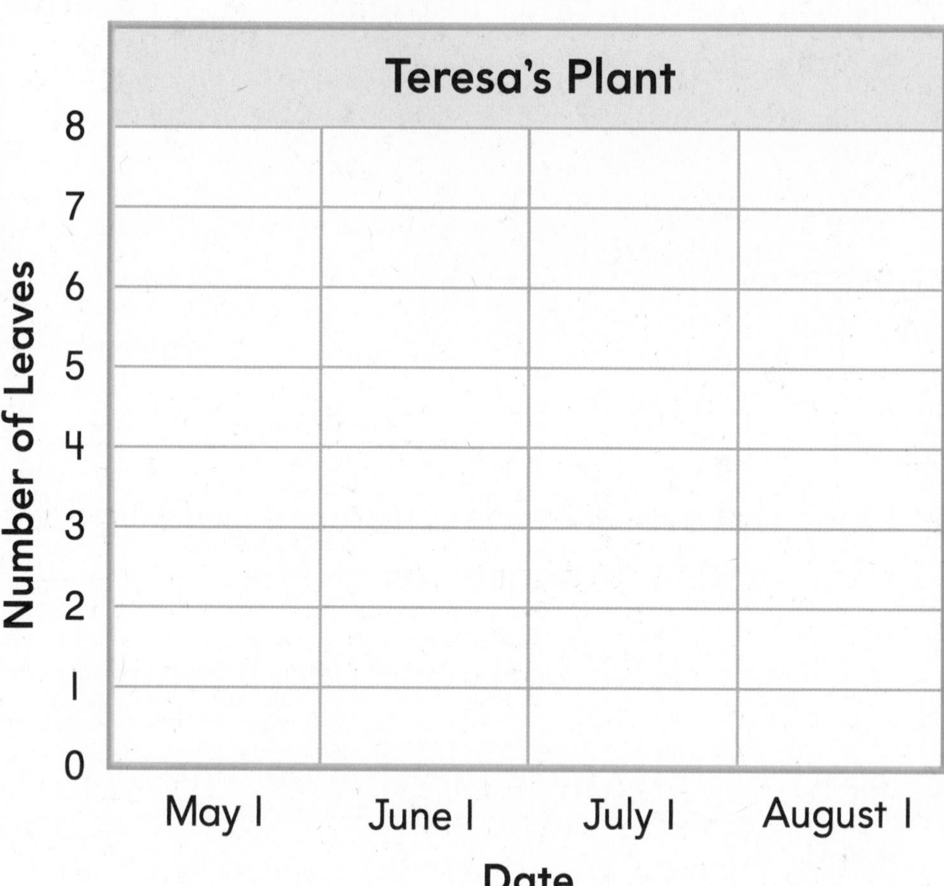

The number of leaves on the plant ________________

____

5. If Teresa counts 9 leaves on September 1, how will the number of leaves change from May 1 to September 1?

____

____

Name ____________________

6. Use the tally chart to complete the picture graph. Draw a ☺ for each child.

Favorite Recess Game	
tag	I
hopscotch	~~IIII~~
kickball	III
jacks	II

Favorite Recess Game					
tag					
hopscotch					
kickball					
jacks					

Key: Each ☺ stands for 1 child.

7. How many children chose hopscotch?

_______ children

8. How many fewer children chose tag than kickball?

_______ fewer children

9. GO DEEPER Which two games were chosen by a total of 4 children?

____

10. Mr. Sanchez asked the children in his class to name their favorite type of book. Use the data to complete the bar graph.

8 children chose fiction
4 children chose science
6 children chose history
9 children chose poetry

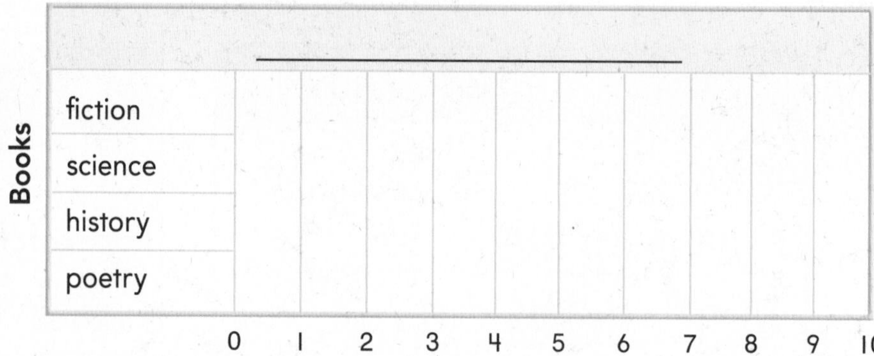

Personal Math Trainer

11. THINK SMARTER+ Fill in the bubble next to all the sentences that describe the data in the bar graph above.

- ○ 8 children chose fiction.
- ○ Fewer children chose fiction than history.
- ○ 3 more children chose history than science.
- ○ More children chose poetry than any other kind of book.

12. Did more children choose science and history books together than poetry books? Explain.

____

____

13. How many children chose a book that is not fiction?

______ children

A Farmer's Job

by Tami Morton

BIG IDEA Describe, analyze, and draw two- and three-dimensional shapes. Develop a conceptual understanding of fractions.

A farmer's job is never done. Farmers are busy during all of the seasons of the year. They grow fruits and vegetables for people to eat.

What shapes do you see?

____

Why is a farmer's work important?

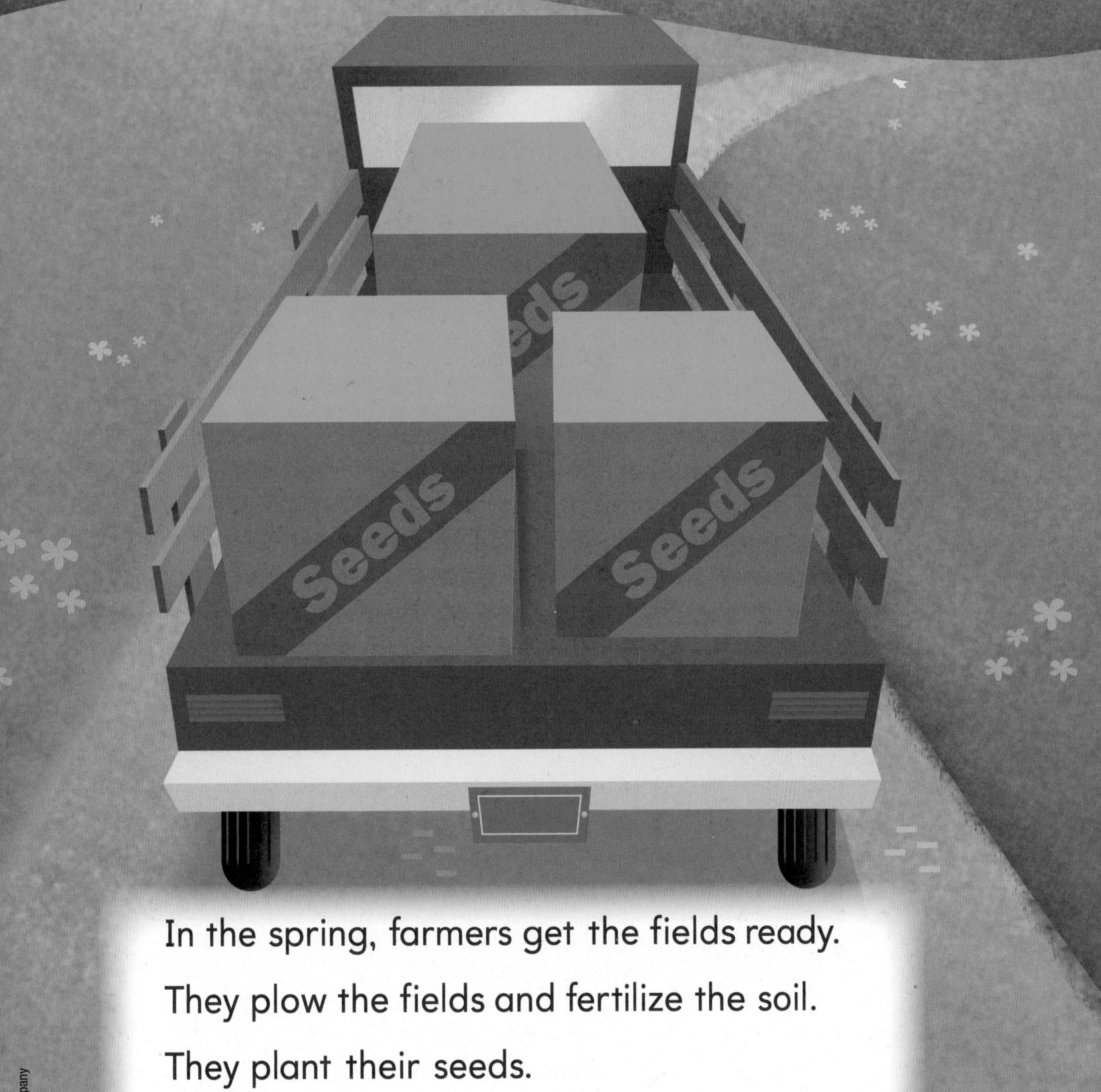

In the spring, farmers get the fields ready.

They plow the fields and fertilize the soil.

They plant their seeds.

What shapes do you see?

____

Social Studies

How is a farmer's work today different from long ago?

In the summer, farmers take care of their crops. They make sure that the plants have enough water when it does not rain. What shapes do you see?

____

Social Studies

Why does a farmer need to know about changes in the weather?

In the fall, farmers harvest many fruits and vegetables. They sell most of these fruits and vegetables to other people. What shapes do you see?

____

Why does a farmer grow more fruits and vegetables than his or her family can eat?

In the winter, farmers clear the fields and get ready for the next season. They plan what they are going to plant. They check their machines. A farmer's job is never done. What shapes do you see?

____

Why are the seasons important to a farmer?

Name ________________________________

Write About the Story

Look at the pictures of the farm objects. Draw a picture and write your own story about the objects. Tell about the shapes that the objects look like.

Vocabulary Review

cylinder	cube
cone	circle
sphere	triangle
square	rectangle
rectangular prism	

WRITE Math

____

____

____

____

____

What shape do you see?

Draw a line to match the shape with the name.

cylinder

rectangular prism

circle

Circle each shape that has a curved surface.

cylinder

rectangular prism

cube

cone

sphere

Write a riddle about a shape. Ask a classmate to read the riddle and name the shape.

Geometry and Fraction Concepts

Curious about Math

Hot air rises. A balloon filled with hot air will float up into the sky.

Some balloons look as though they have two-dimensional shapes on them. Name some two-dimensional shapes. Then draw some examples of them.

Name ________________________________

Equal Parts

Circle the shape that has two equal parts.

1. 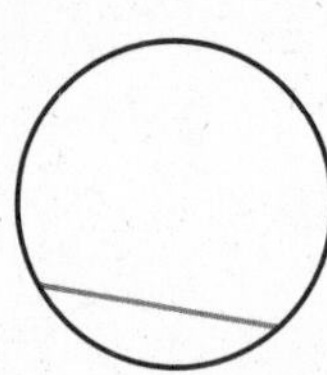 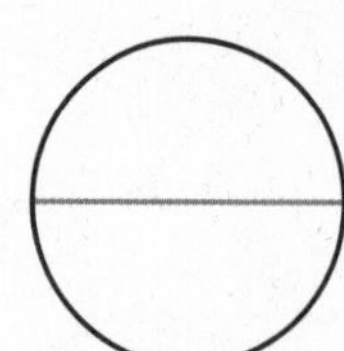

2. 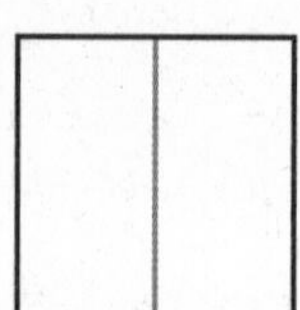 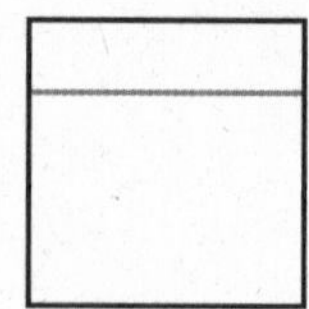

Identify Three-Dimensional Shapes

3. Circle each ● .

4. Circle each ▢ .

Identify Shapes

Circle all the shapes that match the shape name.

5. triangle 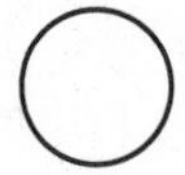 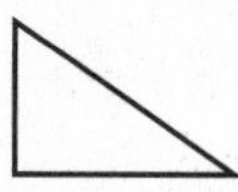 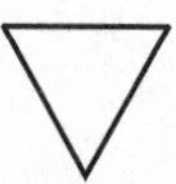 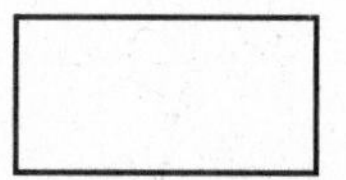

6. rectangle   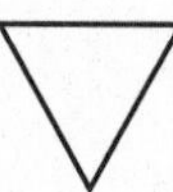 

This page checks understanding of important skills needed for success in Chapter 11.

Name ________________________________

Vocabulary Builder

Review Words
equal parts
shape
rectangle
triangle
square

Visualize It

Draw pictures to complete the graphic organizer.

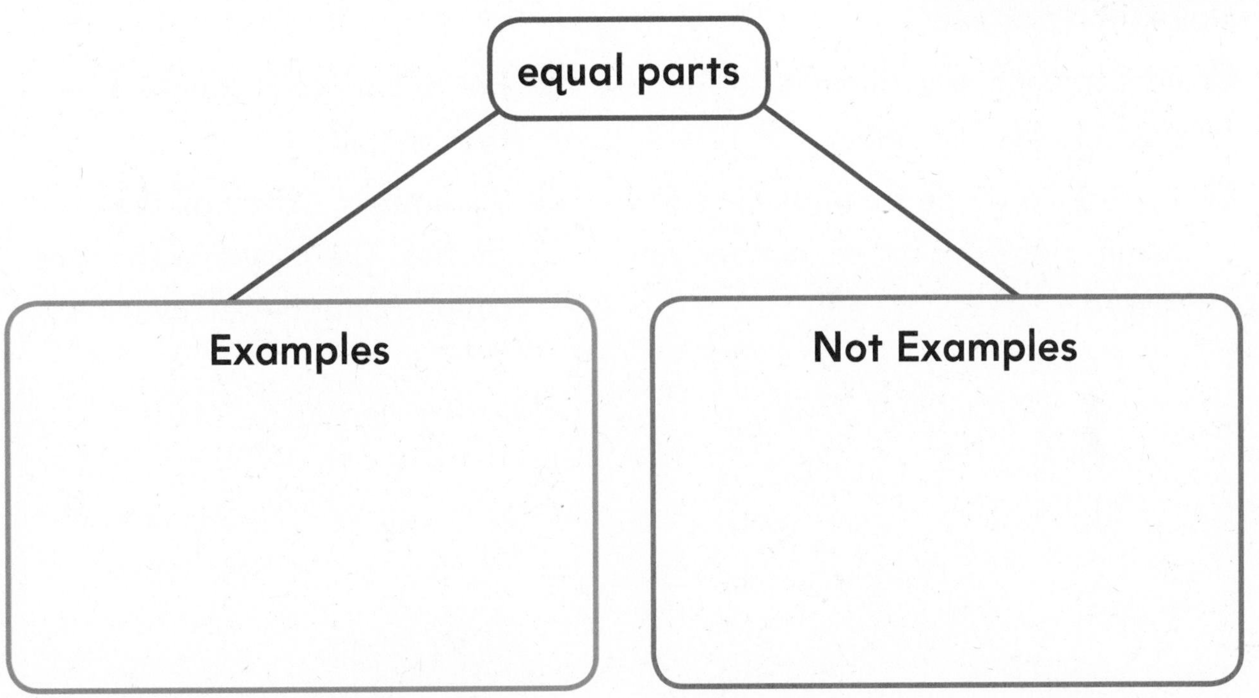

Understand Vocabulary

Draw a **shape** to match the shape name.

rectangle	triangle	square

GO DIGITAL
- Interactive Student Edition
- Multimedia eGlossary

Game

Count the Sides

Materials • 1  • 10  • 10

Play with a partner.

1. Toss the . If you toss a 1 or a 2, toss the again.
2. Look for a shape that has the same number of sides as the number you tossed.
3. Put one of your counters on that shape.
4. Take turns. Cover all the shapes. The player with more counters on the board wins.

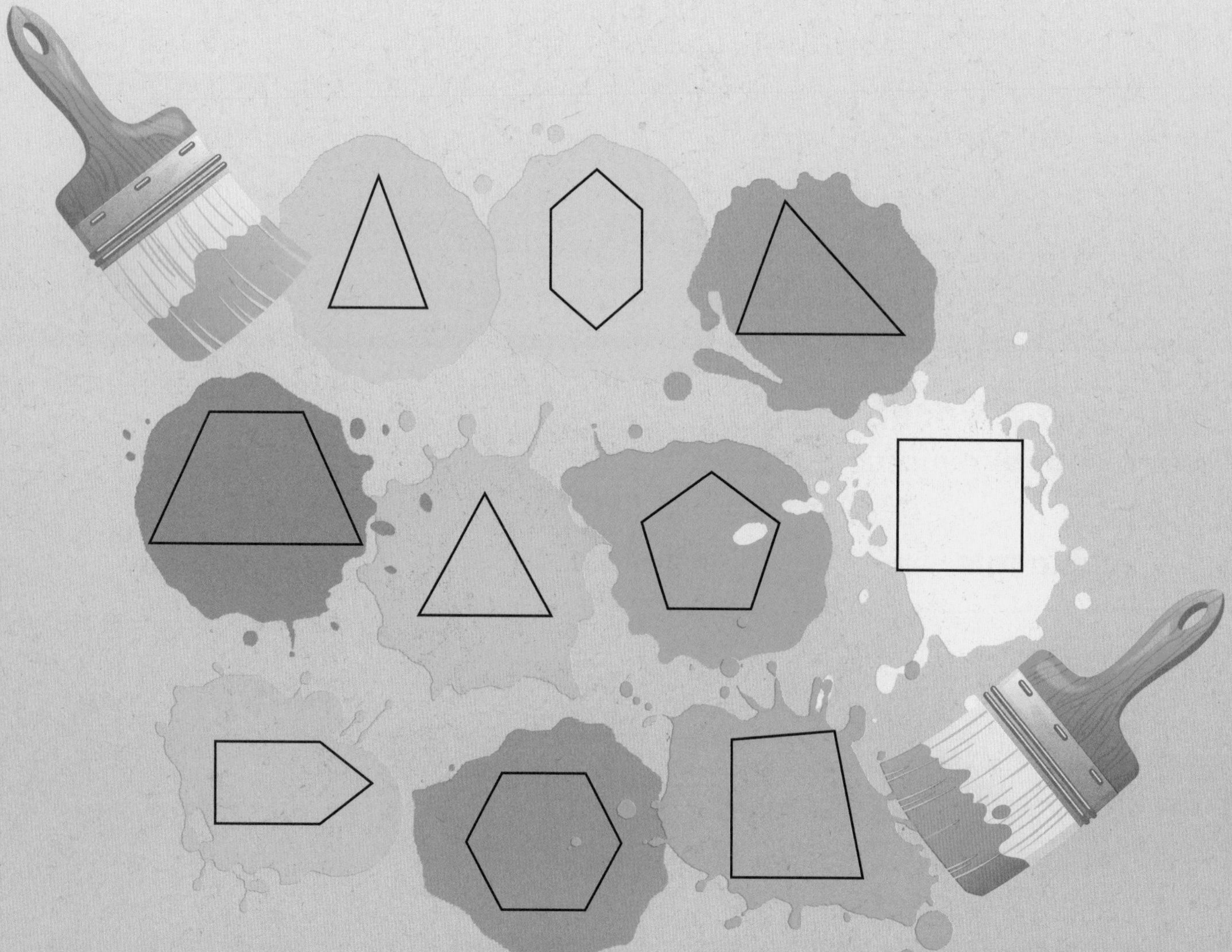

Chapter 11 Vocabulary

angle ángulo 3	**cone** cono 9
cube cubo 10	**cylinder** cilindro 11
edge arista 20	**face** cara 23
fourth of cuarto de 25	**fourths** cuartos 26

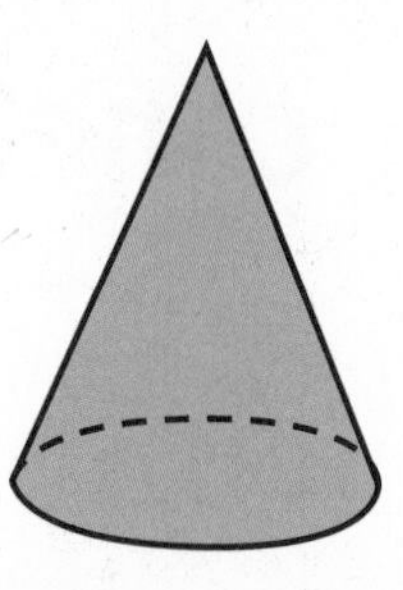

© Houghton Mifflin Harcourt Publishing Company

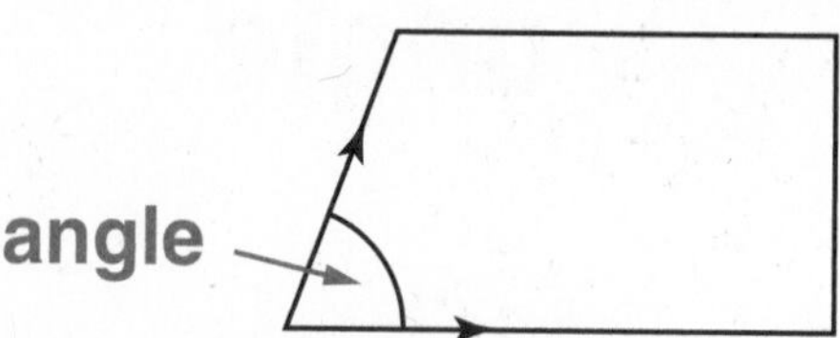

© Houghton Mifflin Harcourt Publishing Company

© Houghton Mifflin Harcourt Publishing Company

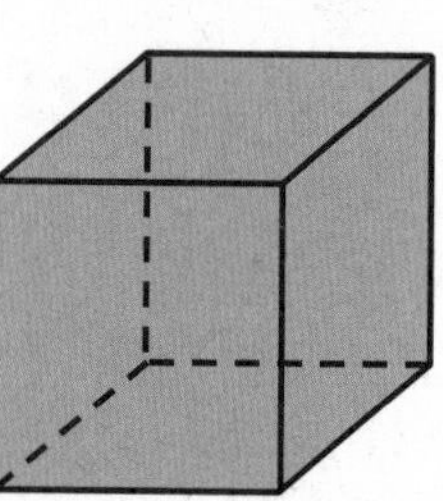

© Houghton Mifflin Harcourt Publishing Company

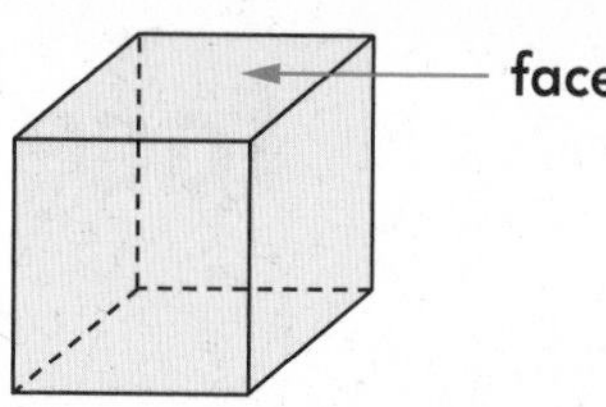

Each flat surface of this cube is a **face**.

© Houghton Mifflin Harcourt Publishing Company

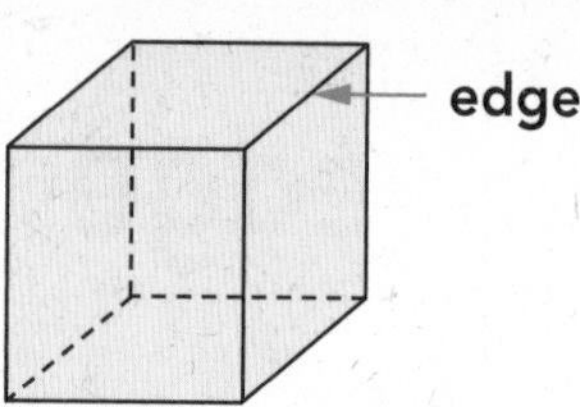

An **edge** is formed where two faces of a three-dimensional shape meet.

© Houghton Mifflin Harcourt Publishing Company

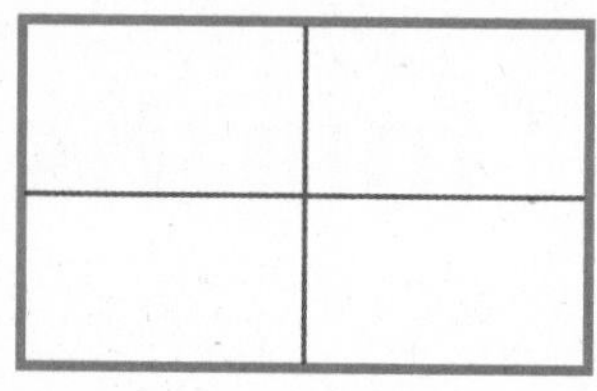

This shape has 4 equal parts. These equal parts are called **fourths**.

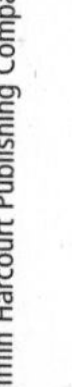

© Houghton Mifflin Harcourt Publishing Company

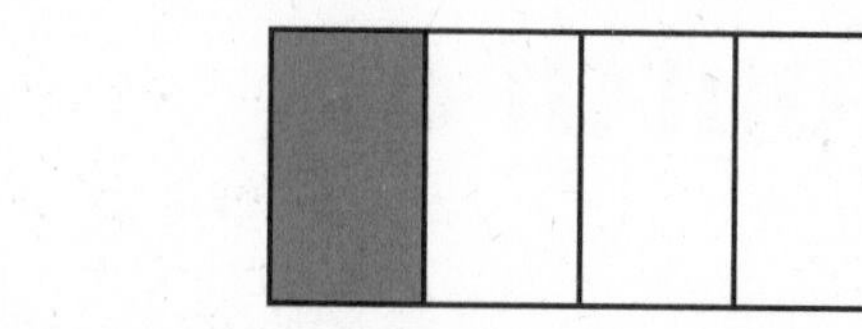

A **fourth of** the shape is green.

half of

mitad de

27

halves

mitades

28

hexagon

hexágono

29

pentagon

pentágono

47

quadrilateral

cuadrilátero

51

quarter of

cuarta parte de

53

rectangular prism

prisma rectangular

55

side

lado

57

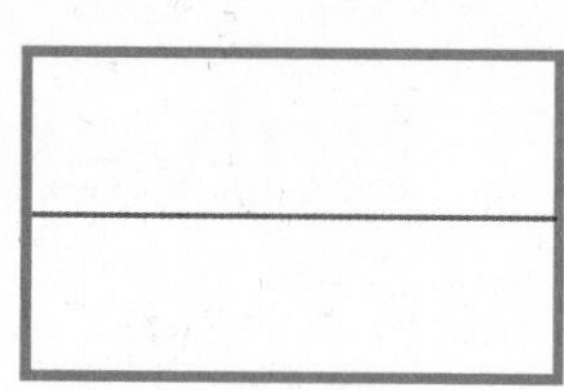

This shape has 2 equal parts. These equal parts are called **halves**.

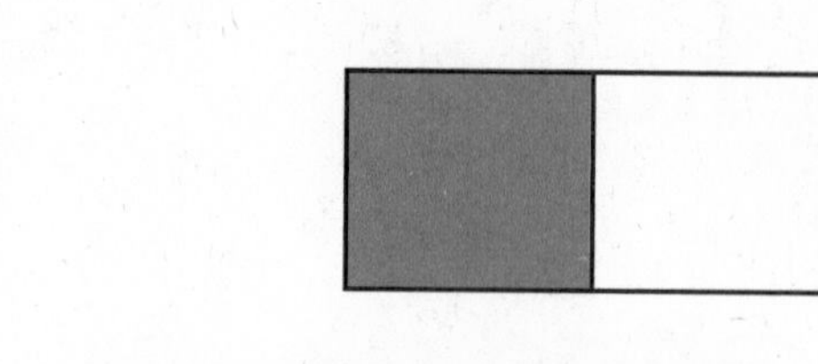

A **half of** the shape is green.

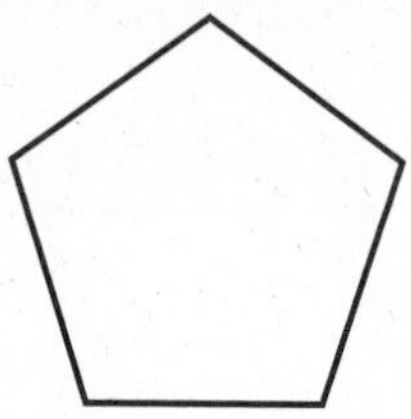

A two-dimensional shape with 5 sides is a **pentagon**.

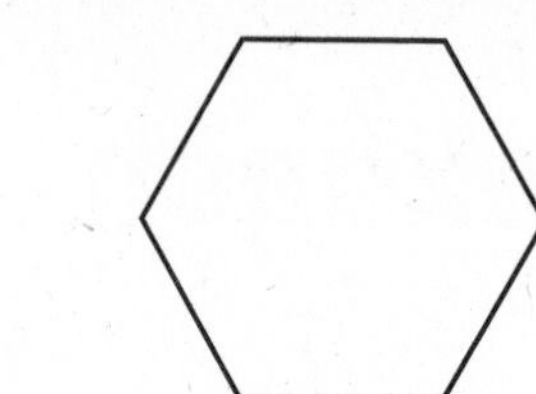

A two-dimensional shape with 6 sides is a **hexagon**.

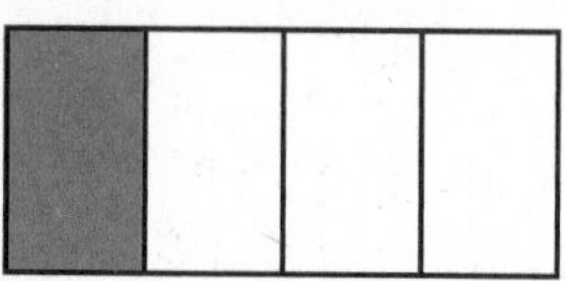

A **quarter of** the shape is green.

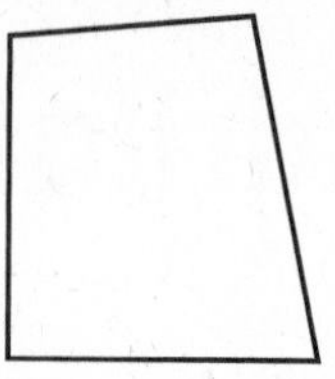

A two-dimensional shape with 4 sides is a **quadrilateral**.

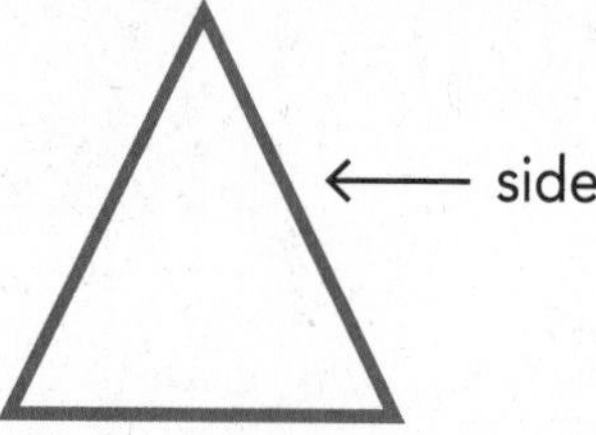

Triangles have 3 sides.

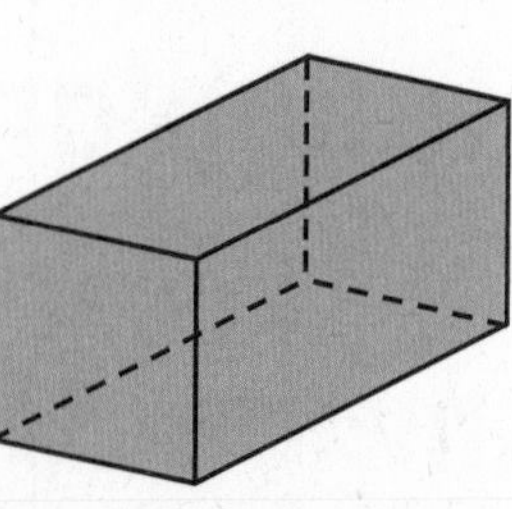

sphere

esfera

58

third of

tercio de

62

thirds

tercios

63

vertex/vertices

vértice/vértices

65

A **third of** the shape is green.

vertex

A corner point of a three-dimensional shape is a vertex.

vertex

This shape has 5 vertices.

This shape has 3 equal parts. These equal parts are called **thirds**.

Going to a Balloon Race

Word Box
angle
cone
cube
cylinder
edge
face
fourths
halves
hexagon
pentagon
quadrilateral
rectangular prism
side
thirds
vertex

For 2 players

Materials

- 1
- 1
- 1
- Clue Cards

How to Play

1. Put your on START.
2. Toss the , and move that many spaces.
3. If you land on these spaces:
   Blue Space Follow the directions.
   Red Space Take a Clue Card from the pile.
   If you answer the question correctly, keep the card.
   If not, return the card to the bottom of the pile.
4. Collect at least 5 Clue Cards. Move around the track as many times as you need to.
5. When you have 5 Clue Cards, follow the closest center path to reach FINISH.
6. The first player to reach FINISH wins.

TAKE A CLUE CARD

Your balloon catches a breeze. Move ahead 1.

FINISH

TAKE A CLUE CARD

Your balloon is blown off course. Go back 1.

START ▶

TAKE A CLUE CARD

Your balloon has a good launch. Move ahead 1.

TAKE A CLUE CARD

Your balloon is getting too close to the ground. Go back 1.

FINISH

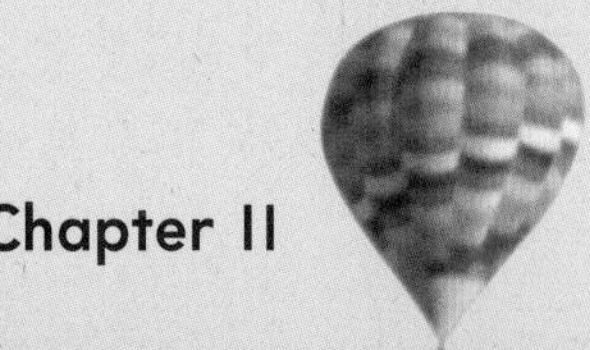

The Write Way

Reflect

Choose one idea. Write about it in the space below.

- Draw and write about all of the words. Use a separate piece of paper for your drawings.

  face edge vertex

- Choose one of these shapes. Write three things you know about it.

  quadrilateral pentagon hexagon

- Explain how you know the difference between halves, thirds, and fourths. Draw pictures on a separate piece of paper if you need to.

Name ______________________________

Three-Dimensional Shapes

Essential Question What objects match three-dimensional shapes?

Learning Objective You will identify and classify three-dimensional shapes.

Listen and Draw Real World

Draw a picture of an object with the same shape shown.

Math Talk Math Processes and Practices 3

Apply Describe how the shapes are alike. Describe how they are different.

FOR THE TEACHER • Have children look at the first shape and name some real objects that have this shape, such as a cereal box. Have each child draw a picture of a real-life object that has the same shape. Repeat for the second shape.

Model and Draw

These are three-dimensional shapes.

cube

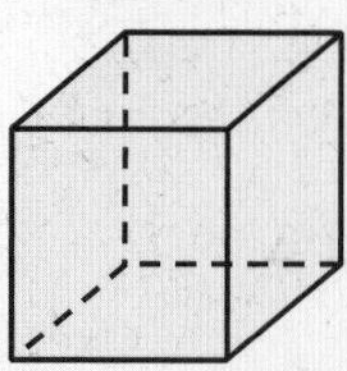

rectangular prism

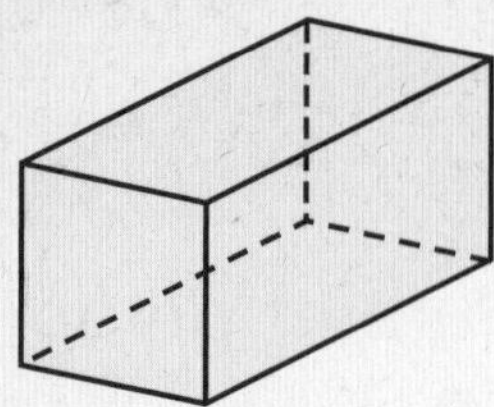

sphere

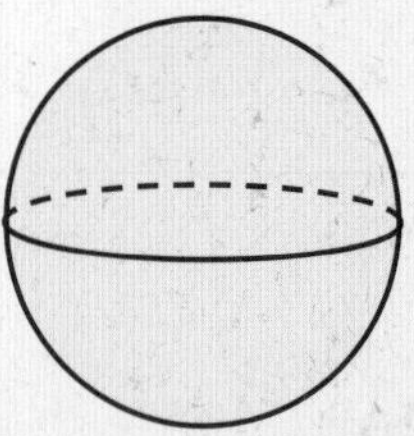

cylinder

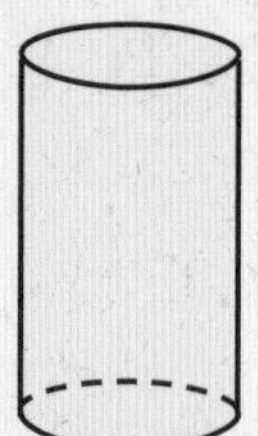

cone

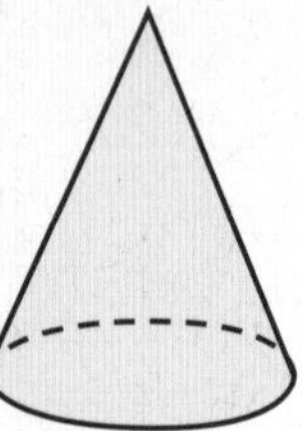

Which of these objects has the shape of a cube?

Share and Show

Circle the objects that match the shape name.

1. sphere

2. cube

Name ___________________________

On Your Own

Circle the objects that match the shape name.

3. cylinder

4. rectangular prism

5. cone

6. GO DEEPER Julio used cardboard squares as the flat surfaces of a cube. How many squares did he use?

_____ squares

7. THINKSMARTER Circle the shapes that have a curved surface. Draw an X on the shapes that do not have a curved surface.

Math on the Spot

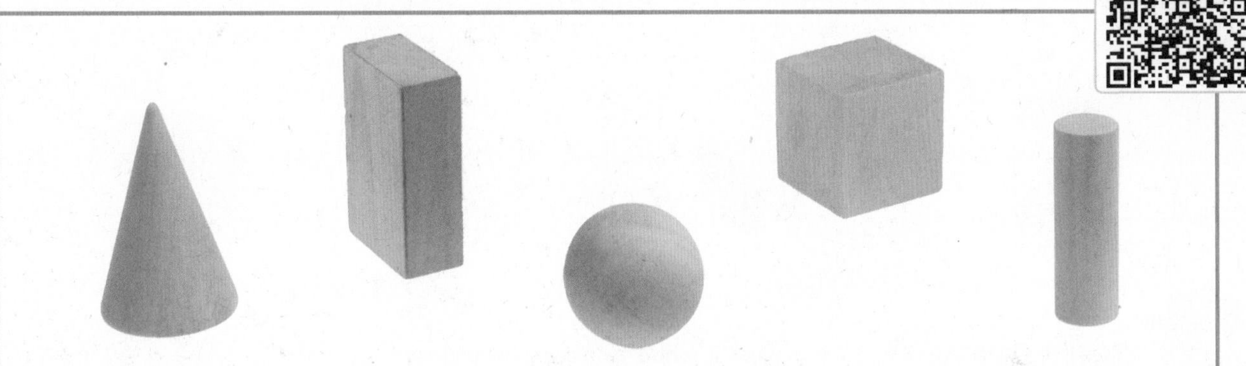

Problem Solving • Applications

8. Math Processes and Practices 6 **Make Connections**
Reba traced around the bottom of each block. Match each block with the shape Reba drew.

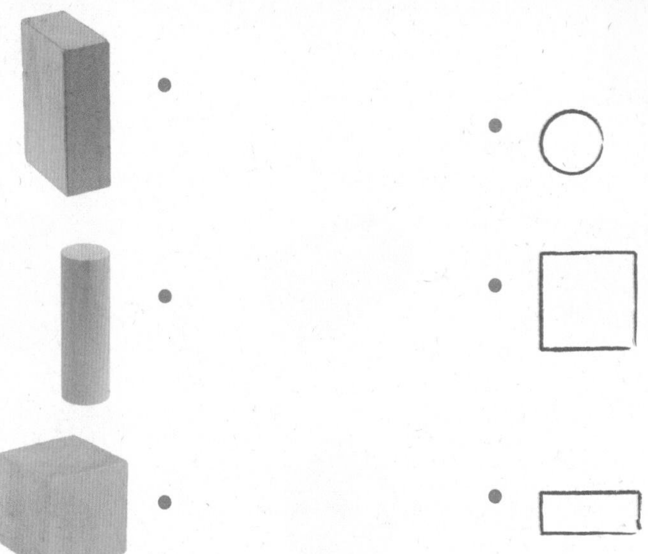

9. THINK SMARTER Match the shapes.

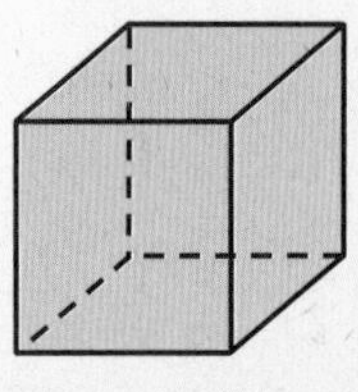
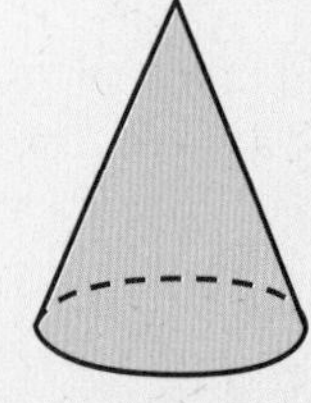
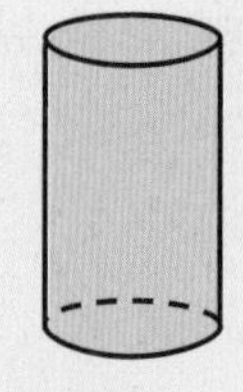
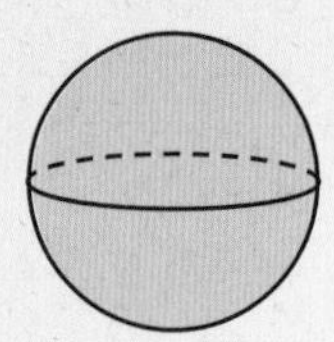

TAKE HOME ACTIVITY • Ask your child to name an object that has the shape of a cube.

Name ______________________________

Three-Dimensional Shapes

Practice and Homework
Lesson 11.1

Learning Objective You will identify and classify three-dimensional shapes.

Circle the objects that match the shape name.

1. cube			
2. cone	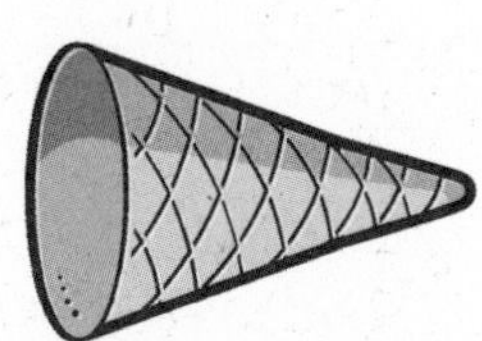		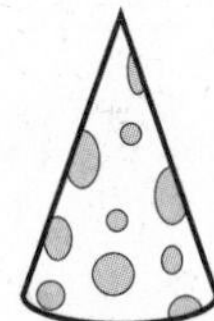
3. rectangular prism			

Problem Solving

4. Lisa draws a circle by tracing around the bottom of a block. Which could be the shape of Lisa's block? Circle the name of the shape.

cone   cube   rectangular prism

5. WRITE Math Describe one way that a cube and a cylinder are alike. Describe one way they are different.

____

Lesson Check

1. What is the name of this shape?

____

2. What is the name of this shape?

____

Spiral Review

3. The string is about 6 centimeters long. Circle the best estimate for the length of the crayon.

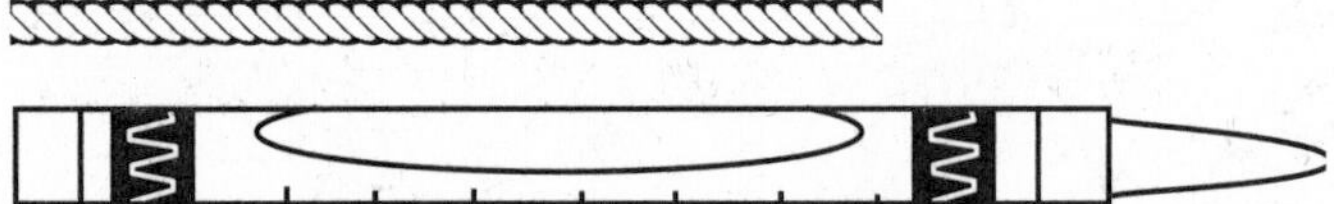

3 centimeters   9 centimeters   14 centimeters

4. What is the total value of this group of coins?

____

5. What time is shown on this clock?

____ : ____

FOR MORE PRACTICE GO TO THE Personal Math Trainer

Name ______________________________

Attributes of Three-Dimensional Shapes

Essential Question How would you describe the faces of a rectangular prism and the faces of a cube?

Learning Objective You will use the number of faces, edges, and vertices to describe three-dimensional shapes.

Listen and Draw

Circle the cones. Draw an X on the sphere.

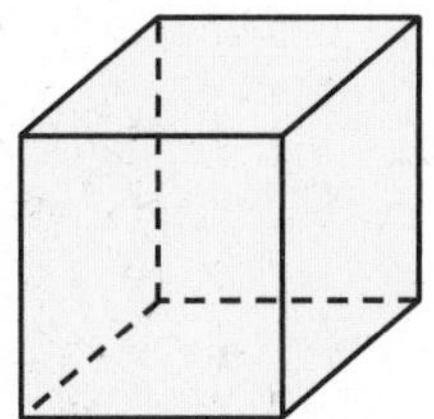
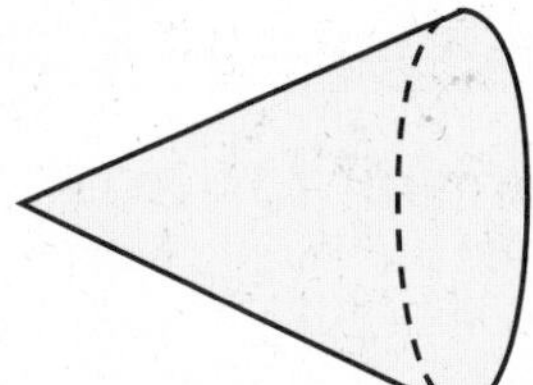
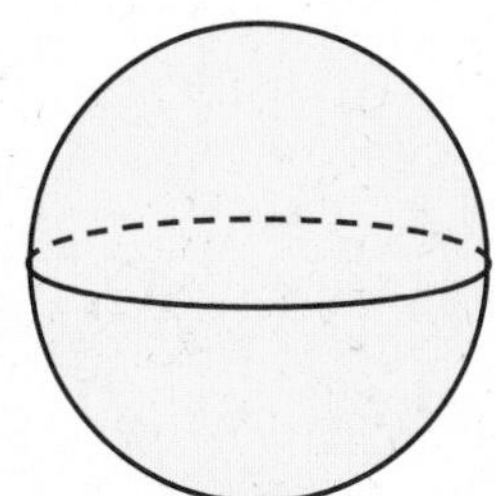

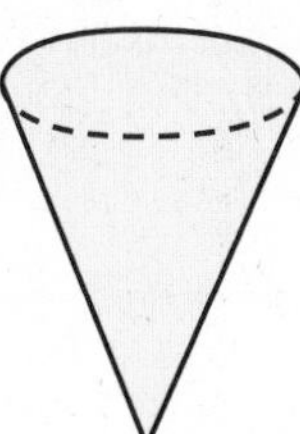
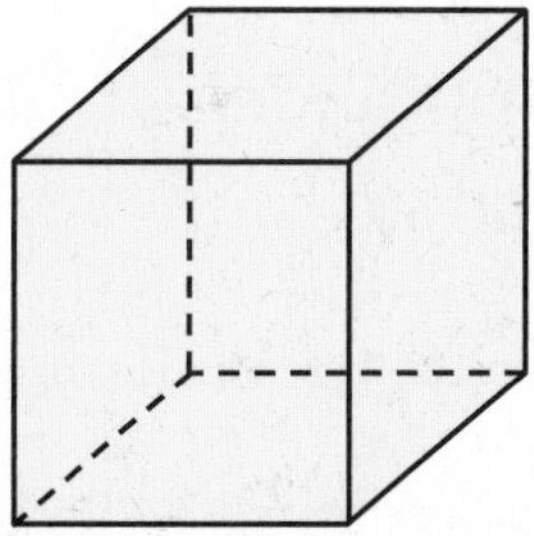

Math Processes and Practices 1

Name the other shapes on this page. **Describe** how they are different.

HOME CONNECTION • Your child identified the shapes on this page to review some of the different kinds of three-dimensional shapes.

Model and Draw

The **faces** of a cube are squares.

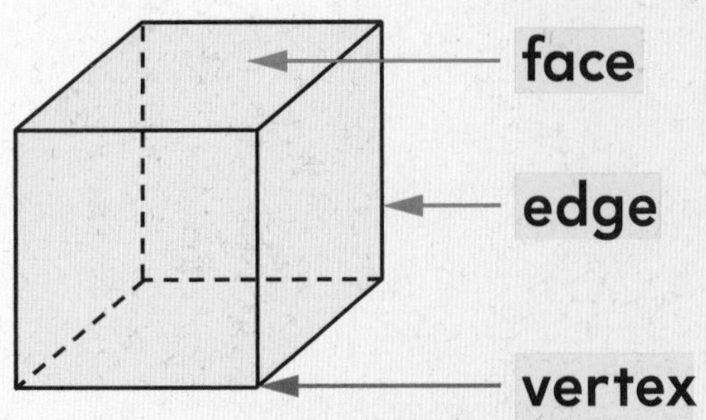

The **vertices** are the corner points of the cube.

Share and Show

Write how many for each.

	faces	edges	vertices
✓ 1. 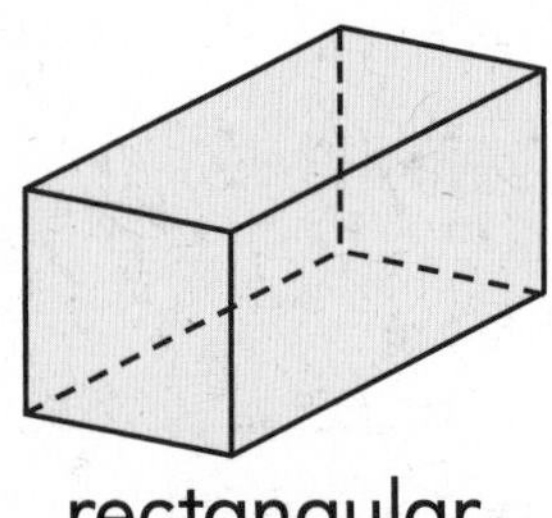 rectangular prism	____	____	____
✓ 2. 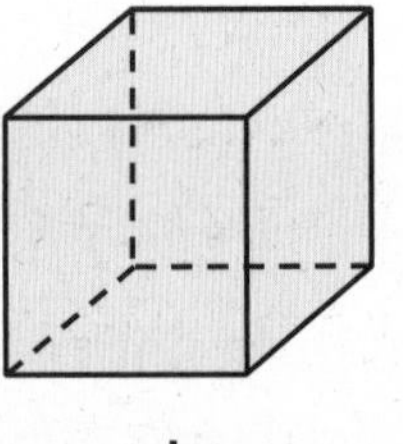 cube	____	____	____

Name ______________________________

On Your Own

3. GO DEEPER Use dot paper.
Follow these steps to draw a cube.

Step 1 Draw a square. Make each side 4 units long.

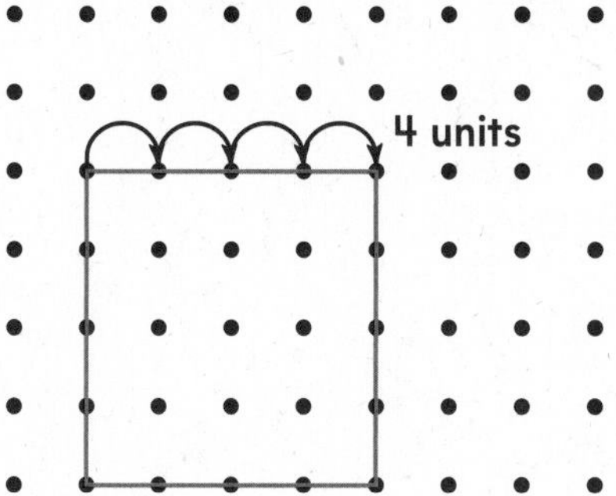

Step 2 Draw edges from 3 vertices, like this.

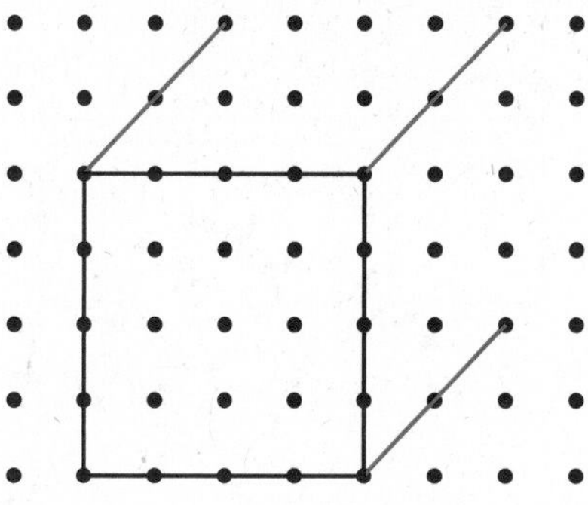

Step 3 Draw 2 more edges.

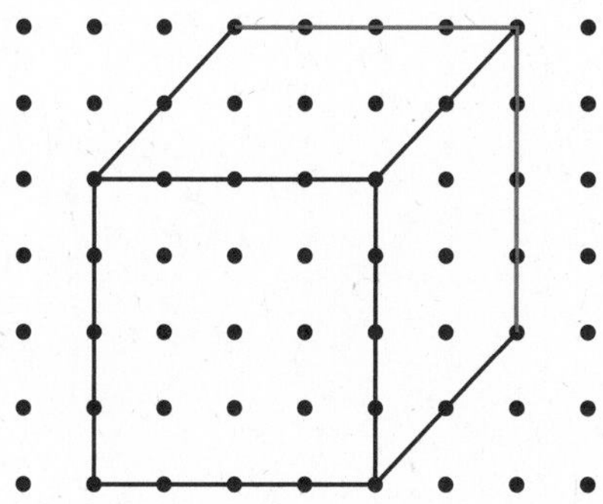

Step 4 Draw 3 dashed edges to show the faces that are not seen.

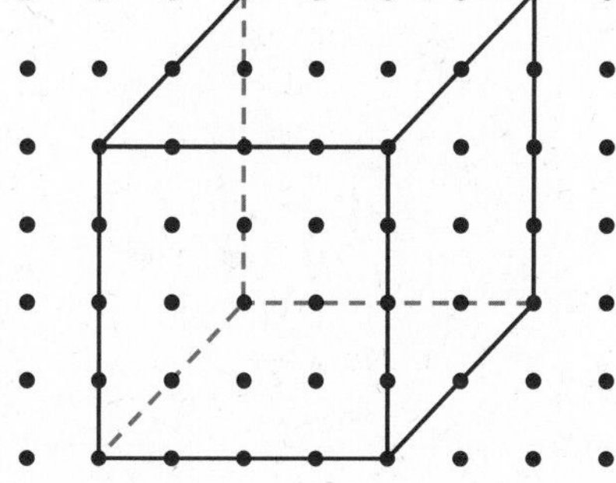

4. THINK SMARTER Trace all the faces of a rectangular prism on a sheet of paper. Write to tell about the shapes that you drew.

____

____

Problem Solving • Applications

5. Math Processes and Practices 6 **Make Connections** Marcus traced around the faces of a three-dimensional shape. Circle the name of the shape he used.

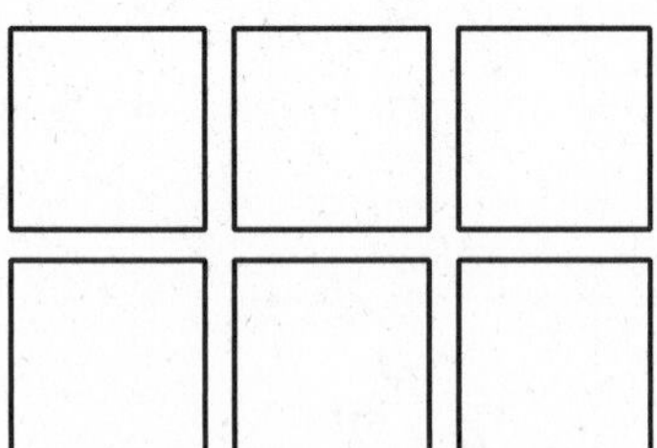

cylinder
cube
sphere
cone

6. THINKSMARTER Use the words on the tiles to label the parts of the cube.

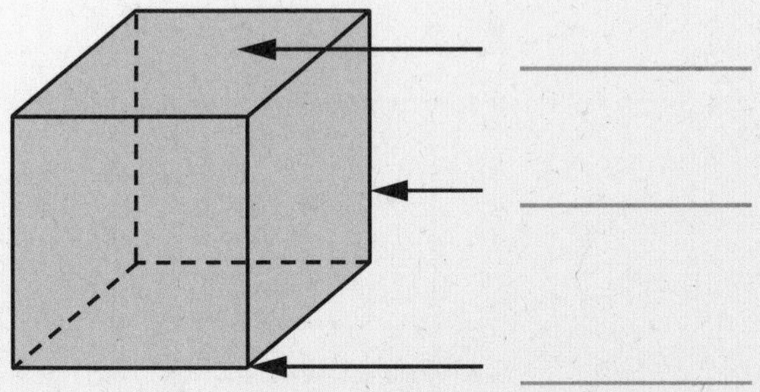

edge | face | vertex

Describe the faces of a cube.

____

____

TAKE HOME ACTIVITY • Have your child tell you about the faces on a cereal box or another kind of box.

Name ______________________________

Attributes of Three-Dimensional Shapes

Learning Objective You will use the number of faces, edges, and vertices to describe three-dimensional shapes.

Circle the set of shapes that are the faces of the three-dimensional shape.

1.

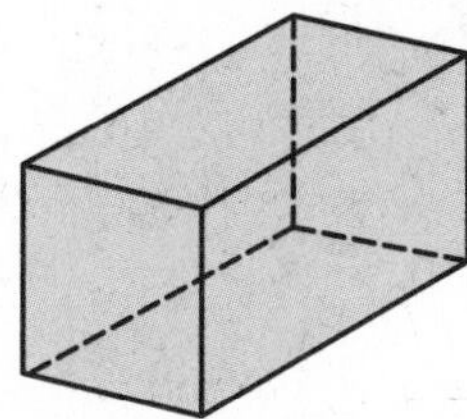

rectangular prism

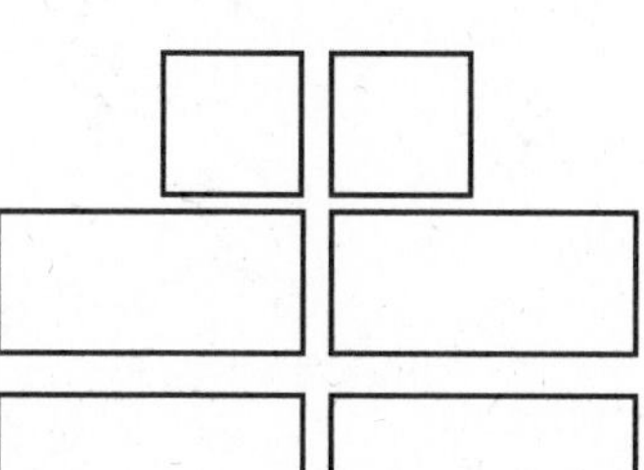

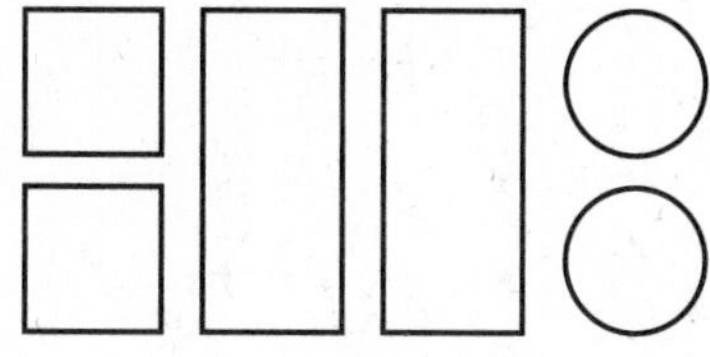

2.

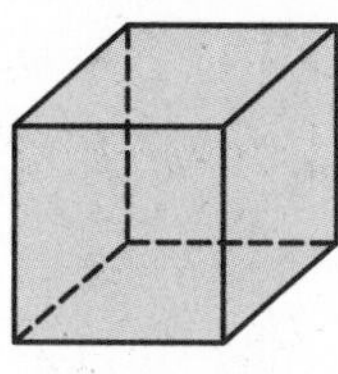

cube

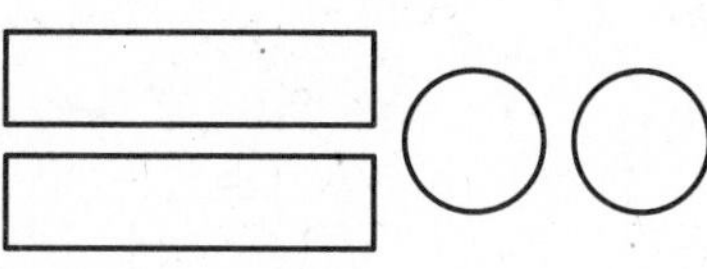

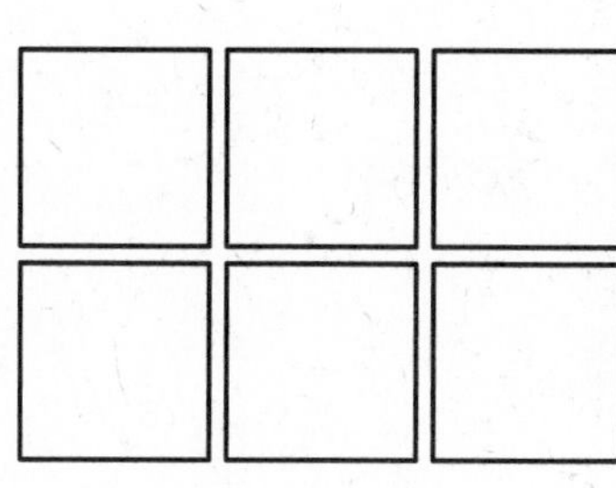

Problem Solving

3. Kevin keeps his marbles in a container that has the shape of a cube. He wants to paint each face a different color. How many different paint colors does he need?

_____ different paint colors

4. WRITE Math Describe a cube. Use the words *faces*, *edges*, and *vertices* in your description.

____

____

Lesson Check

1. How many faces does a cube have?

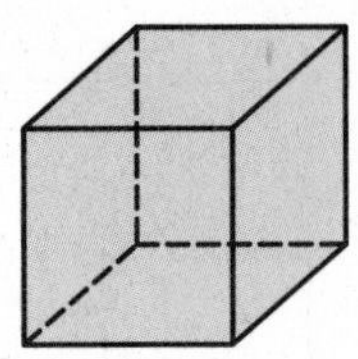

____ faces

2. How many faces does a rectangular prism have?

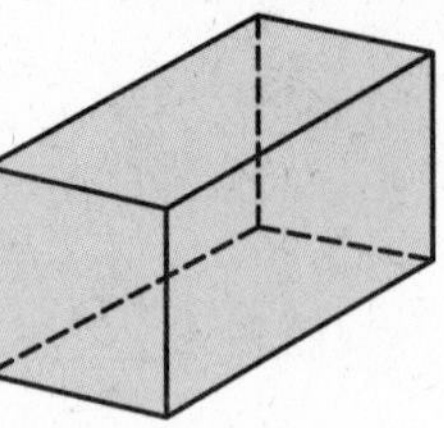

____ faces

Spiral Review

3. What time is shown on this clock?

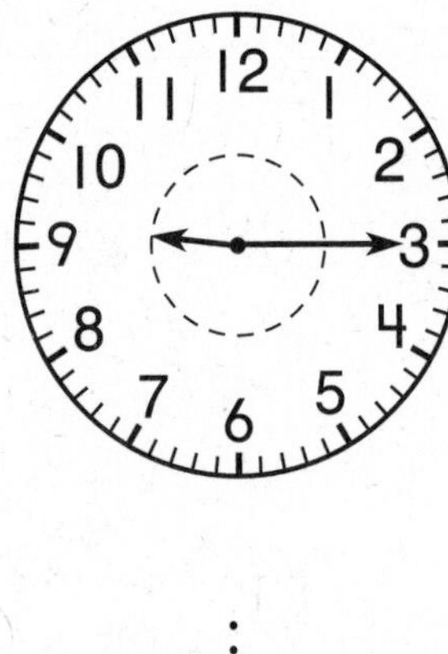

____ : ____

4. Circle the cone.

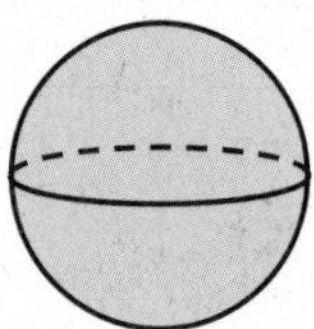
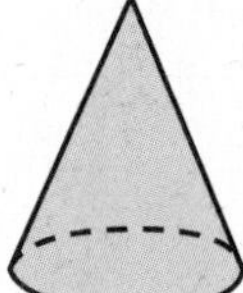
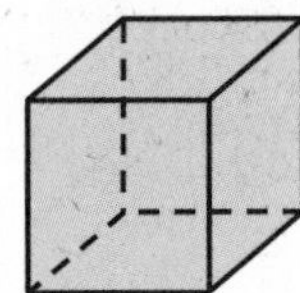
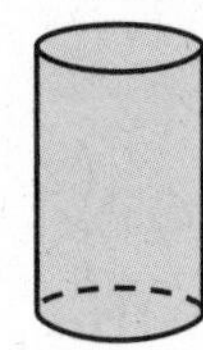

5. Use the line plot. How many books are 8 inches long?

____ books

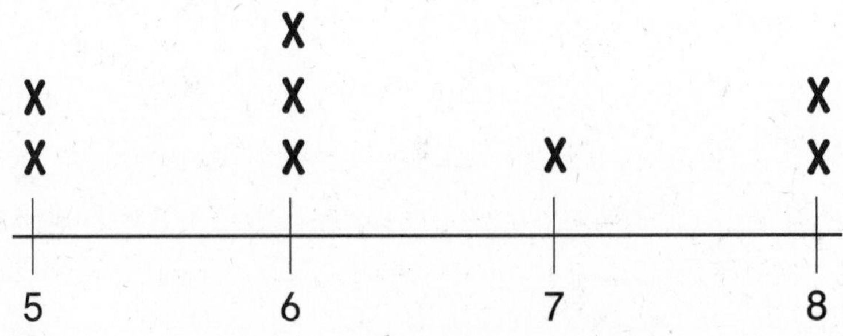

FOR MORE PRACTICE GO TO THE **Personal Math Trainer**

Name ______________________

Build Three-Dimensional Shapes

Essential Question How can you build a rectangular prism?

Learning Objective You will create rectangular prisms using unit cubes.

Listen and Draw (Real World)

Circle the shapes with curved surfaces. Draw an X on the shapes with flat surfaces.

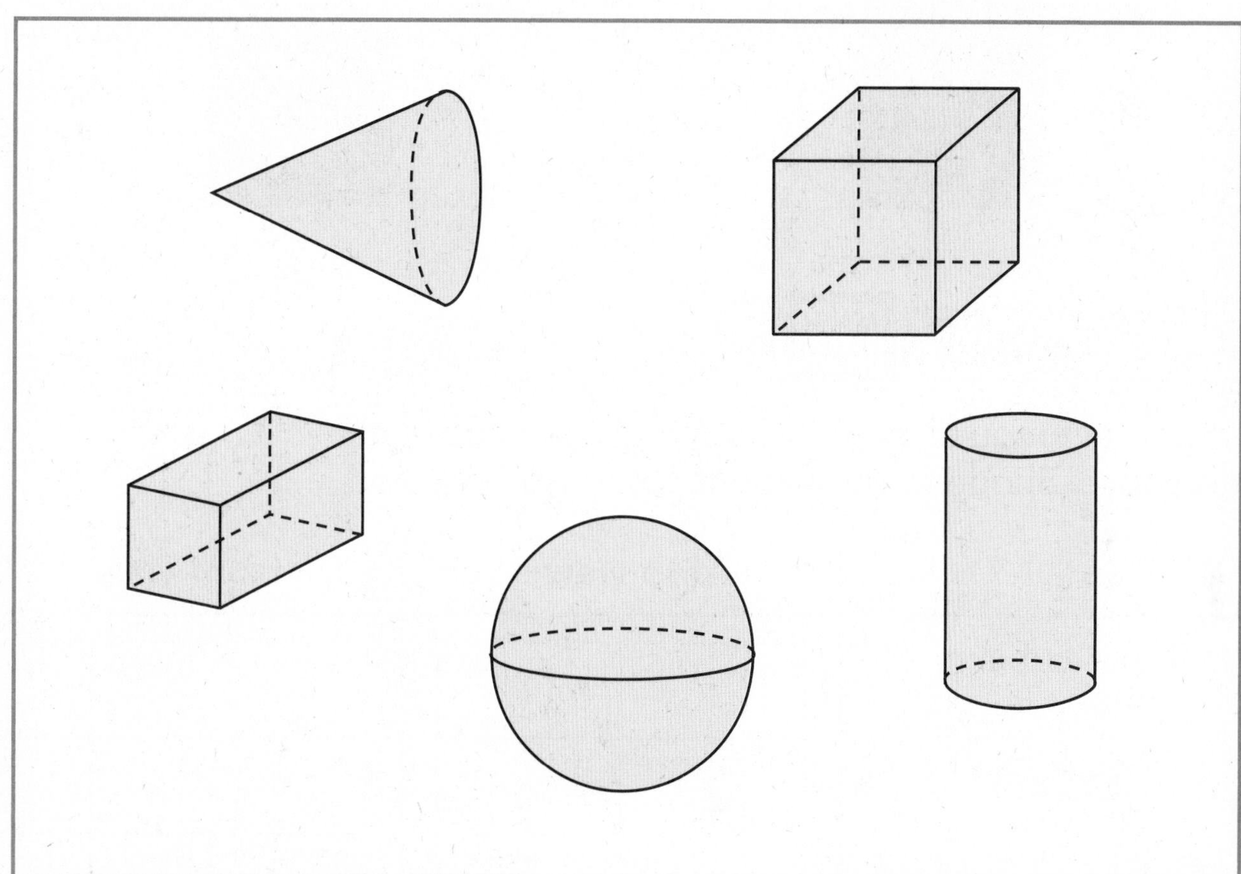

Math Talk Math Processes and Practices 3

Name the shapes you drew an X on. **Describe** how they are different.

HOME CONNECTION • Your child sorted the shapes on this page using the attributes of the shapes.

Model and Draw

Build this rectangular prism using 12 unit cubes.

The shading shows the top and front views.

top view

front view

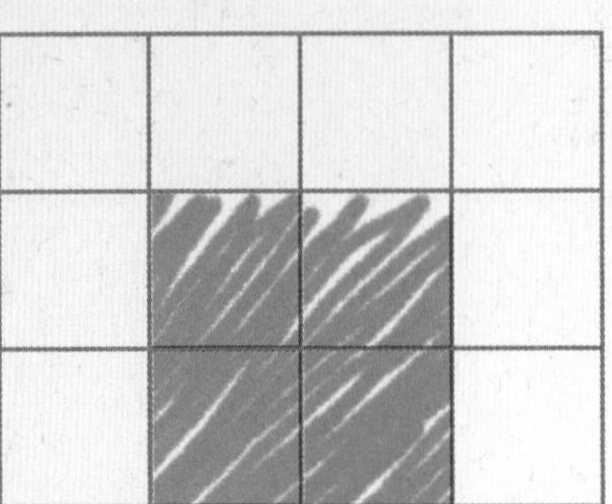

Share and Show

Build a rectangular prism with the given number of unit cubes. Shade to show the top and front views.

	top view	front view
1. 9 unit cubes		
2. 16 unit cubes		

Name ______________________________

On Your Own

Build a rectangular prism with the given number of unit cubes. Shade to show the top and front views.

	top view	front view
3. 24 unit cubes	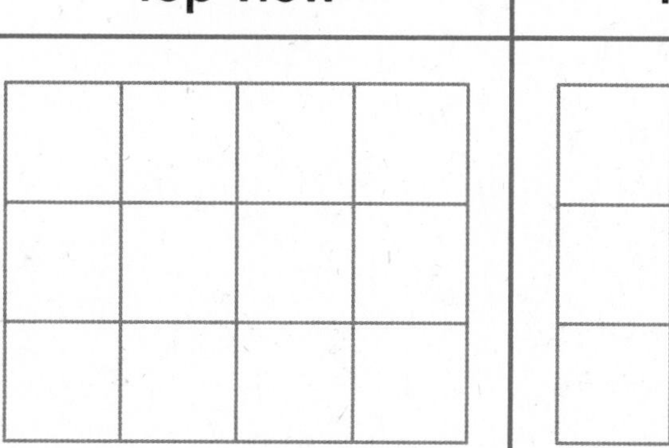	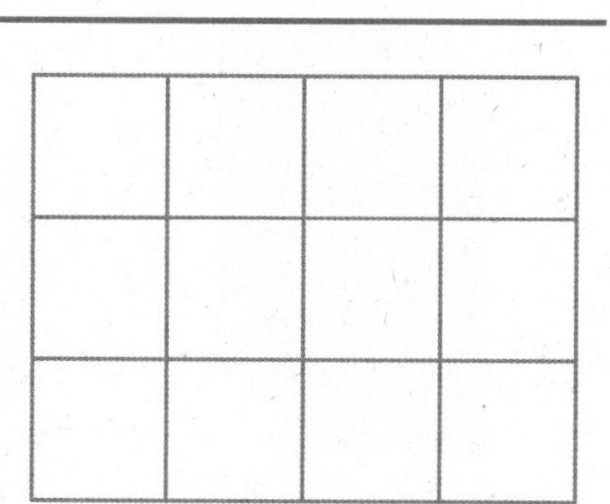

4. THINK SMARTER The top, side, and front views of a rectangular prism are shown. Build the prism. How many unit cubes are used to build the solid?

top view   front view   side view

______ unit cubes

5. Math Processes and Practices 1 **Analyze** Jen uses 18 unit cubes to build a rectangular prism. The top and front views are shown. Shade to show the side view.

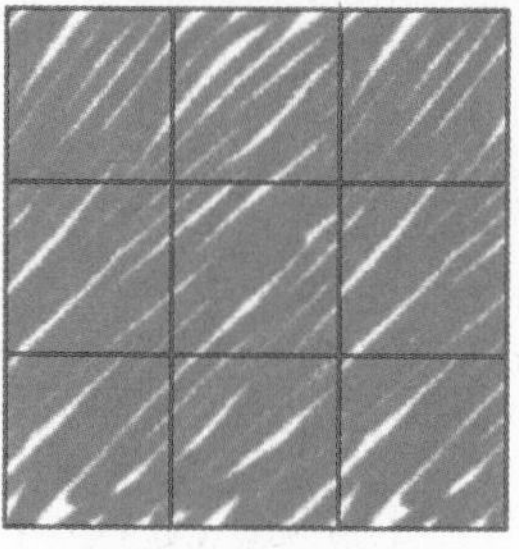
top view

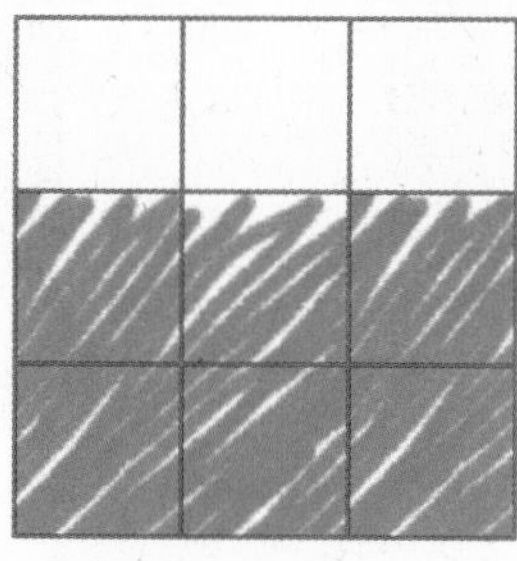
front view

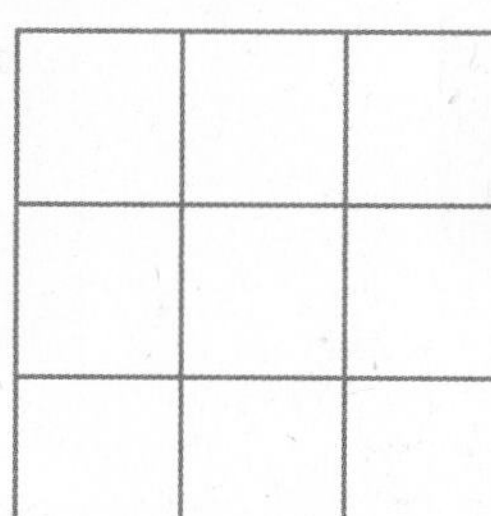
side view

Problem Solving • Applications

Solve. Write or draw to explain.

6. GO DEEPER Tomas built this rectangular prism. How many unit cubes did he use?

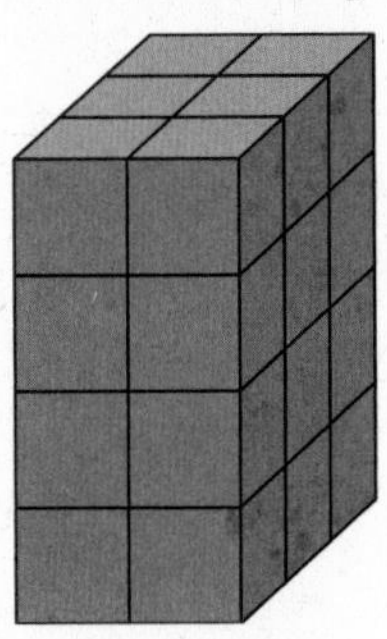

_____ unit cubes

7. Math Processes and Practices 7 **Look for Structure** Theo builds the first layer of a rectangular prism using 4 unit cubes. He adds 3 more layers of 4 unit cubes each. How many unit cubes does he use for the prism?

_____ unit cubes

8. THINK SMARTER + Tyler built this rectangular prism using unit cubes. Then he took it apart and used all of the cubes to build two new prisms. Fill in the bubble next to the two prisms he built.

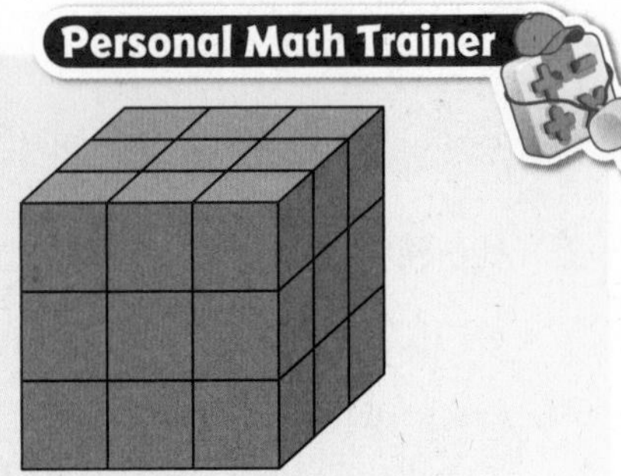

○ 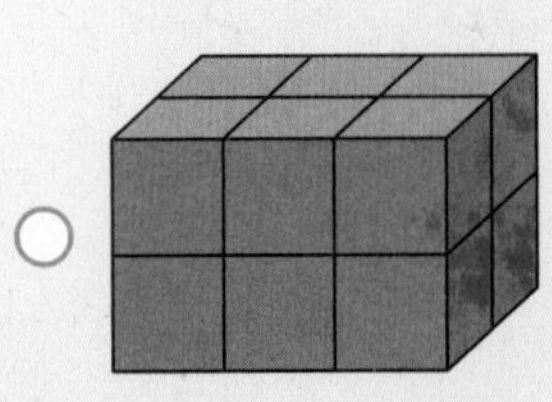

○ 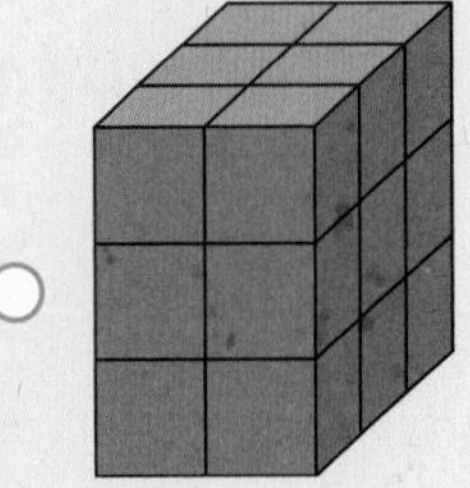

○ 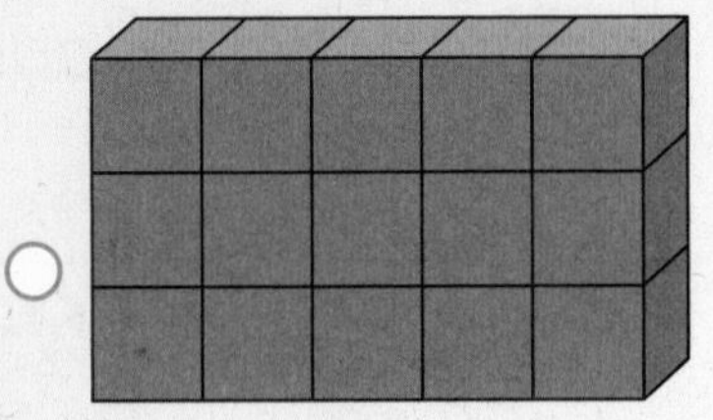

TAKE HOME ACTIVITY • Ask your child to show how he or she solved a problem in the lesson.

Name ____________________________________

Build Three-Dimensional Shapes

Learning Objective You will create rectangular prisms using unit cubes.

Build a rectangular prism with the given number of unit cubes. Shade to show the top and front views.

	top view	**front view**
1. 12 unit cubes		

Problem Solving

Solve. Write or draw to explain.

2. Rosie built this rectangular prism. How many unit cubes did she use?

_____ unit cubes

3. WRITE Math Build a rectangular prism using cubes. Then, draw in your journal the top, side, and bottom views of your prism.

Lesson Check

1. Milt builds the first layer of a rectangular prism using 3 unit cubes. He adds 2 more layers of 3 unit cubes each. How many unit cubes are used for the prism?

____ unit cubes

2. Thea builds the first layer of a rectangular prism using 4 unit cubes. Raj adds 4 more layers of 4 unit cubes each. How many unit cubes are used for the prism?

____ unit cubes

Spiral Review

3. Patti's dance class starts at quarter past 4. At what time does her dance class start?

____ : ____

4. Nicole has 56 beads. Charles has 34 beads. How many more beads does Nicole have than Charles?

____ more beads

Use the bar graph.

5. Which fruit got the fewest votes?

____

6. How many more votes did grape get than apple?

____ more votes

FOR MORE PRACTICE GO TO THE Personal Math Trainer

Name ___________________________

Two-Dimensional Shapes

Essential Question What shapes can you name just by knowing the number of sides and vertices?

Learning Objective You will use the number of sides and vertices to describe two-dimensional shapes.

Listen and Draw

Use a ruler. Draw a shape with 3 straight sides.
Then draw a shape with 4 straight sides.

Math Processes and Practices 7

Describe how your shapes are different from the shapes a classmate drew.

FOR THE TEACHER • Have children use rulers as straight edges for drawing the sides of shapes. Have children draw a two-dimensional shape with 3 sides and then a two-dimensional shape with 4 sides.

Model and Draw

You can count **sides** and **vertices** to name two-dimensional shapes. Look at how many sides and vertices each shape has.

triangle

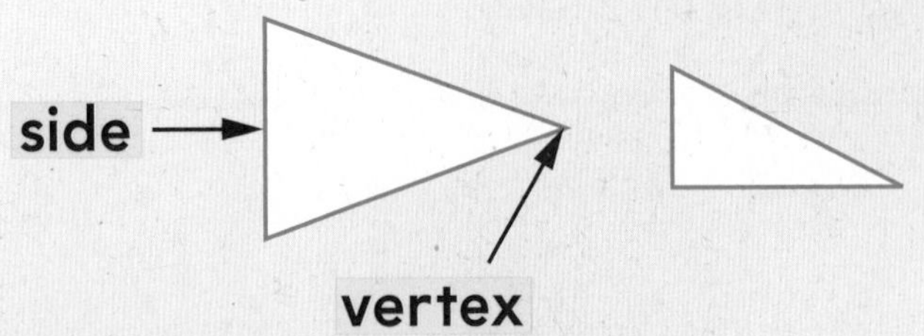

3 sides

3 vertices

quadrilateral

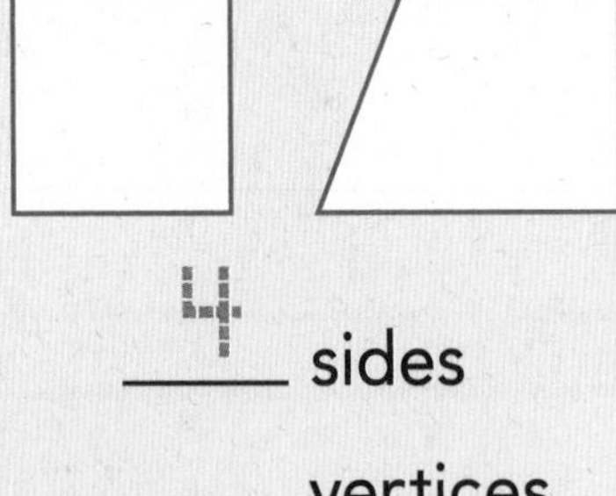

4 sides

_____ vertices

pentagon

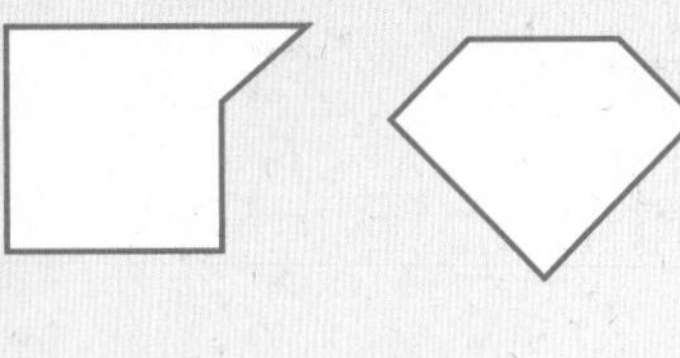

_____ sides

_____ vertices

hexagon

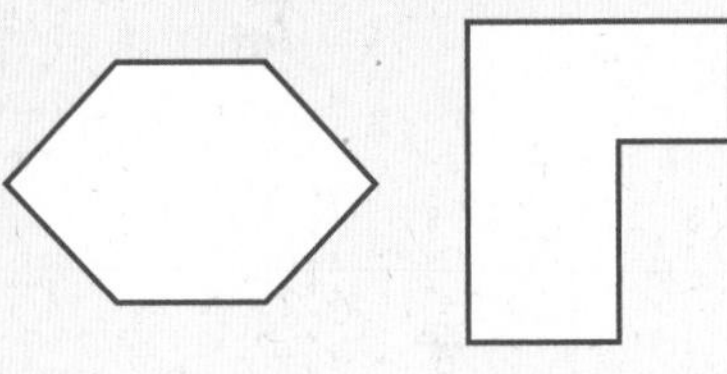

_____ sides

_____ vertices

Share and Show

Write the number of sides and the number of vertices.

1. triangle

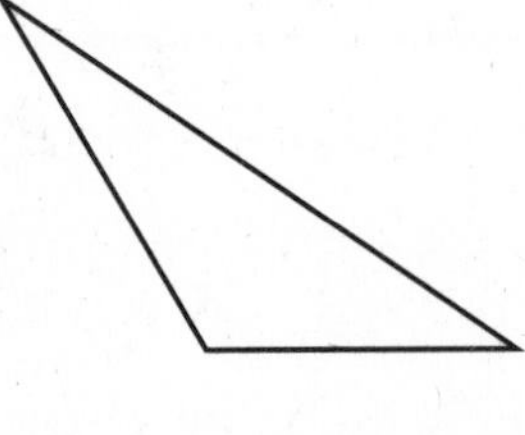

_____ sides

_____ vertices

✓ 2. hexagon

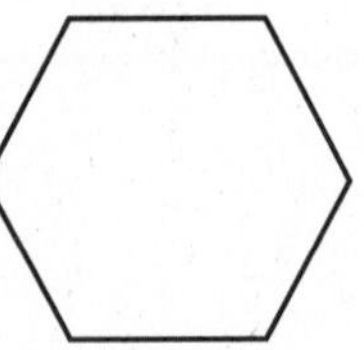

_____ sides

_____ vertices

✓ 3. pentagon

_____ sides

_____ vertices

Name ______________________________

On Your Own

pentagon
triangle
hexagon
quadrilateral

Write the number of sides and the number of vertices. Then write the name of the shape.

4.

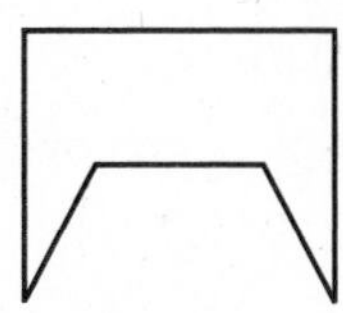

_____ sides

_____ vertices

____

5.

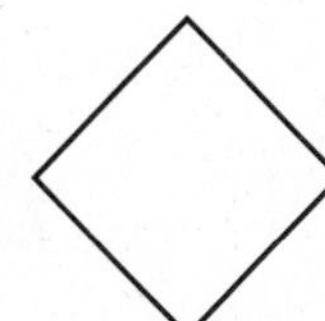

_____ sides

_____ vertices

____

6.

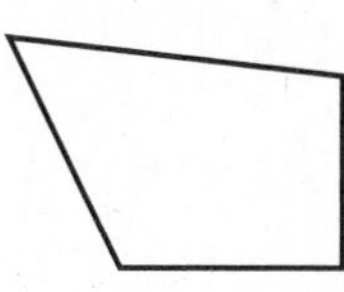

_____ sides

_____ vertices

____

7.

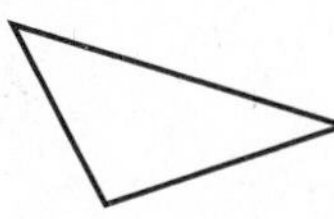

_____ sides

_____ vertices

____

8.

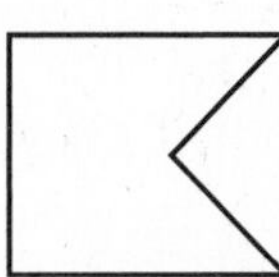

_____ sides

_____ vertices

____

9.

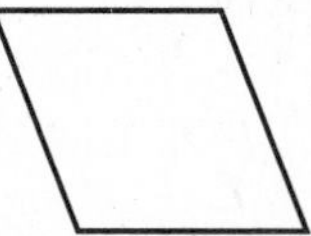

_____ sides

_____ vertices

____

GO DEEPER Draw more sides to make the shape.

10. pentagon

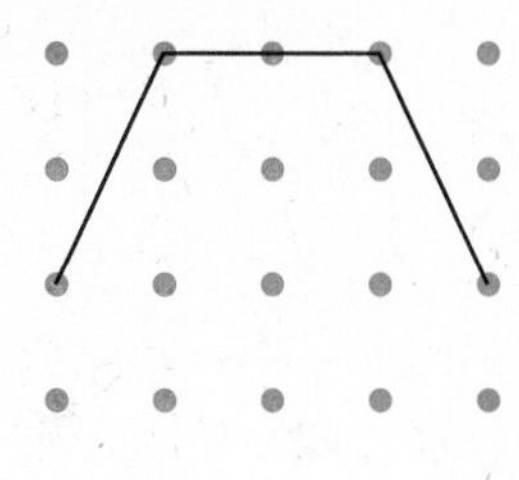

11. quadrilateral

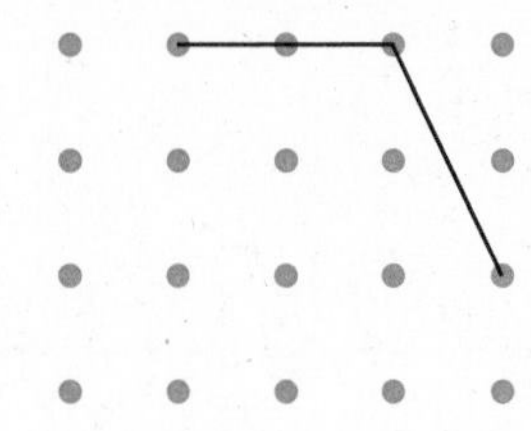

12. hexagon

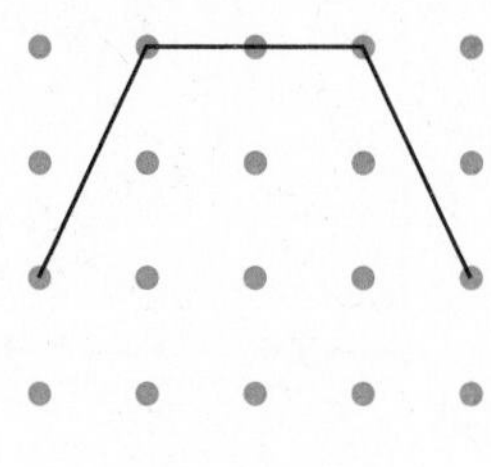

Problem Solving • Applications

Solve. Draw or write to explain.

13. THINKSMARTER Alex draws a hexagon and two pentagons. How many sides does Alex draw altogether?

_____ sides

14. Math Processes and Practices 4 **Use Diagrams** Ed draws a shape that has 4 sides. It is not a square. It is not a rectangle. Draw a shape that could be Ed's shape.

15. THINKSMARTER Count the sides and vertices of each two-dimensional shape. Draw each shape where it belongs in the chart.

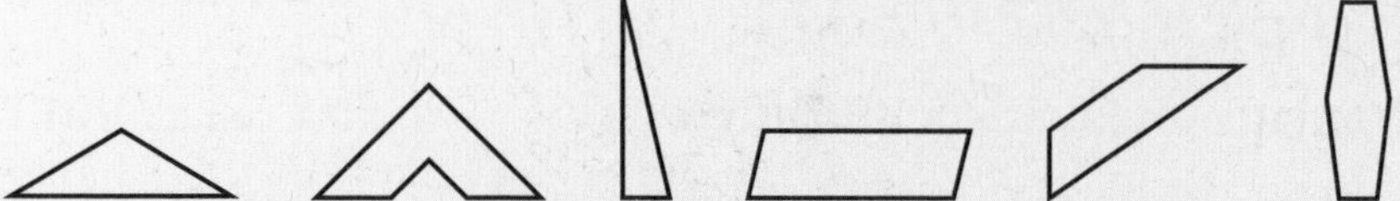

Quadrilateral	Hexagon	Triangle

TAKE HOME ACTIVITY • Ask your child to draw a shape that is a quadrilateral.

Name ______________________________

Two-Dimensional Shapes

Learning Objective You will use the number of sides and vertices to describe two-dimensional shapes.

Write the number of sides and the number of vertices. Then write the name of the shape.

pentagon | triangle | hexagon | quadrilateral

1.

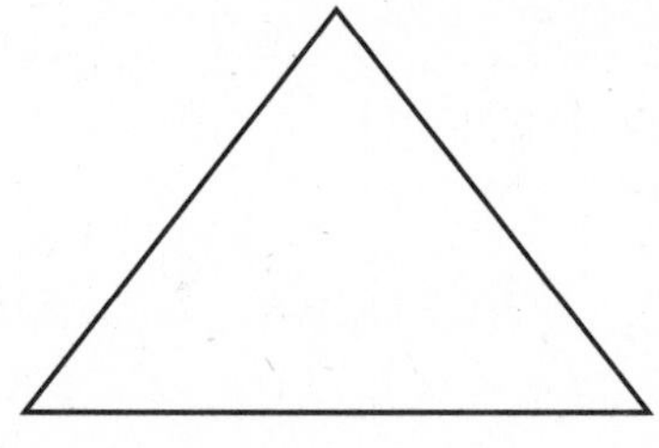

_____ sides

_____ vertices

____

2.

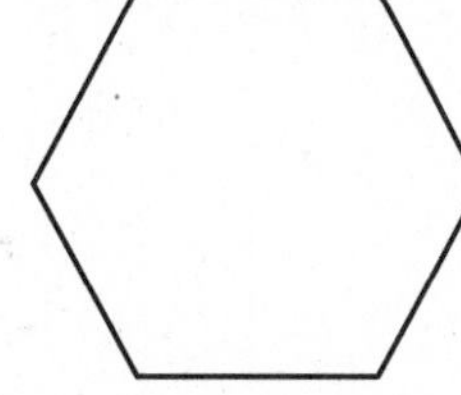

_____ sides

_____ vertices

____

3.

_____ sides

_____ vertices

____

Problem Solving

Solve. Draw or write to explain.

4. Oscar is drawing a picture of a house. He draws a pentagon shape for a window. How many sides does his window have?

_____ sides

5. WRITE Math Draw and label a pentagon and a quadrilateral.

Lesson Check

1. How many sides does a hexagon have?

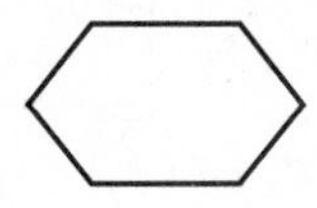

____ sides

2. How many vertices does a quadrilateral have?

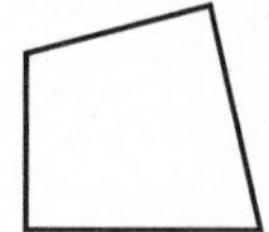

____ vertices

Spiral Review

3. Use a centimeter ruler. What is the length of the ribbon to the nearest centimeter?

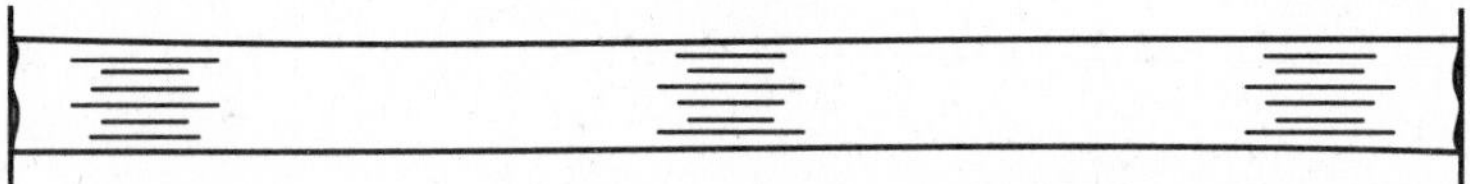

____ centimeters

4. Look at the picture graph. How many more children chose apples than oranges?

____ more children

Favorite Fruit					
apples	☺	☺	☺	☺	
oranges	☺	☺			
grapes	☺	☺	☺		
peaches	☺	☺			

Key: Each ☺ stands for 1 child.

Name ______________________

Angles in Two-Dimensional Shapes

Essential Question How do you find and count angles in two-dimensional shapes?

Learning Objective You will find and count angles in two-dimensional shapes.

Listen and Draw

Use a ruler. Draw two different triangles. Then draw two different rectangles.

Math Processes and Practices 1

Describe a triangle and a rectangle. Tell about their sides and vertices.

FOR THE TEACHER • Have children use pencils and rulers (or other straight edges) to draw the shapes. Have them draw two different triangles in the green box and two different rectangles in the purple box.

Model and Draw

When two sides of a shape meet, they form an **angle**.

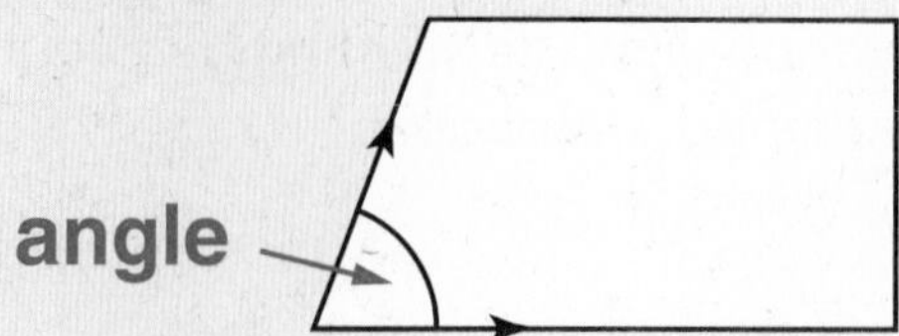

This shape has 3 angles.

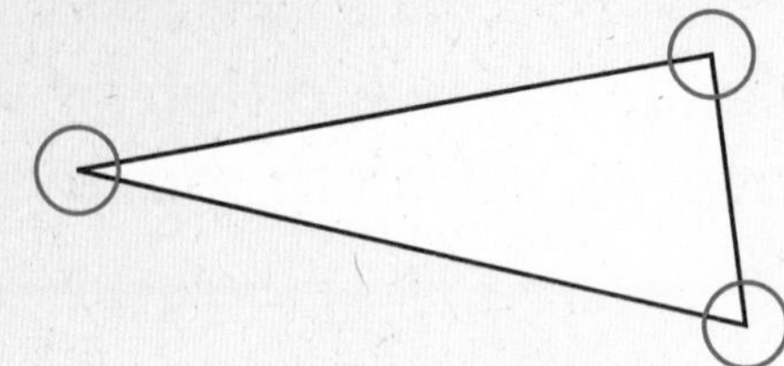

Share and Show

Circle the angles in each shape. Write how many.

1.

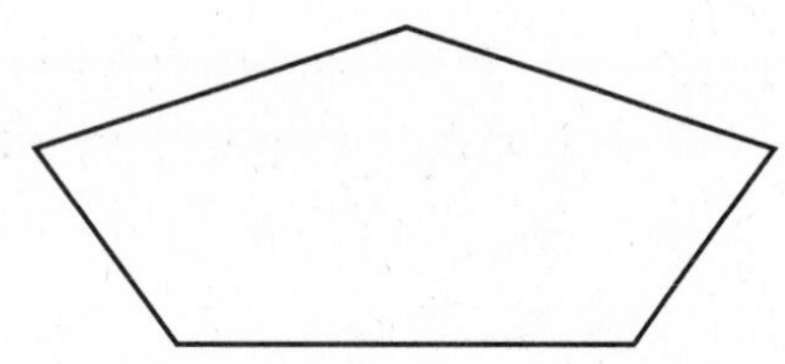

______ angles

2.

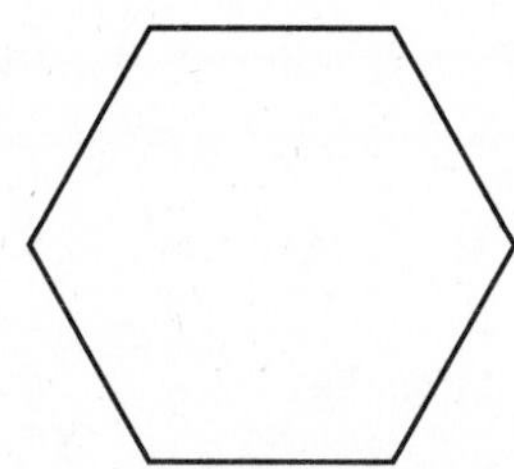

______ angles

✓3.

______ angles

✓4.

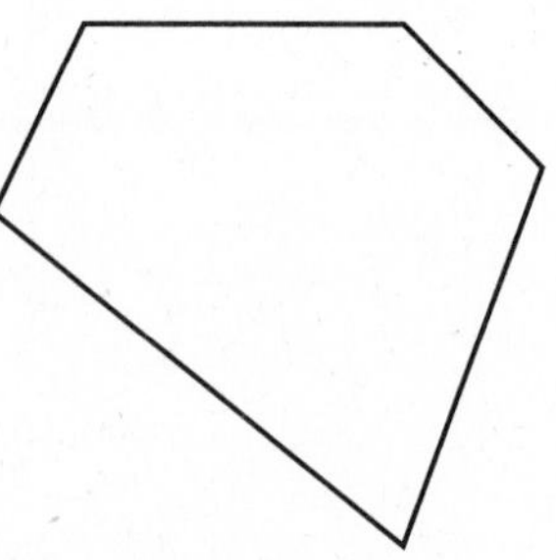

______ angles

Name ______________________________

On Your Own

Circle the angles in each shape. Write how many.

5.

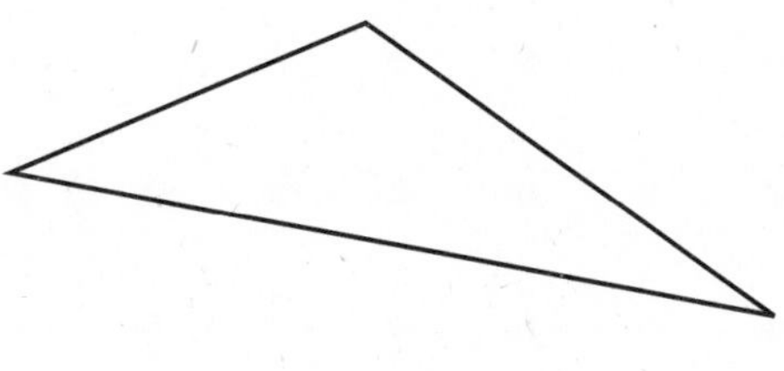

_____ angles

6.

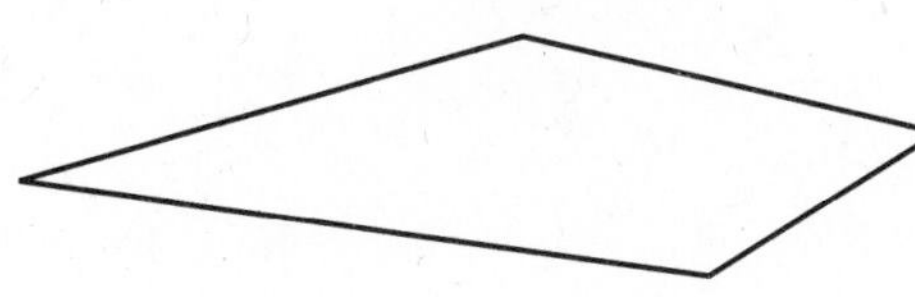

_____ angles

7.

_____ angles

8.

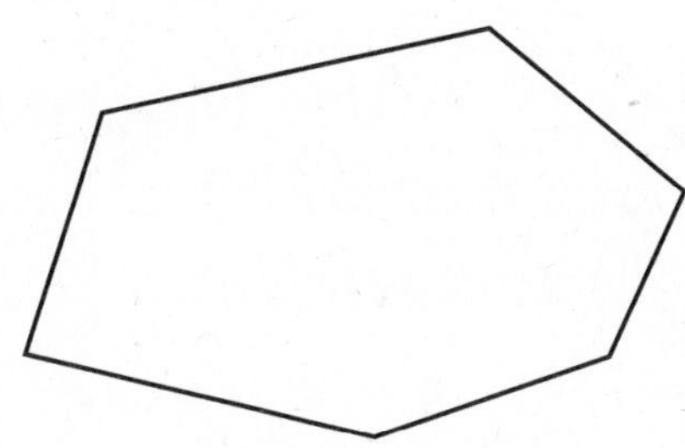

_____ angles

9. THINKSMARTER Draw more sides to make the shape. Write how many angles.

pentagon

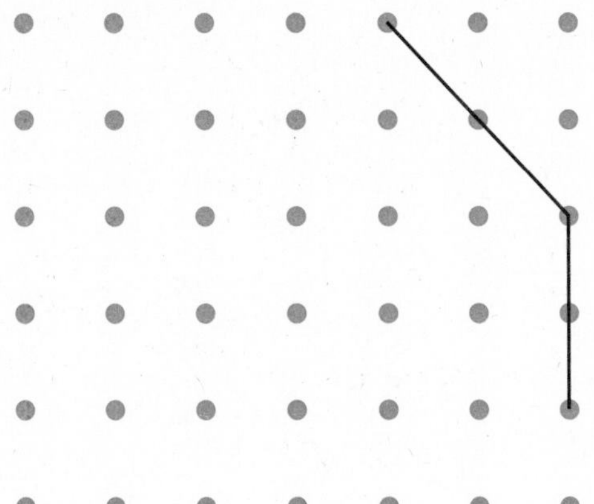

_____ angles

quadrilateral

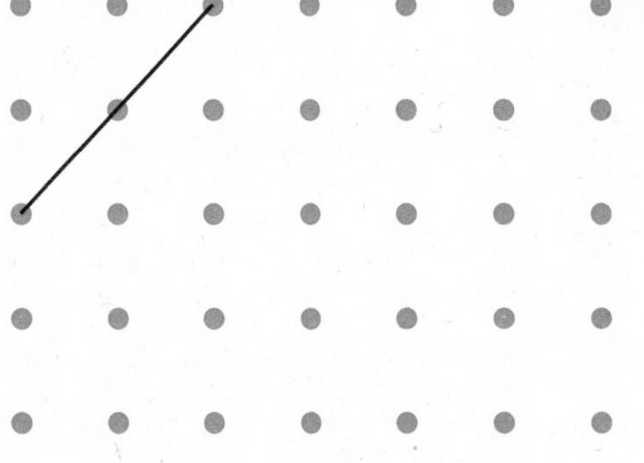

_____ angles

Problem Solving • Applications

10. Draw two shapes that have 7 angles in all.

11. Math Processes and Practices 4 **Use Diagrams** Ben drew 3 two-dimensional shapes that had 11 angles in all. Draw shapes Ben could have drawn.

12. THINKSMARTER Fill in the bubble next to all the shapes that have 5 angles.

○ 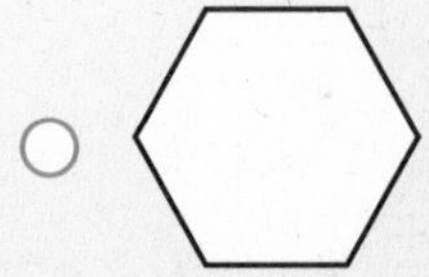
○ 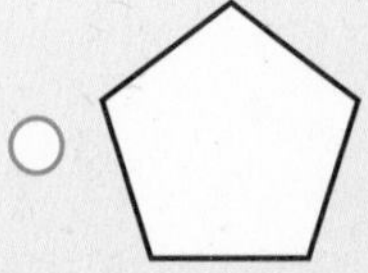
○ 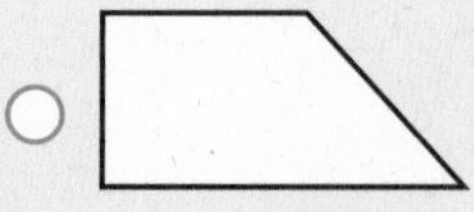
○ 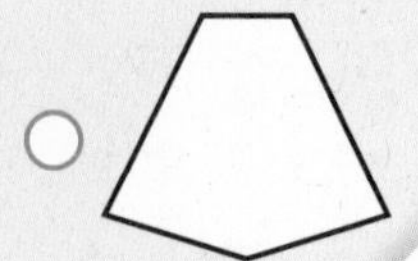

TAKE HOME ACTIVITY • Ask your child to draw a shape with 4 sides and 4 angles.

Name ________________________________

Angles in Two-Dimensional Shapes

Learning Objective You will find and count angles in two-dimensional shapes.

Circle the angles in each shape. Write how many.

1.

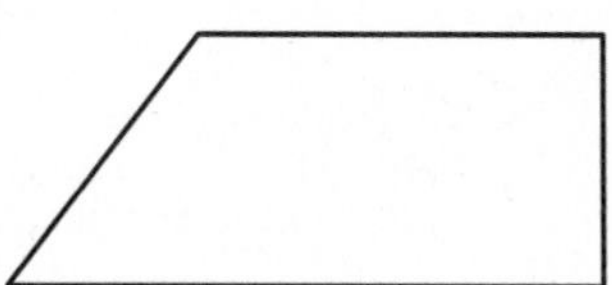

____ angles

2.

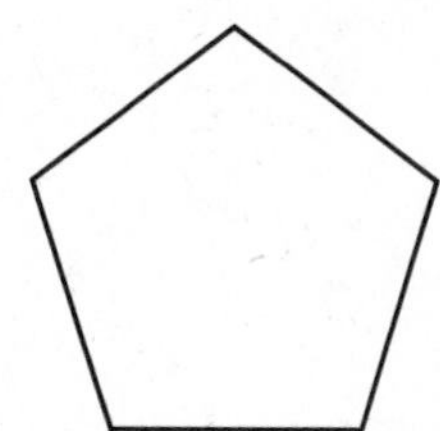

____ angles

Problem Solving

3. Logan drew 2 two-dimensional shapes that had 8 angles in all. Draw shapes Logan could have drawn.

4. WRITE Math Draw a two-dimensional shape with 4 angles. Circle the angles. Write the name of the two-dimensional shape you drew.

____

Lesson Check

1. How many angles does this shape have?

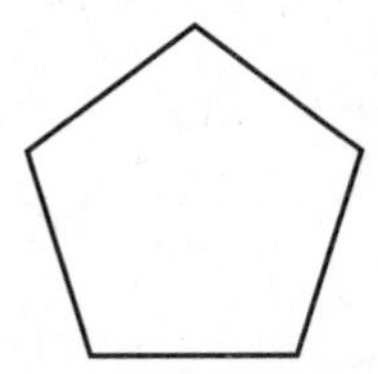

____ angles

2. How many angles does this shape have?

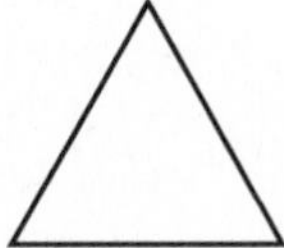

____ angles

Spiral Review

3. Use an inch ruler. What is the length of the string to the nearest inch?

____ inches

4. Look at the picture graph. How many children chose daisies?

____ children

Favorite Flower						
roses	☺	☺	☺	☺		
tulips	☺	☺	☺			
daisies	☺	☺	☺	☺	☺	
lillies	☺	☺				

Key: Each ☺ stands for 1 child.

Name ______________________________

Sort Two-Dimensional Shapes

Essential Question How do you use the number of sides and angles to sort two-dimensional shapes?

Learning Objective You will use the number of sides and angles to classify two-dimensional shapes.

Listen and Draw

Make the shape with pattern blocks. Draw and color the blocks you used.

Use one block.

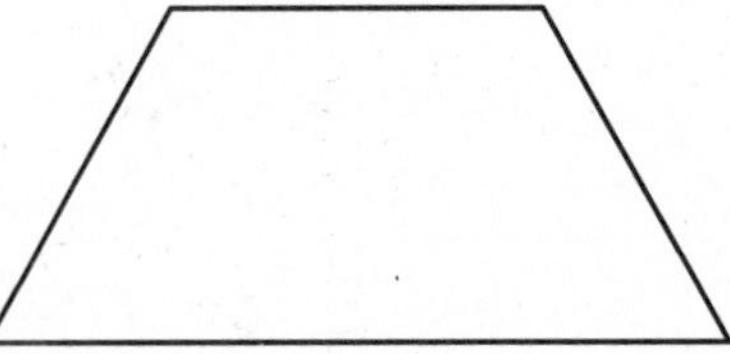

Use two blocks.

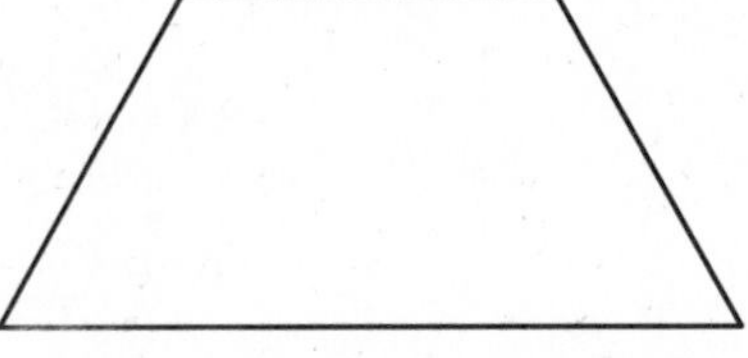

Use three blocks.

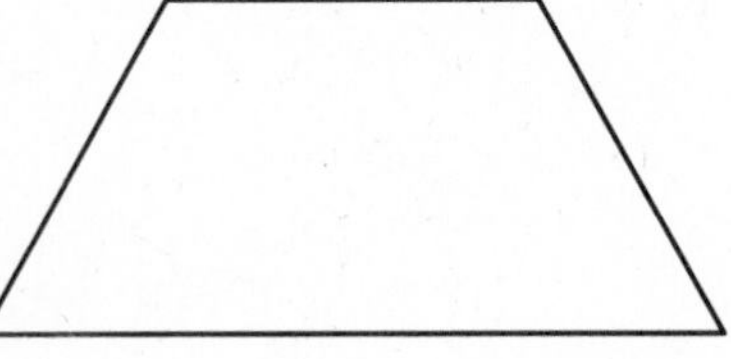

Math Processes and Practices 6

Describe how you could sort the blocks you used.

FOR THE TEACHER • Tell children that the shape shown three times on the page is a trapezoid. Have children use pattern blocks to make the trapezoid three times: with one pattern block, with two pattern blocks, and then with three pattern blocks.

Model and Draw

Which shapes match the rule?

Shapes with more than 3 sides

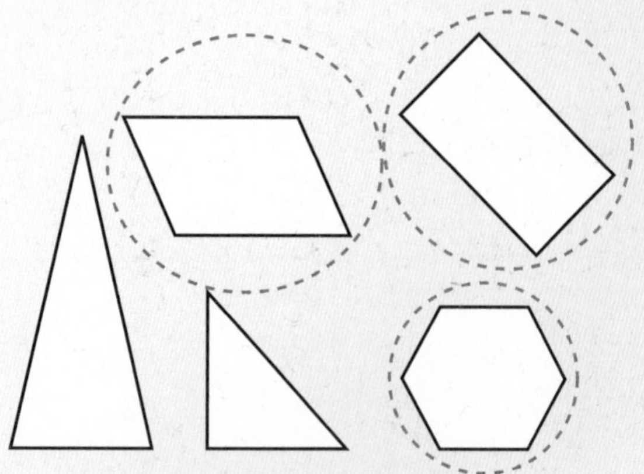

Shapes with fewer than 5 angles

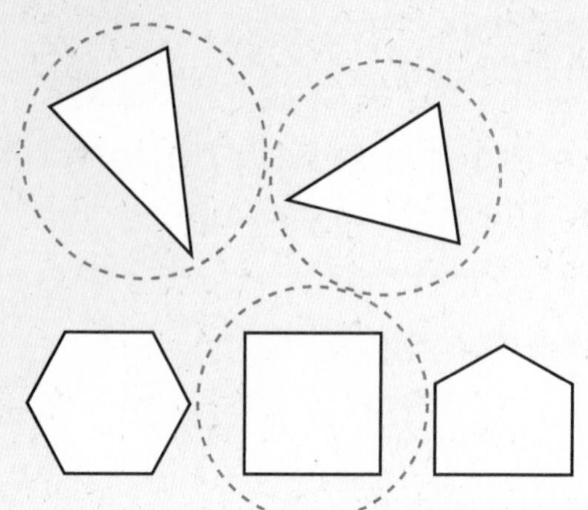

Share and Show

Circle the shapes that match the rule.

1. Shapes with 5 sides

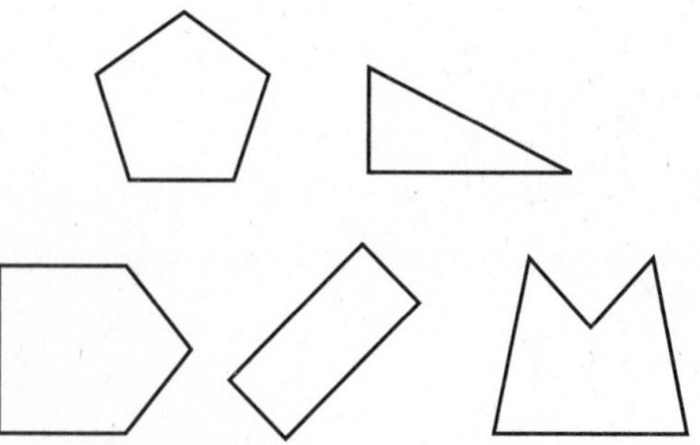

2. Shapes with more than 3 angles

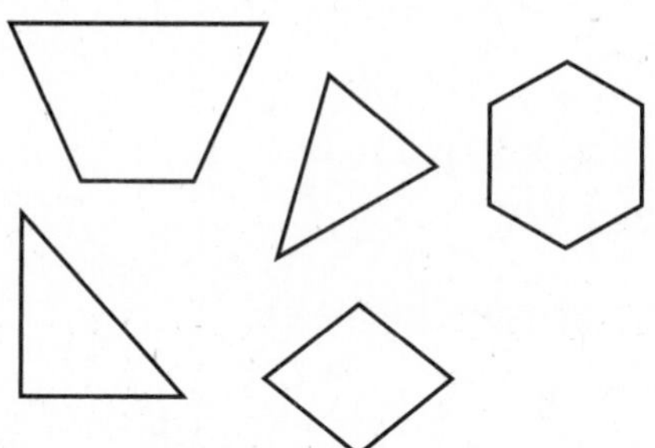

3. Shapes with fewer than 4 angles

4. Shapes with fewer than 5 sides

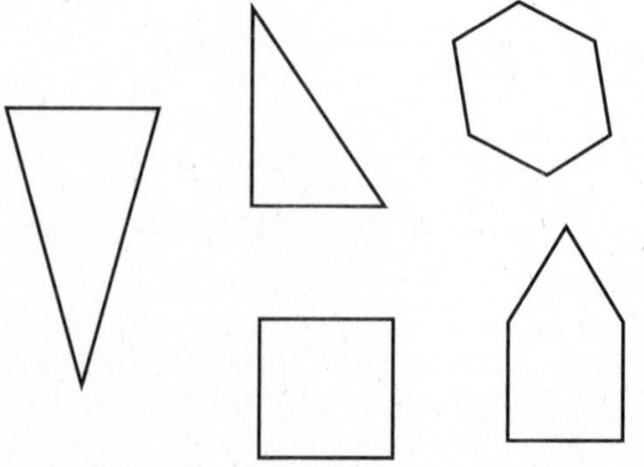

Name ______________________________

On Your Own

Circle the shapes that match the rule.

5. Shapes with 4 sides

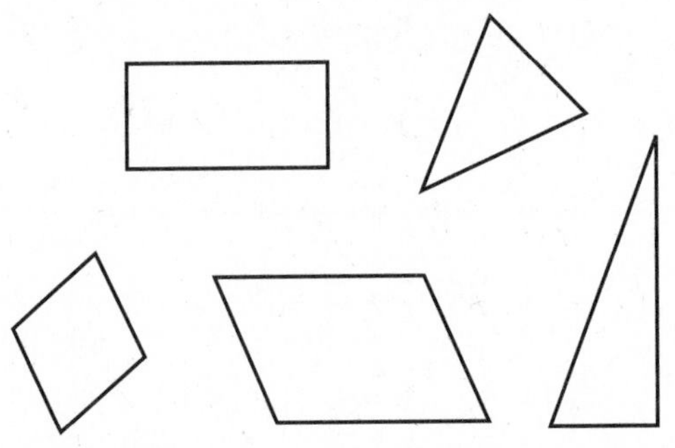

6. Shapes with more than 4 angles

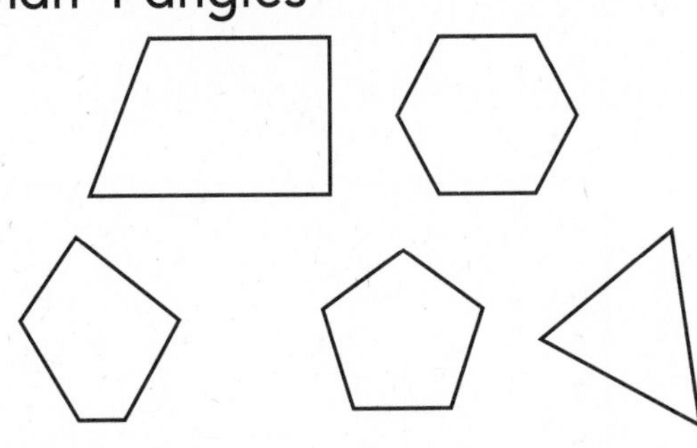

7. Shapes with fewer than 4 angles

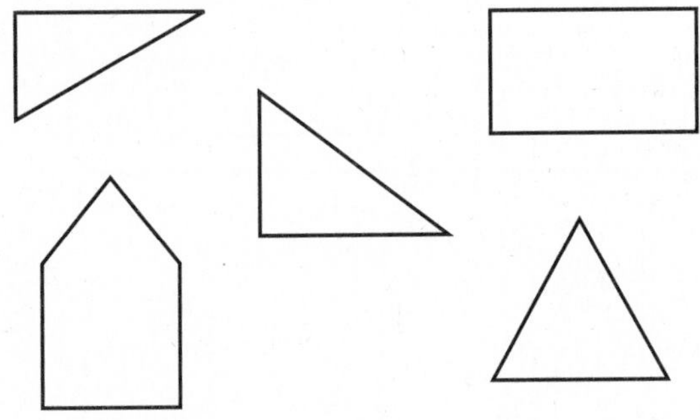

8. Shapes with fewer than 5 sides

9. THINK SMARTER Draw three shapes that match the rule. Circle them. Then draw two shapes that do not match the rule.

Shapes with fewer than 5 angles

Problem Solving • Applications

10. 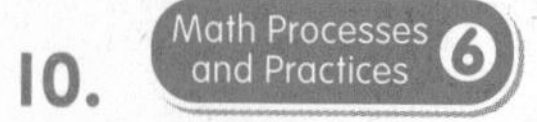

Make Connections

Sort the shapes.

- Use red to color the shapes with more than 4 sides.
- Use blue to color the shapes with fewer than 5 angles.

11. THINKSMARTER Draw each shape where it belongs in the chart.

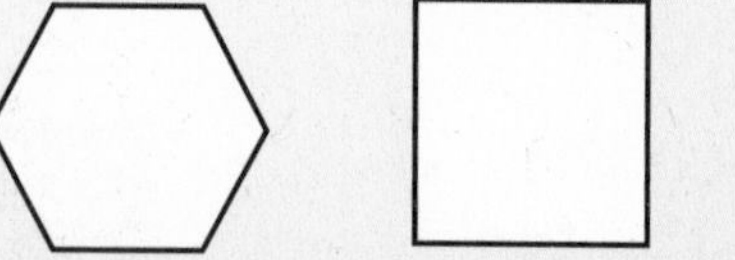

Shapes with fewer than 5 sides	Shapes with more than 4 sides

TAKE HOME ACTIVITY • Ask your child to draw some shapes that each have 4 angles.

Name ___________________________

Sort Two-Dimensional Shapes

Practice and Homework
Lesson 11.6

Learning Objective You will use the number of sides and angles to classify two-dimensional shapes.

Circle the shapes that match the rule.

1. Shapes with fewer than 5 sides

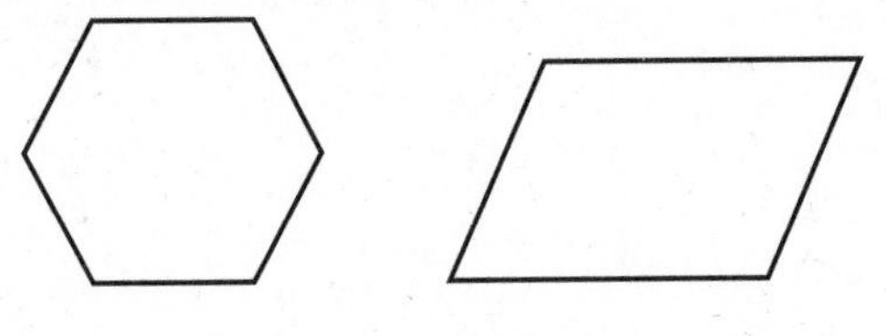
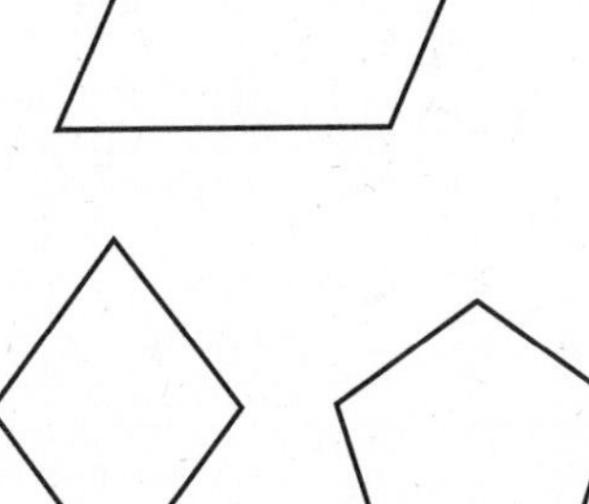
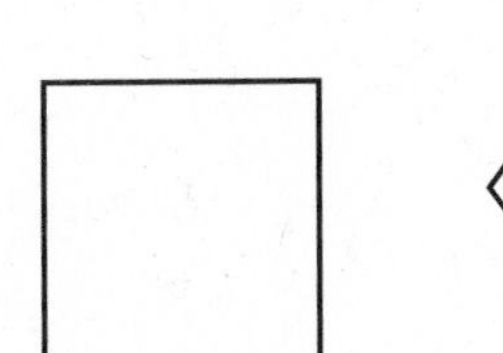

2. Shapes with more than 4 sides

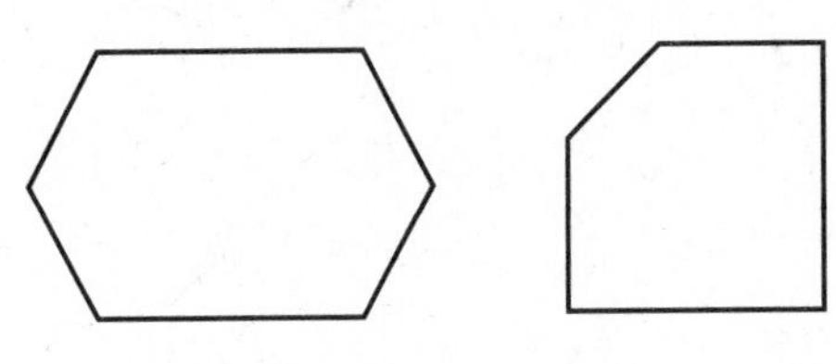
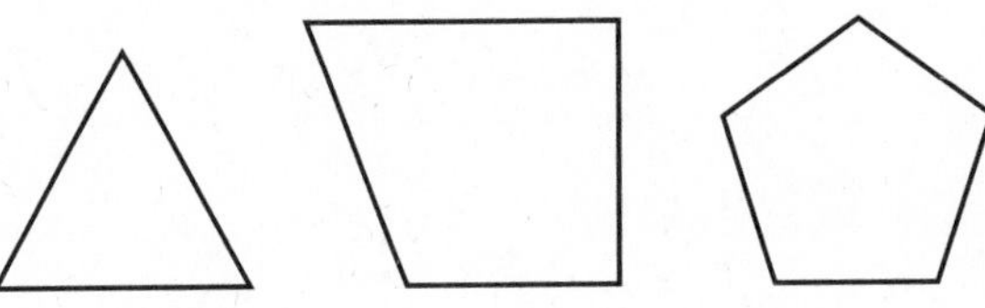

Problem Solving Real World

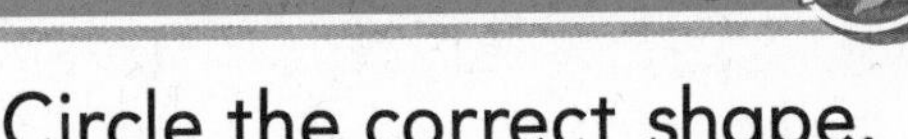

Circle the correct shape.

3. Tammy drew a shape with more than 3 angles. It is not a hexagon. Which shape did Tammy draw?

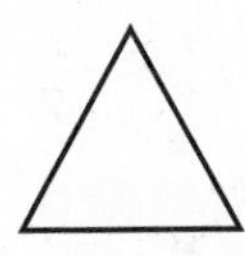
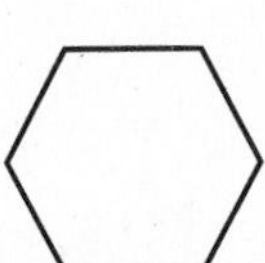

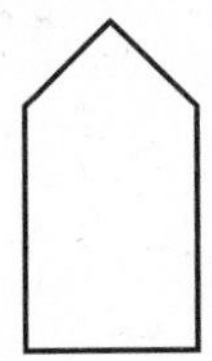

4. WRITE Math Draw three shapes that match the rule.
Shapes with more than 3 angles.

Lesson Check

1. Which shape has fewer than 4 sides?

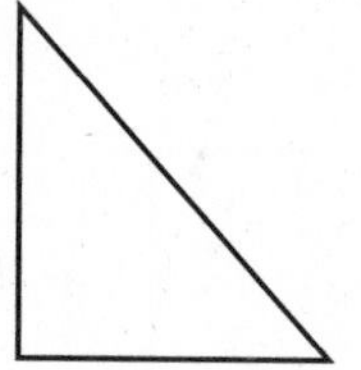
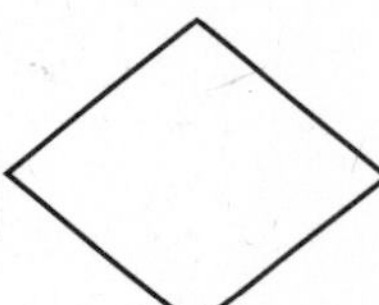
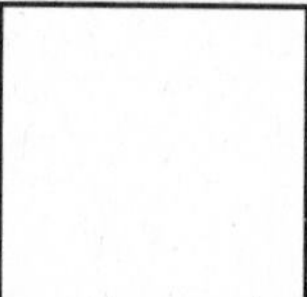
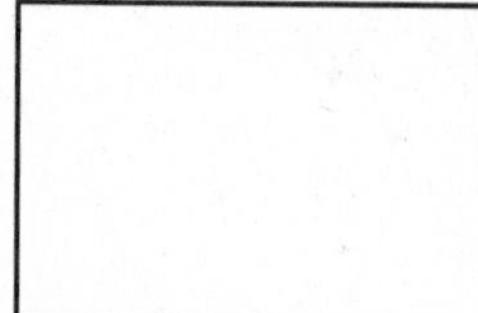

Spiral Review

2. Use an inch ruler. What is the length of the pencil to the nearest inch?

____ inches

3. Use the tally chart. How many children chose basketball as their favorite sport?

____ children

Favorite Sport	
Sport	**Tally**
soccer	𝍸
basketball	𝍸 II
football	IIII
baseball	IIII

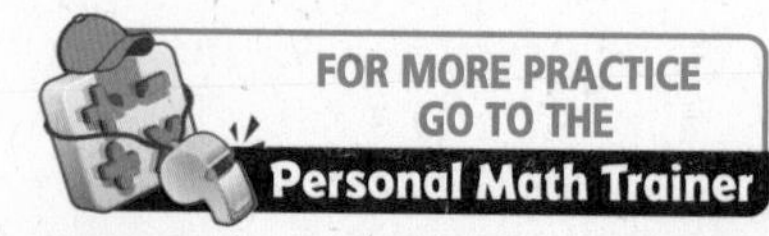

Name ______________________________

Partition Rectangles

Essential Question How do you find the total number of same-size squares that will cover a rectangle?

Learning Objective You will find the total number of same-size squares that will cover a rectangle.

Listen and Draw

Put several color tiles together. Trace around the shape to draw a two-dimensional shape.

Math Talk — Math Processes and Practices 

Is there a different shape that can be made with the same number of tiles? **Explain.**

HOME CONNECTION • After putting together tiles, your child traced around them to draw a two-dimensional shape. This activity is an introduction to partitioning a rectangle into several same-size squares.

Model and Draw

Trace around color tiles. How many square tiles cover this rectangle?

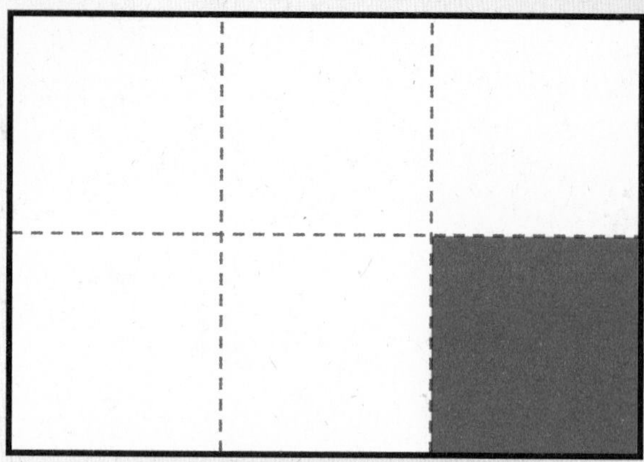

Number of rows: 2

Number of columns: 3

Total: ____ square tiles

Share and Show

Use color tiles to cover the rectangle.
Trace around the square tiles. Write how many.

1.

Number of rows: ____

Number of columns: ____

Total: ____ square tiles

2.

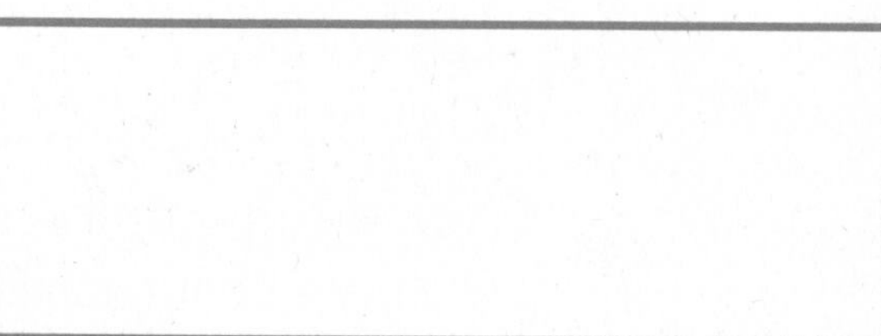

Number of rows: ____

Number of columns: ____

Total: ____ square tiles

Name ___________________________

On Your Own

Use color tiles to cover the rectangle.
Trace around the square tiles. Write how many.

3. 

Number of rows: _____

Number of columns: _____

Total: _____ square tiles

4. 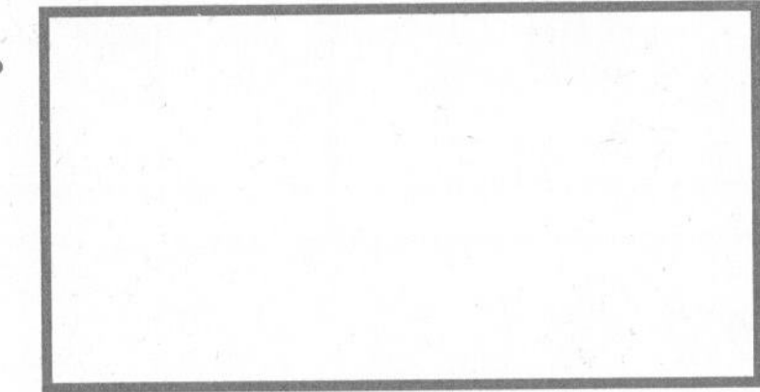

Number of rows: _____

Number of columns: _____

Total: _____ square tiles

5. THINK SMARTER Mary started to cover this rectangle with ones blocks. **Explain** how you would estimate the number of ones blocks that would cover the whole rectangle.

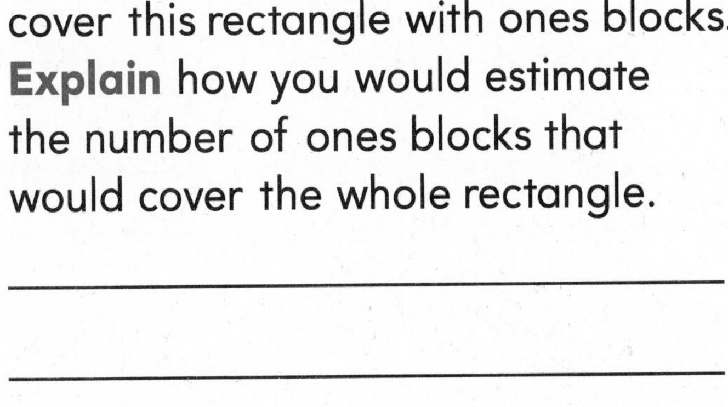

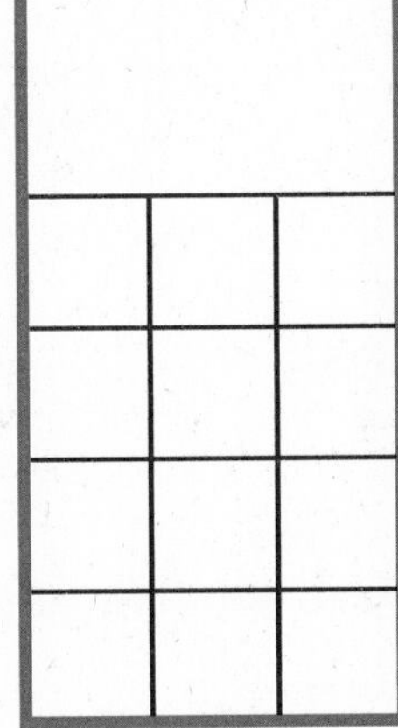

TAKE HOME ACTIVITY • Have your child describe what he or she did in this lesson.

Name ____________________

Mid-Chapter Checkpoint

Concepts and Skills

Circle the objects that match the shape name.

1. cylinder				
2. cube				

Write the number of sides and the number of vertices.

3. quadrilateral

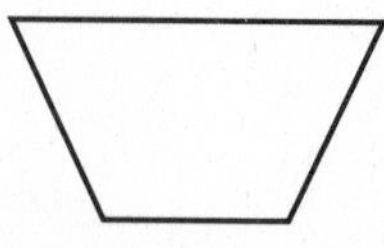

_____ sides

_____ vertices

4. pentagon

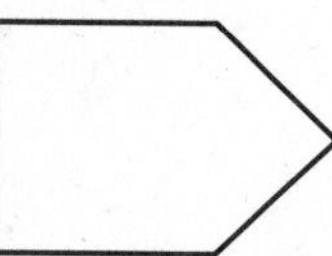

_____ sides

_____ vertices

5. hexagon

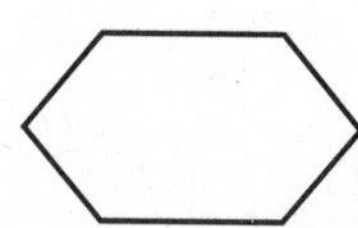

_____ sides

_____ vertices

6. THINK SMARTER How many angles does this shape have?

_____ angles

Name ______________________________

Partition Rectangles

Learning Objective You will find the total number of same-size squares that will cover a rectangle.

Use color tiles to cover the rectangle. Trace around the square tiles. Write how many.

1.

Number of rows: ____

Number of columns: ____

Total: ____ square tiles

2.

Number of rows: ____

Number of columns: ____

Total: ____ square tiles

Problem Solving Real World

Solve. Write or draw to explain.

3. Nina wants to put color tiles on a square. 3 color tiles fit across the top of the square. How many rows and columns of tiles will Nina need? How many square tiles will she use in all?

Number of rows: _____

Number of columns: _____

Total: _____ square tiles

4. WRITE Math Look at Exercise 1 above. Is there a different rectangle that you could cover with 6 color tiles? Explain.

____

Lesson Check

1. Gina uses color tiles to cover the rectangle. How many square tiles does she use?

____ square tiles

Spiral Review

2. How many faces does a cube have?

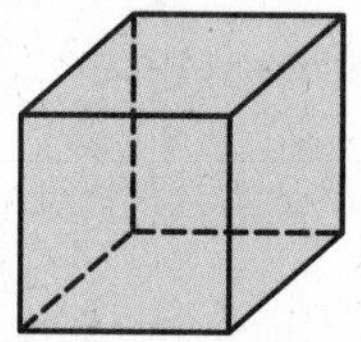

____ faces

3. How many angles does this shape have?

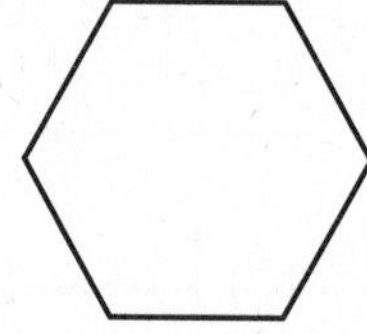

____ angles

4. Use the tally chart. How many more children chose art than reading?

____ more children

Favorite Subject	
Subject	**Tally**
reading	HHH III
math	HHH IIII
science	HHH
art	HHH HHH

Name ______________________________

Equal Parts

Essential Question What are halves, thirds, and fourths of a whole?

Learning Objective You will identify and describe equal parts of circles and rectangles as halves, thirds, or fourths.

Listen and Draw

Put pattern blocks together to match the shape of the hexagon. Trace the shape you made.

Math Processes and Practices 

Compare models
Describe how the shapes you used are different from the shapes a classmate used.

FOR THE TEACHER • Have children place a yellow hexagon pattern block on the workspace and make the same shape by using any combination of pattern blocks. Discuss how they know if the outline of the blocks they used is the same shape as the yellow hexagon.

Model and Draw

The green rectangle is the whole.
It can be divided into equal parts.

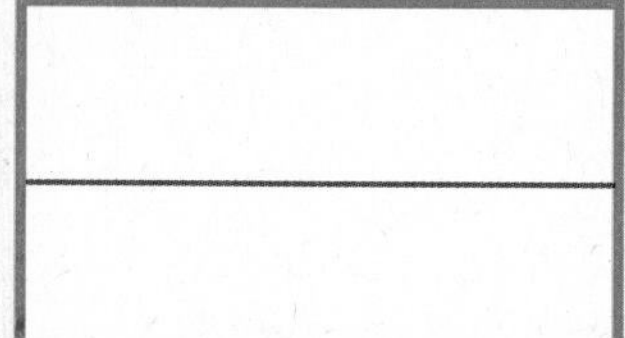

There are 2 halves.
Each part is a half.

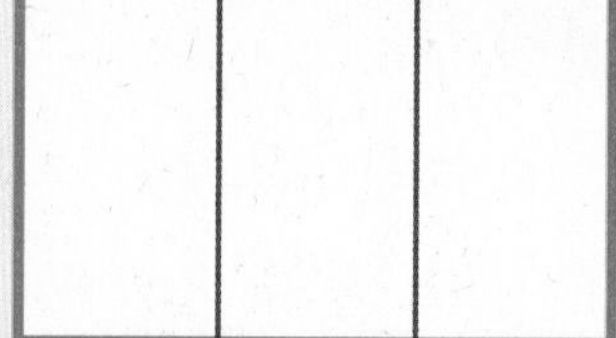

There are 3 thirds.
Each part is a third.

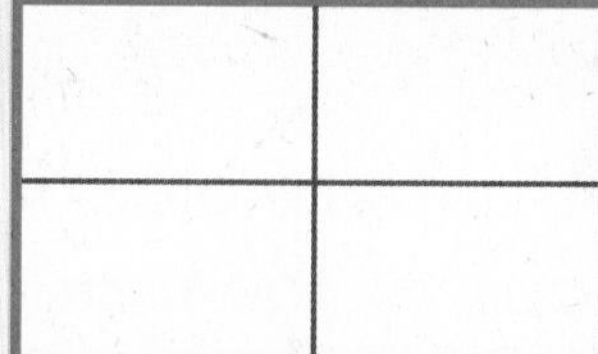

There are 4 fourths.
Each part is a fourth.

Share and Show

Write how many equal parts there are in the whole.
Write **halves**, **thirds**, or **fourths** to name the equal parts.

1.

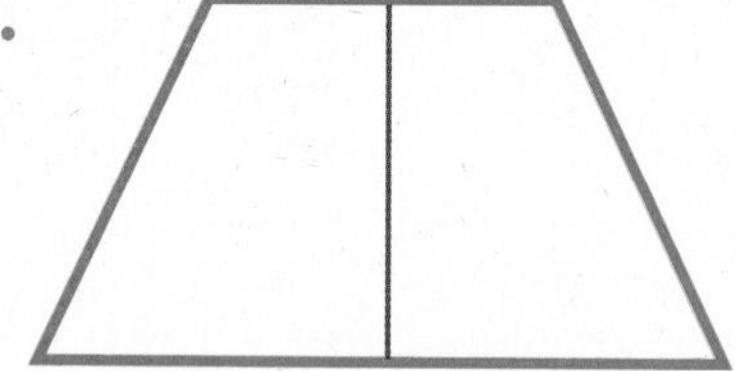

_____ equal parts

____

2.

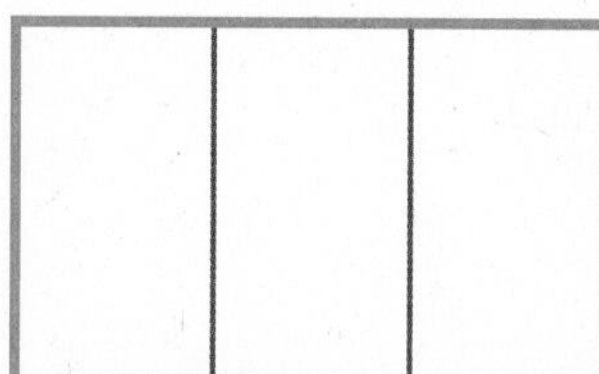

_____ equal parts

____

3.

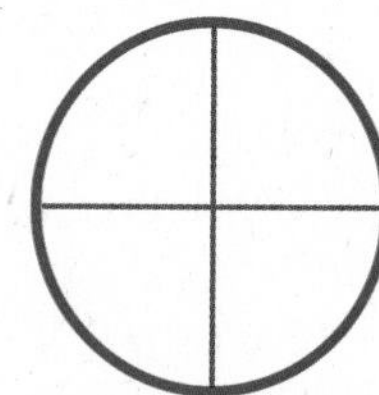

_____ equal parts

____

4.

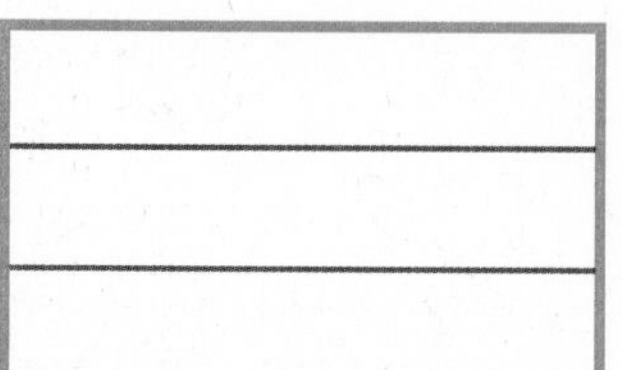

_____ equal parts

____

5.

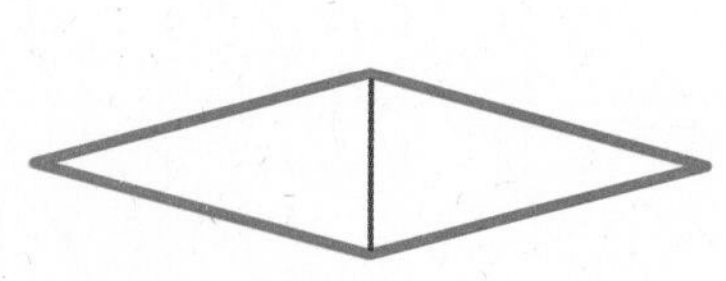

_____ equal parts

____

6.

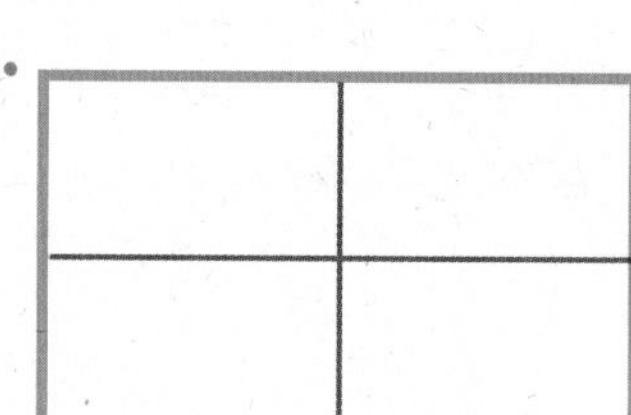

_____ equal parts

____

Name ____________________

On Your Own

Write how many equal parts there are in the whole.
Write **halves**, **thirds**, or **fourths** to name the equal parts.

7. 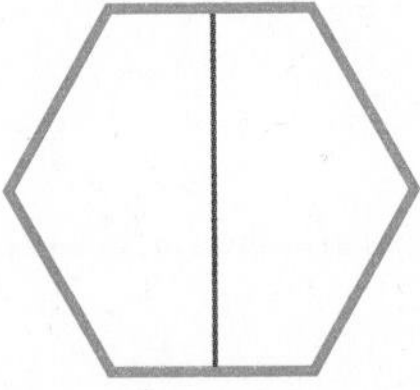

____ equal parts

____

8. 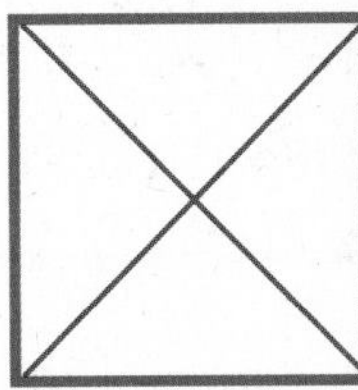

____ equal parts

____

9. 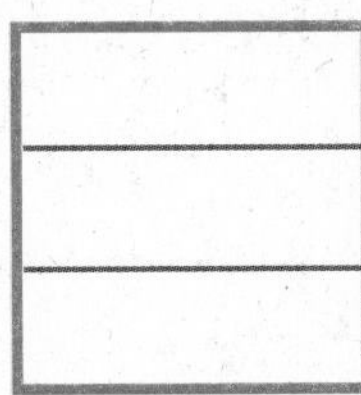

____ equal parts

____

10. 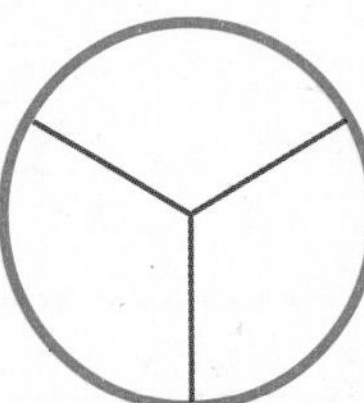

____ equal parts

____

11. 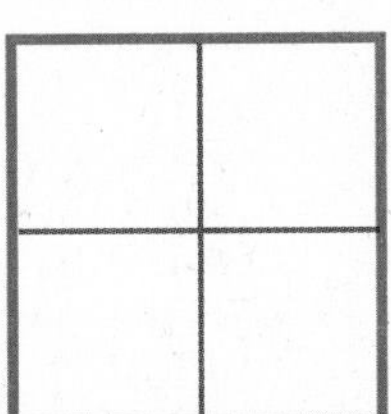

____ equal parts

____

12. 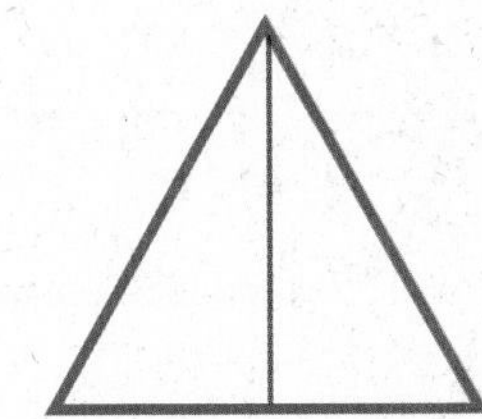

____ equal parts

____

13. THINK SMARTER Draw to show halves. Explain how you know that the parts are halves.

Problem Solving • Applications

14. Math Processes and Practices 6 **Make Connections** Sort the shapes.

- Draw an X on shapes that do **not** show equal parts.
- Use red to color the shapes that show thirds.
- Use blue to color the shapes that show fourths.

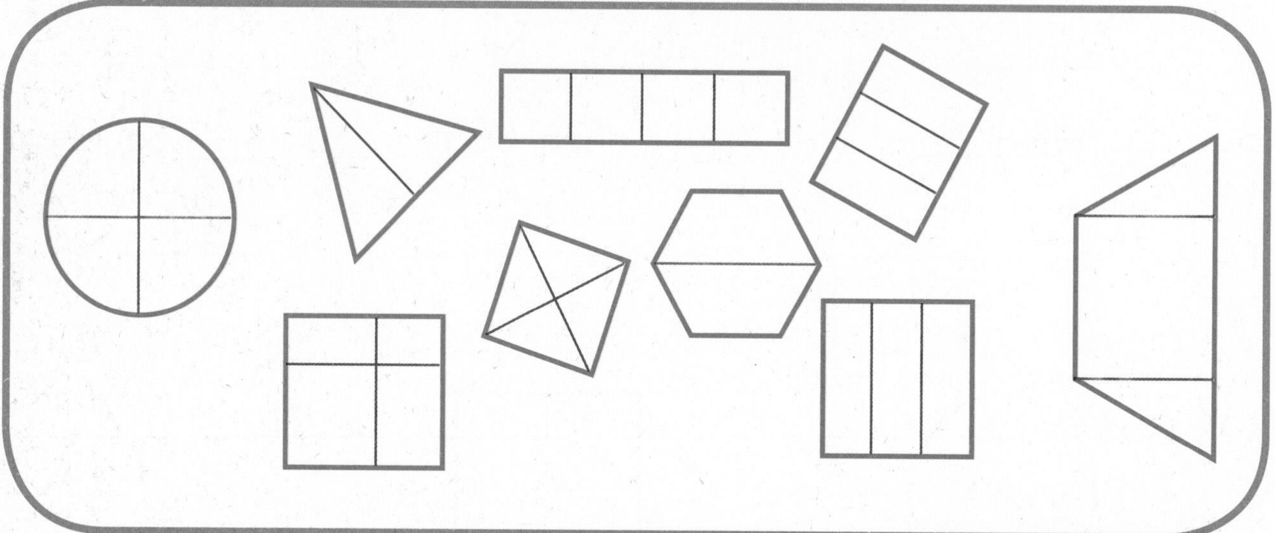

Personal Math Trainer

15. THINK SMARTER + Draw lines to show fourths three different ways.

Explain how you know that the parts are fourths.

___

___

TAKE HOME ACTIVITY • Ask your child to fold one sheet of paper into halves and another sheet of paper into fourths.

Name ________________________________

Equal Parts

Learning Objective You will identify and describe equal parts of circles and rectangles as halves, thirds, or fourths.

Write how many equal parts there are in the whole.
Write halves, thirds, or fourths to name the equal parts.

1. 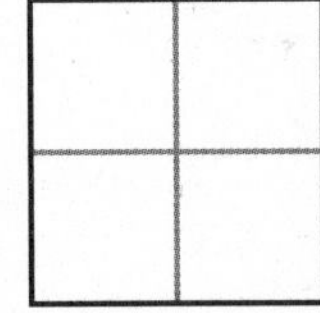

_____ equal parts

____

2. 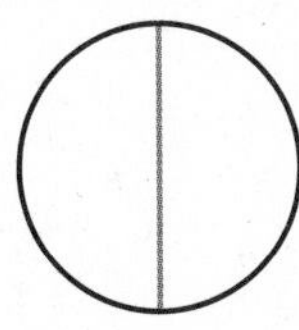

_____ equal parts

____

3. 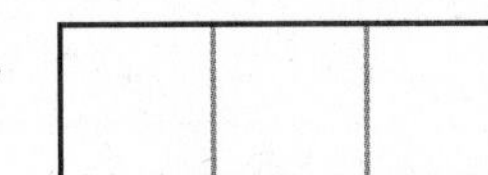

_____ equal parts

____

Problem Solving Real World

4. Sort the shapes.
   - Draw an X on the shapes that do not show equal parts.
   - Circle the shapes that show halves.

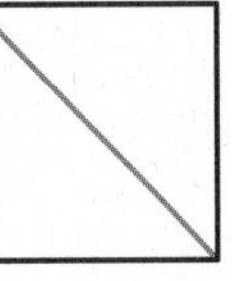
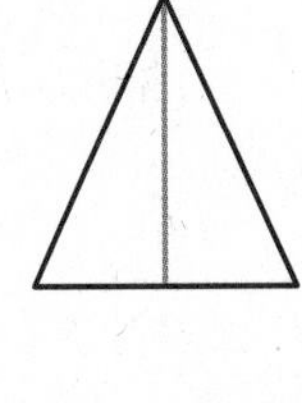

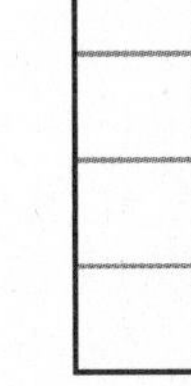

5. WRITE Math Look at the shapes in Exercise 4.
Describe the shapes that you did not put an X on or circle.

____

____

____

Lesson Check

1. What are the 3 equal parts of the shape called?

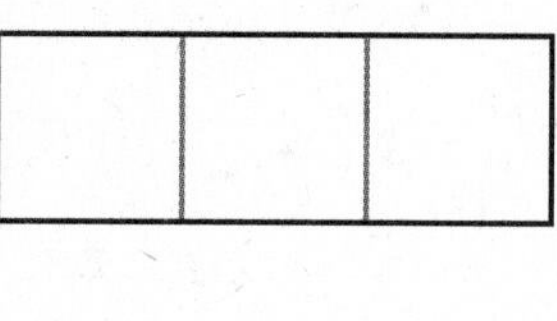

____

2. What are the 4 equal parts of the shape called?

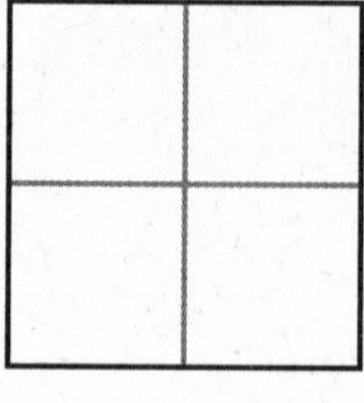

____

Spiral Review

3. What is the sum?

$$\begin{array}{r} 87 \\ +\ 45 \\ \hline \end{array}$$

4. What is the difference?

$$\begin{array}{r} 59 \\ -\ 15 \\ \hline \end{array}$$

5. Circle the quadrilateral.

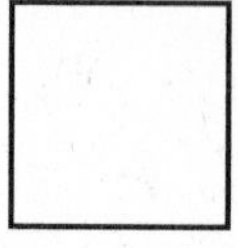
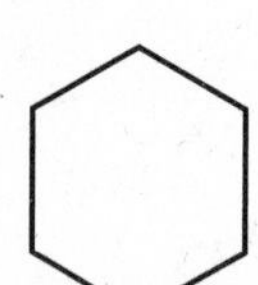

6. Circle the hexagon.

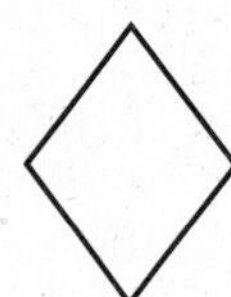
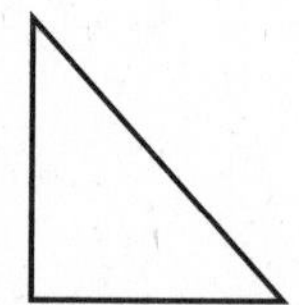

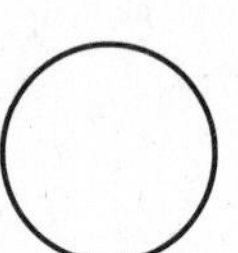

FOR MORE PRACTICE GO TO THE **Personal Math Trainer**

Name ______________________________

Show Equal Parts of a Whole

Essential Question How do you know if a shape shows halves, thirds, or fourths?

Learning Objective You will draw to show halves, thirds, or fourths of a whole.

Listen and Draw

Circle the shapes that show equal parts.

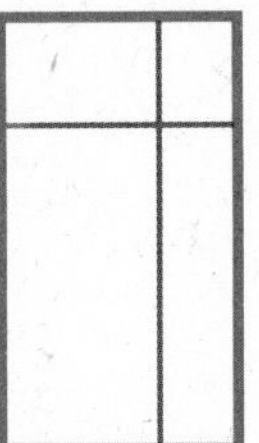

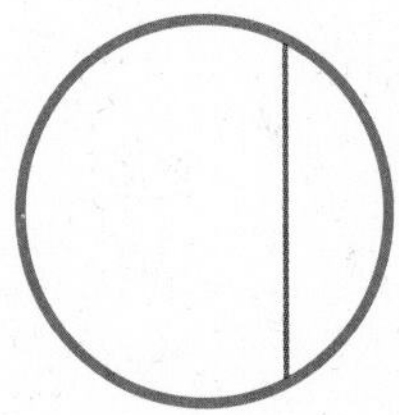

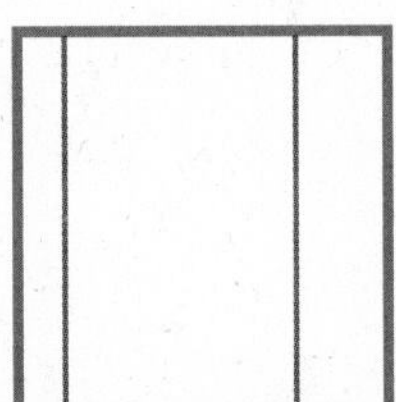

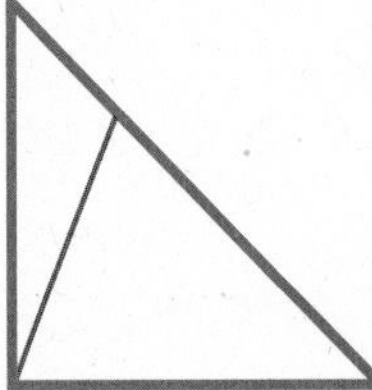

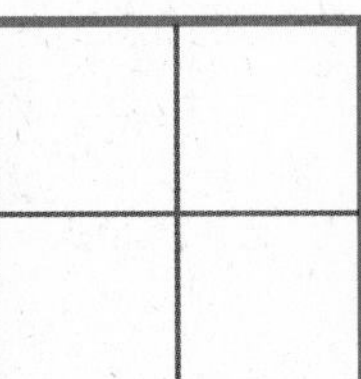

Math Talk Math Processes and Practices 6

Does the triangle show halves? **Explain.**

HOME CONNECTION • Your child completed this sorting activity with shapes to review the concept of equal parts.

Model and Draw

You can draw to show equal parts of a whole.

halves
2 equal parts

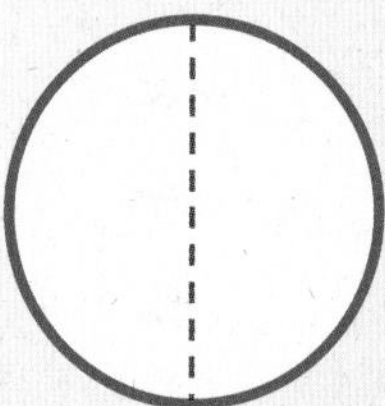

There are 2 halves in a whole.

thirds
3 equal parts

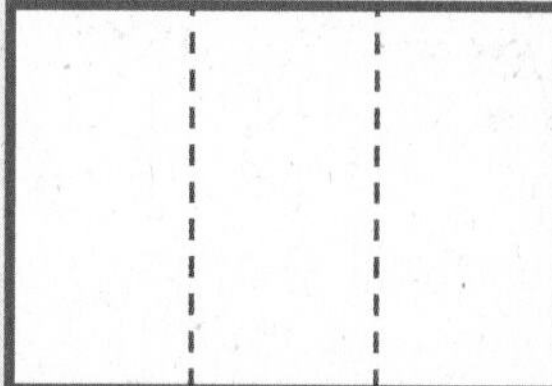

There are 3 thirds in a whole.

fourths
4 equal parts

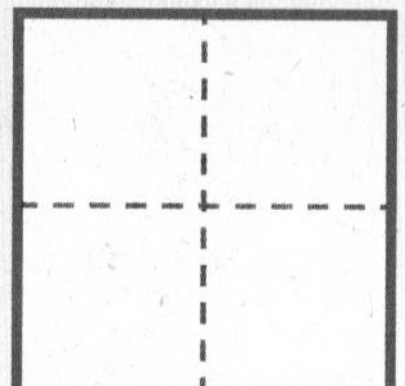

There are 4 fourths in a whole.

Share and Show

Draw to show equal parts.

1. thirds

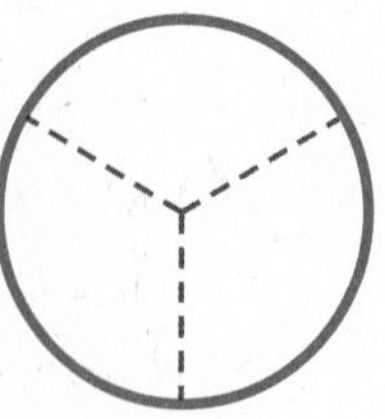

2. halves

3. fourths

4. halves

✓5. fourths

✓6. thirds

Name ______________________________

On Your Own

Draw to show equal parts.

7. halves

8. fourths

9. thirds

10. thirds

11. halves

12. fourths

13. halves

14. thirds

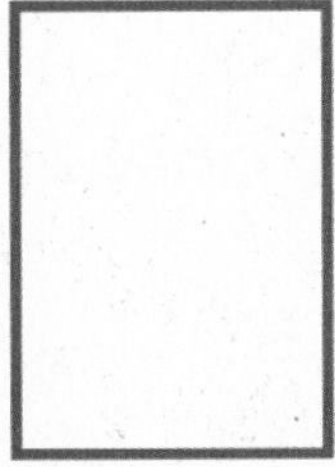

15. fourths

16. Does this shape show thirds?
Explain.

____

____

____

____

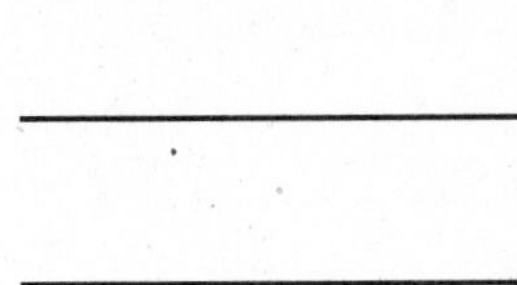

Problem Solving • Applications

17. Colton and three friends want to share a pizza equally. Draw to show how the pizza should be divided.

18. GO DEEPER There are two square pizzas. Each pizza is cut into fourths. How many pieces of pizza are there?

_______ pieces

19. THINK SMARTER Fill in the bubble next to the shapes that show thirds. Explain your answer.

○ 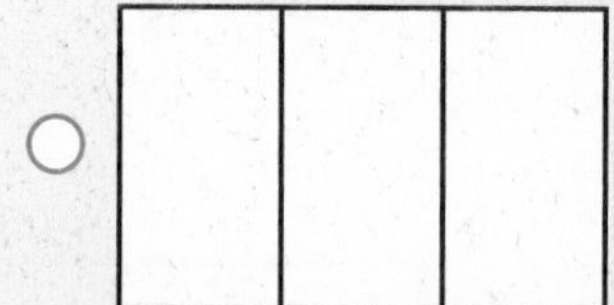 ○ 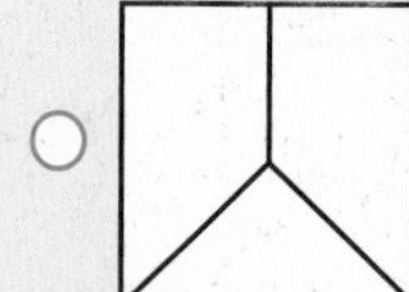 ○ 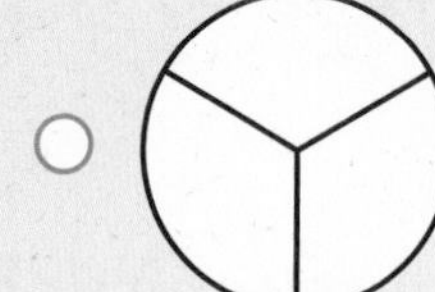 ○ 

____

____

TAKE HOME ACTIVITY • Have your child describe how to show equal parts of a shape.

Name ______________________________

Show Equal Parts of a Whole

Learning Objective You will draw to show halves, thirds, or fourths of a whole.

Draw to show equal parts.

1. halves

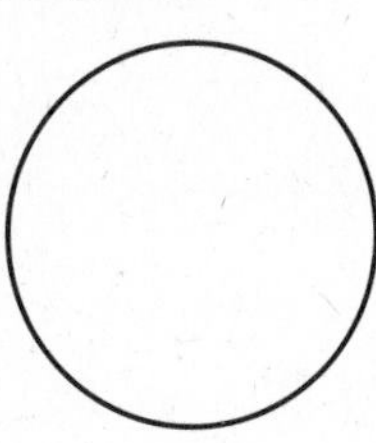

2. fourths

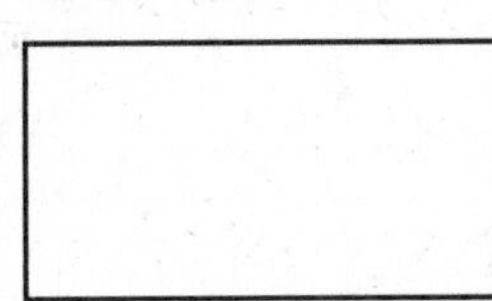

3. thirds

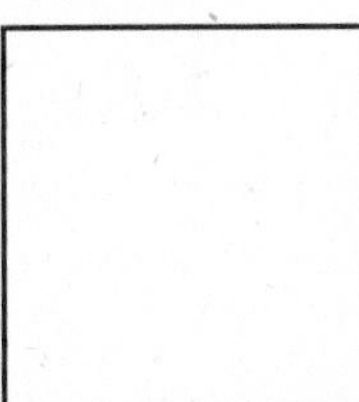

4. thirds

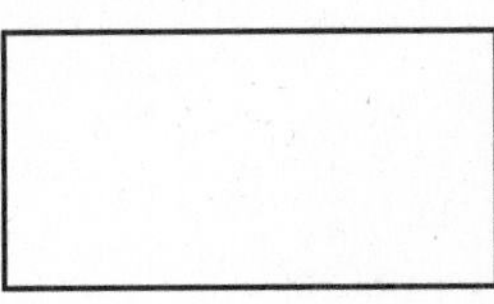

5. halves

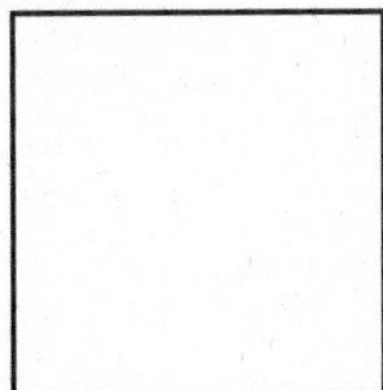

6. fourths

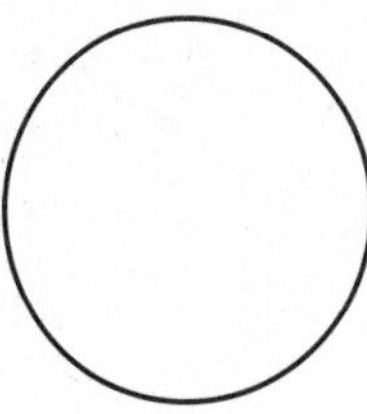

Problem Solving

Solve. Write or draw to explain.

7. Joe has one sandwich. He cuts the sandwich into fourths. How many pieces of sandwich does he have?

_____ pieces

8. WRITE Math Draw three rectangles. Then draw to show halves, thirds, and fourths. Write about each whole that you have drawn.

____

Lesson Check

1. Circle the shape divided into fourths.

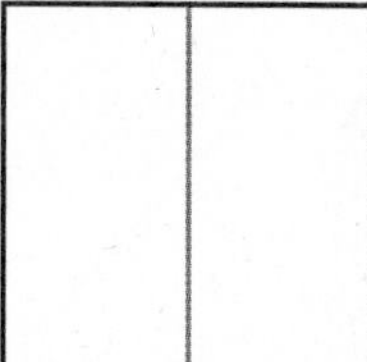
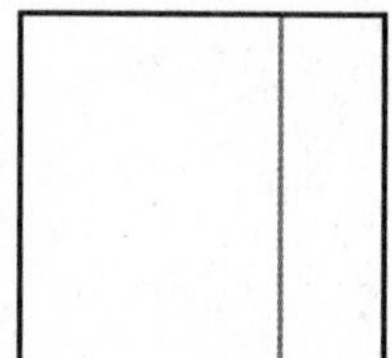
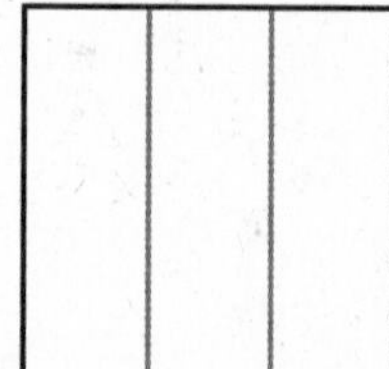
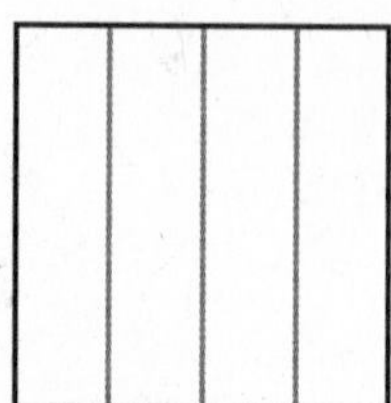

Spiral Review

2. How many angles does this shape have?

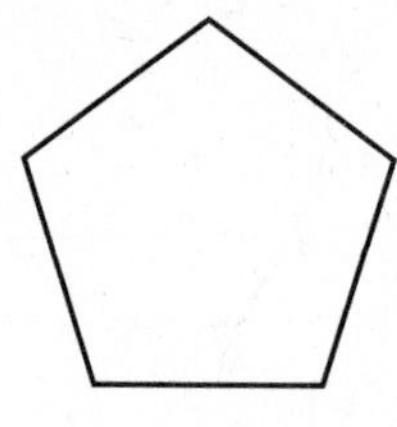

____ angles

3. How many faces does a rectangular prism have?

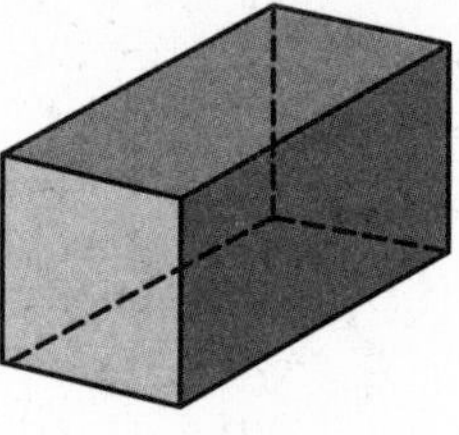

____ faces

4. Use a centimeter ruler. Measure the length of each object. How much longer is the ribbon than the string?

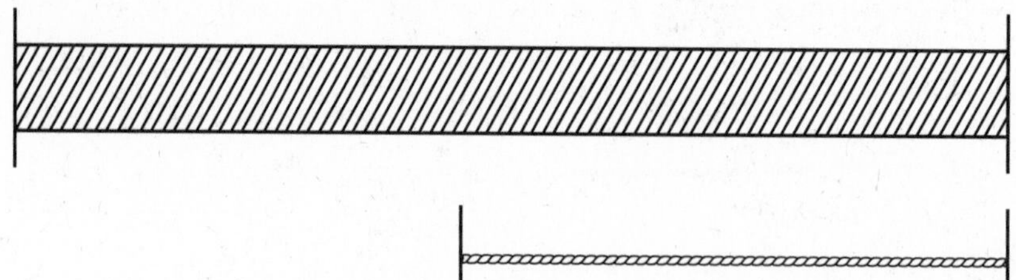

____ centimeters longer

FOR MORE PRACTICE GO TO THE Personal Math Trainer

Name ______________________________

Describe Equal Parts

Essential Question How do you find a half of, a third of, or a fourth of a whole?

Learning Objective You will find a half of, a third of, or a fourth of a whole.

Listen and Draw

Find shapes that show fourths and color them green.
Find shapes that show halves and color them red.

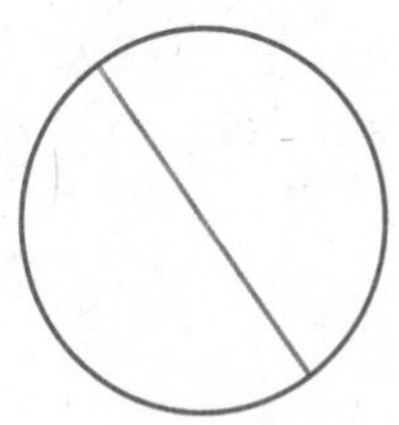

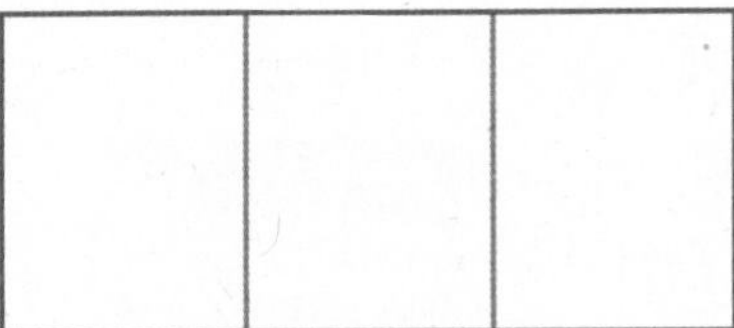

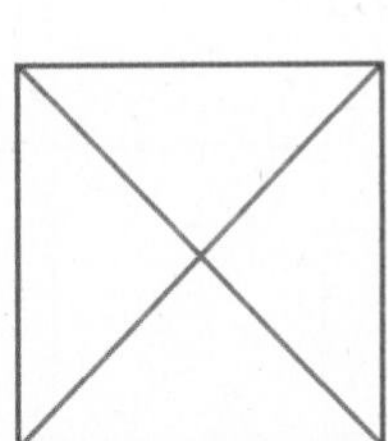

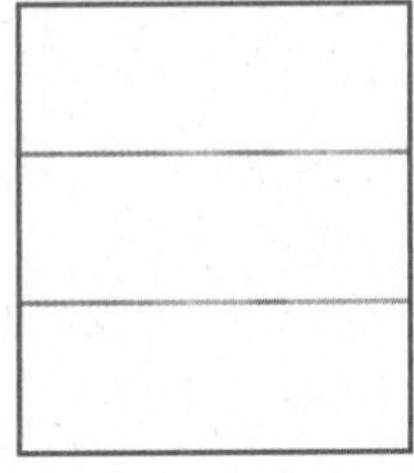

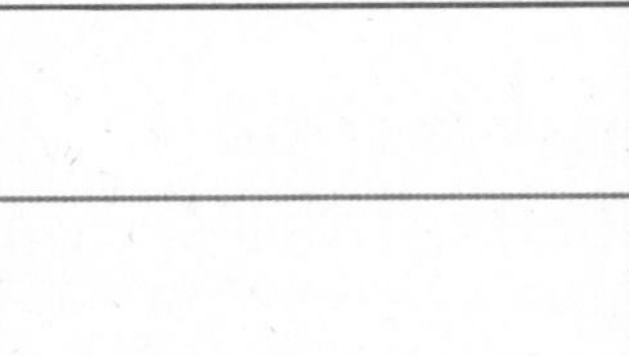

Math Processes and Practices 3

Describe how the thirds in the unshaded shapes compare to each other.

HOME CONNECTION • Your child identified the number of equal parts in shapes to review describing equal parts of a whole.

Model and Draw

These are some ways to show and describe an equal part of a whole.

1 of 4 equal parts is called a **quarter of** that shape.

2 equal parts

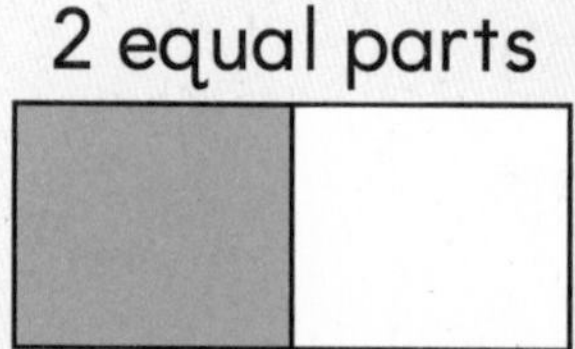

A **half of** the shape is green.

3 equal parts

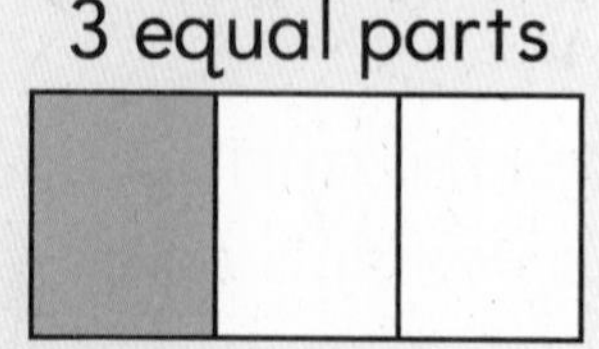

A **third of** the shape is green.

4 equal parts

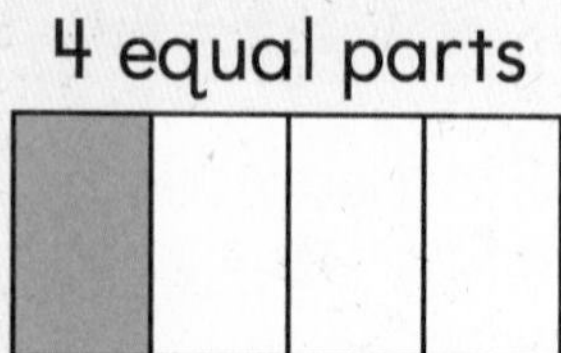

A **fourth of** the shape is green.

Share and Show

Draw to show thirds.
Color a third of the shape.

1.

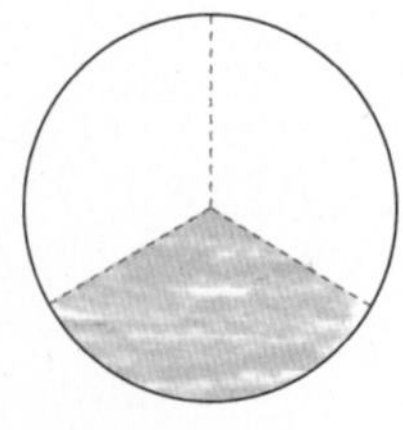

2.

3.

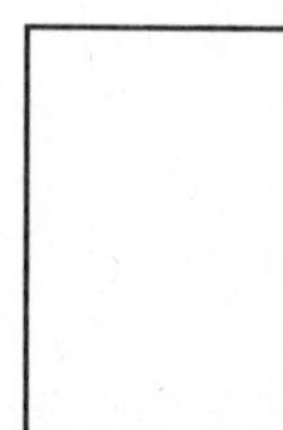

Draw to show fourths.
Color a fourth of the shape.

4.

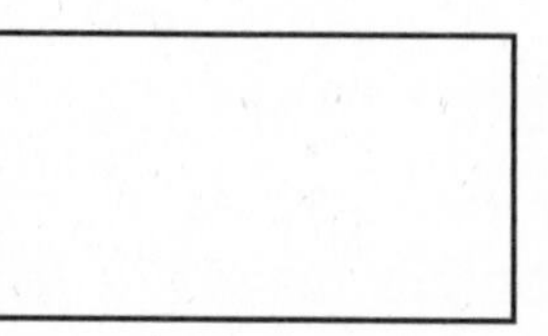

5.

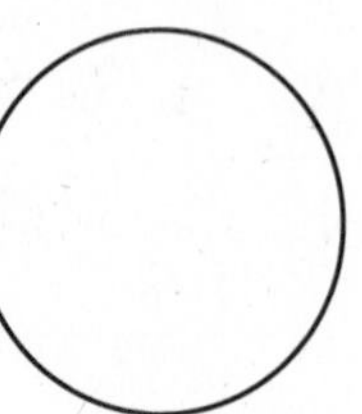

6.

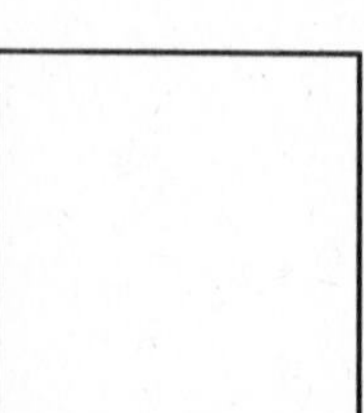

Name ____________________

On Your Own

Draw to show halves.
Color a half of the shape.

7.

8.

9.

10.

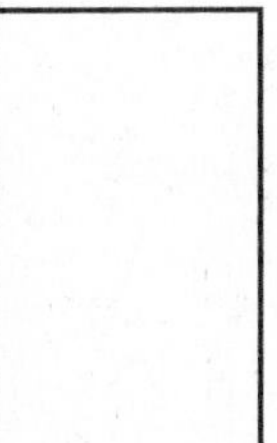

11.

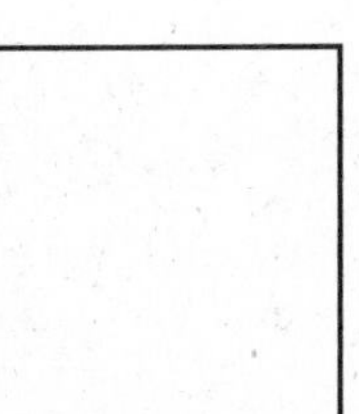

12.

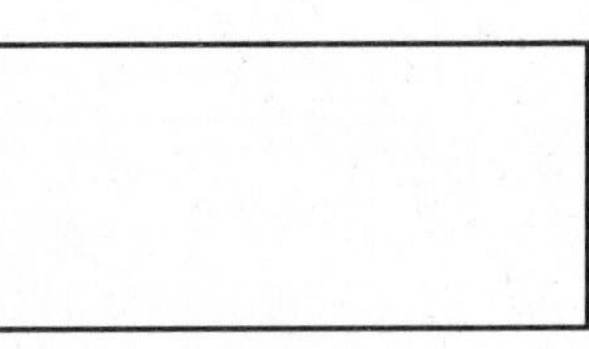

Draw to show fourths.
Color a fourth of the shape.

13.

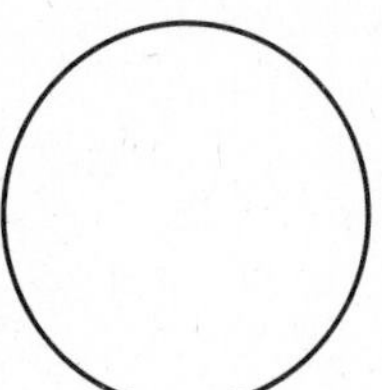

14.

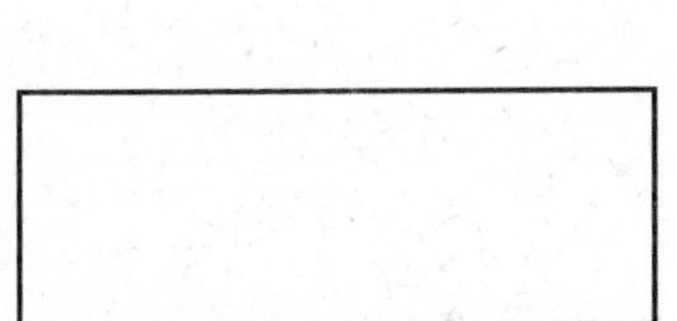

15.

Problem Solving • Applications

16. THINK SMARTER Two posters are the same size. A third of one poster is red, and a fourth of the other poster is blue.

Is the red part or the blue part larger? Draw and write to explain.

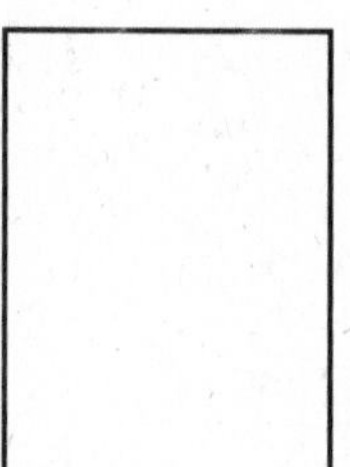

____

____

____

____

____

17. THINK SMARTER Draw to show halves, thirds, and fourths. Color a half of, a third of, or a fourth of the shape.

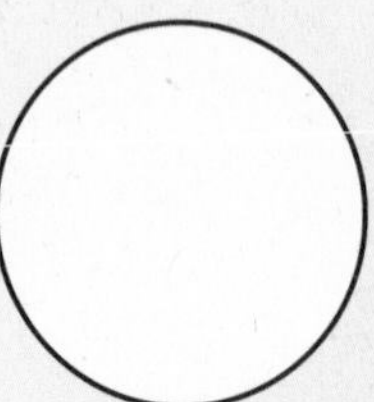

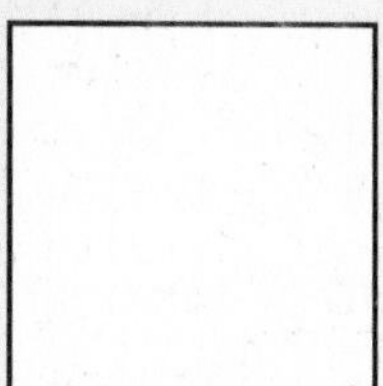

TAKE HOME ACTIVITY • Draw a square. Have your child draw to show thirds and color a third of the square.

Name ______________________________

Describe Equal Parts

Learning Objective You will find a half of, a third of, or a fourth of a whole.

Draw to show halves.
Color a half of the shape.

1. 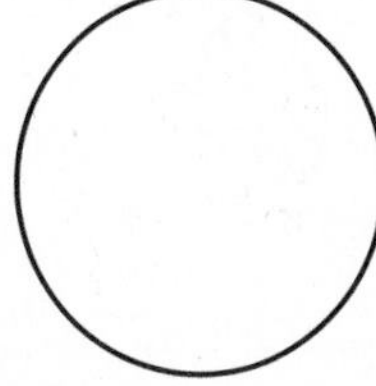

2. 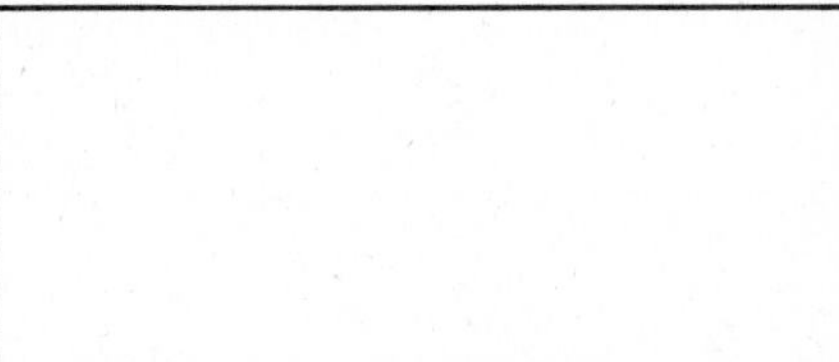

Draw to show thirds.
Color a third of the shape.

3. 

4. 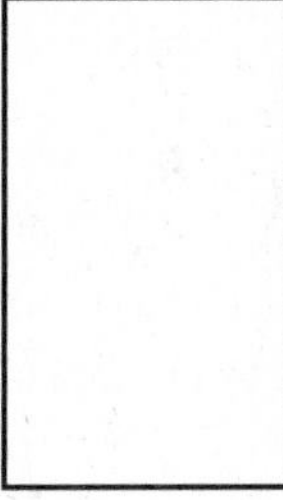

Problem Solving

5. Circle all the shapes that have a third of the shape shaded.

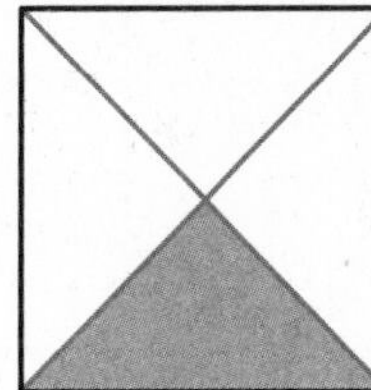
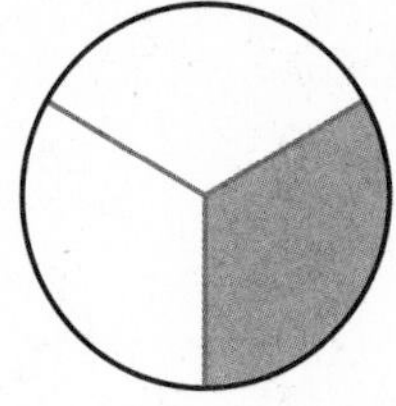

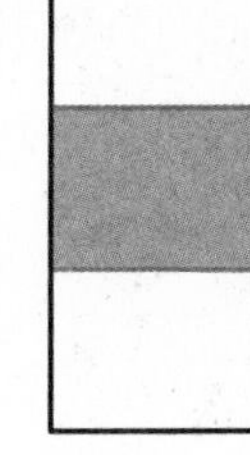
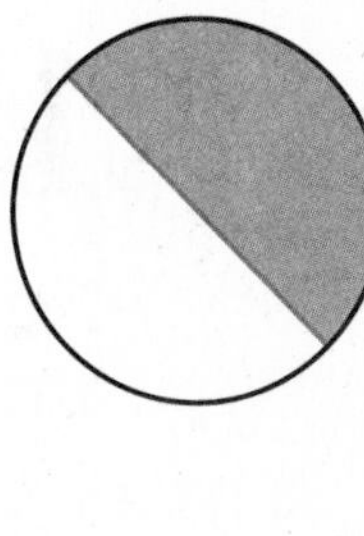

6. WRITE Math Draw pictures to show a third of a whole and a fourth of a whole. Label each picture.

Lesson Check

1. Circle the shape that has a half of the shape shaded.

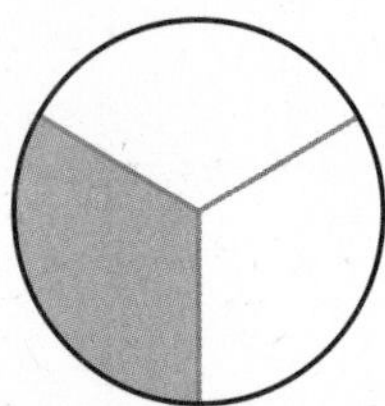 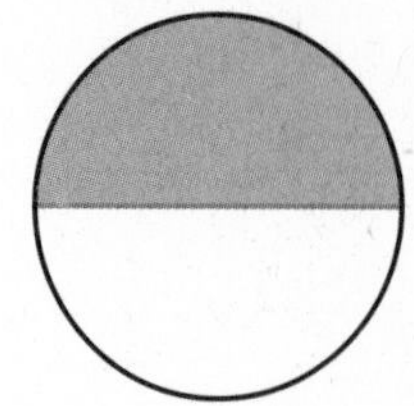 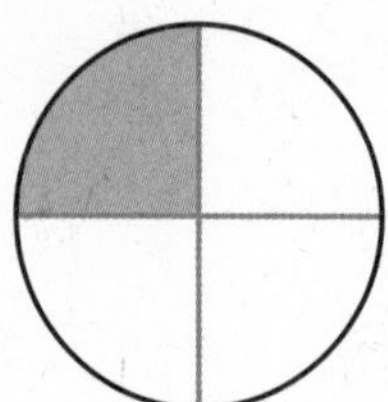 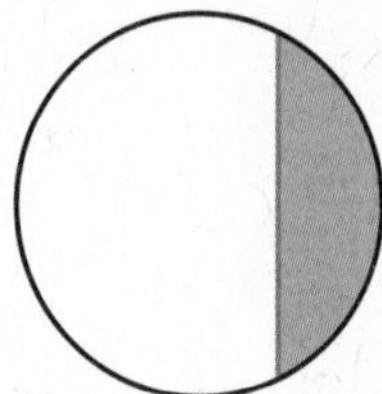

Spiral Review

2. What is the name of this shape?

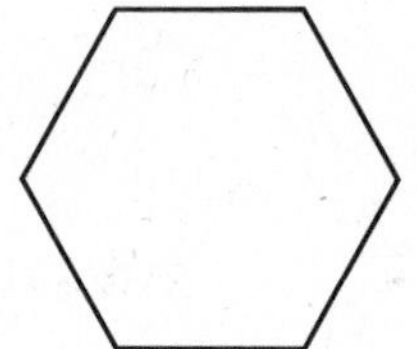

____

3. Use a centimeter ruler. What is the length of the string to the nearest centimeter?

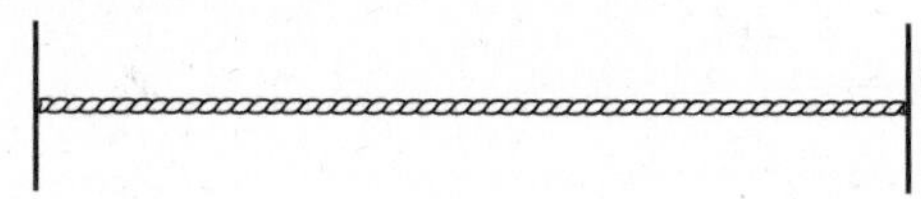

____ centimeters

4. The clock shows the time Chris finished his homework. Write the time. Then circle a.m. or p.m.

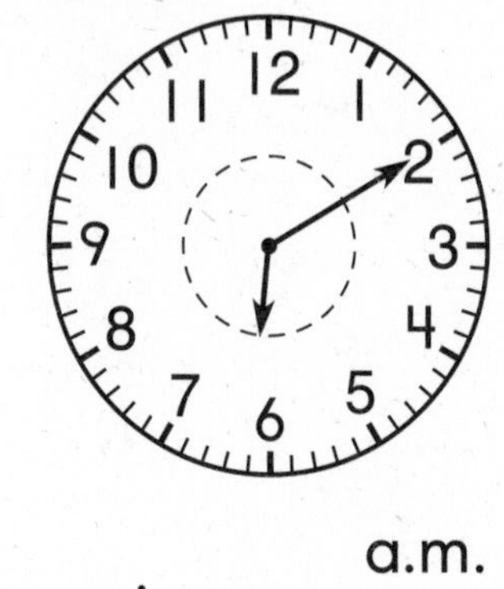

____ : ____ a.m. / p.m.

5. What time is shown on this clock?

____ : ____

FOR MORE PRACTICE GO TO THE Personal Math Trainer

Name ______________________________

Problem Solving • Equal Shares

Essential Question How can drawing a diagram help when solving problems about equal shares?

Learning Objective You will use the strategy *draw a diagram* to solve problems about equal shares by drawing two different ways to divide a shape.

There are two sandwiches that are the same size. Each sandwich is divided into fourths, but the sandwiches are cut differently. How might the two sandwiches be cut?

Unlock the Problem (Real World)

What do I need to find?

how the sandwiches could be cut

What information do I need to use?

There are ____ sandwiches. Each sandwich is divided into ______________.

Show how to solve the problem.

HOME CONNECTION • Your child drew a diagram to represent and solve a problem about dividing a whole in different ways to show equal shares.

Try Another Problem

Draw to show your answer.

- What do I need to find?
- What information do I need to use?

1. Marquis has two square sheets of paper that are the same size. He wants to cut each sheet into halves. What are two different ways he can cut the sheets of paper?

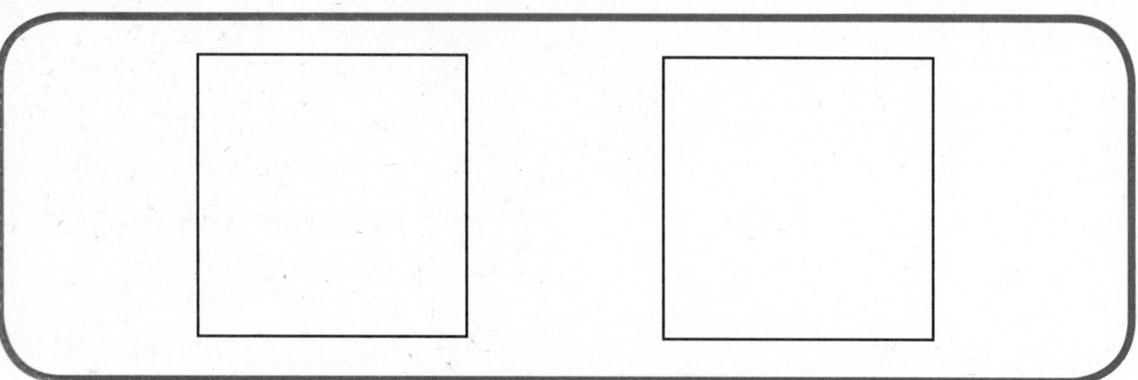

2. Shanice has two pieces of cloth that are the same size. She needs to divide each piece into thirds. What are two different ways she can divide the pieces of cloth?

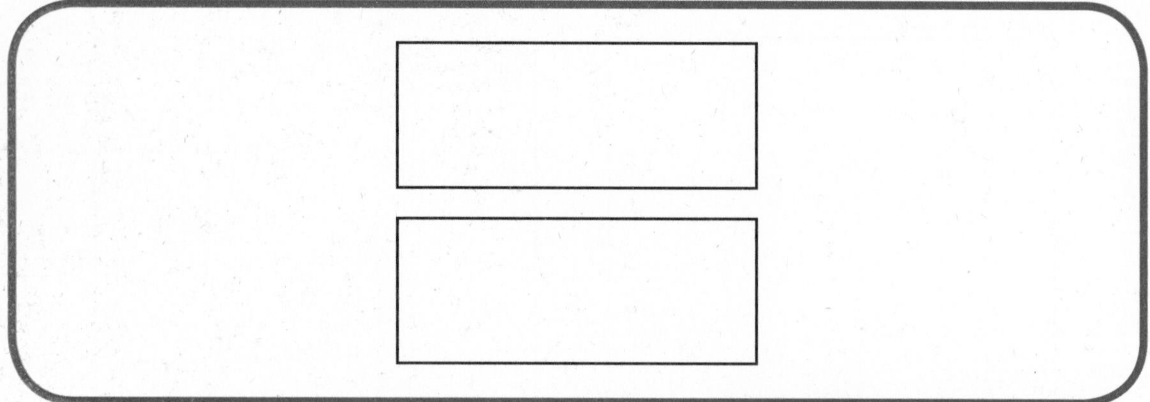

Math Talk Math Processes and Practices 1

In Problem 2, **explain** how a third of the two pieces of cloth are alike and how they are different.

Name ___________________________________

Share and Show

Draw to show your answer.

3. Brandon has two pieces of toast that are the same size. What are two different ways he can divide the pieces of toast into halves?

4. Mr. Rivera has two small trays of pasta that are the same size. What are two different ways he can cut the pasta into fourths?

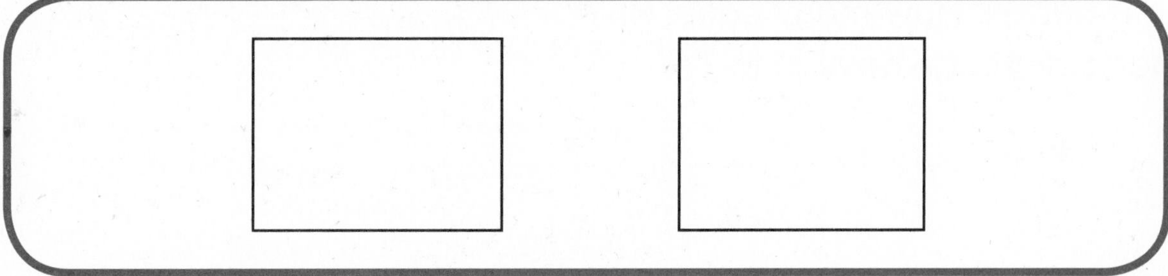

5. THINK SMARTER Erin has two ribbons that are the same size. What are two different ways she can divide the ribbons into thirds?

Problem Solving • Applications

Solve. Write or draw to explain.

6. Math Processes and Practices 4 **Use Diagrams** David needs to divide two pieces of paper into the same number of equal parts. Look at how the first piece of paper is divided. Show how to divide the second piece of paper a different way.

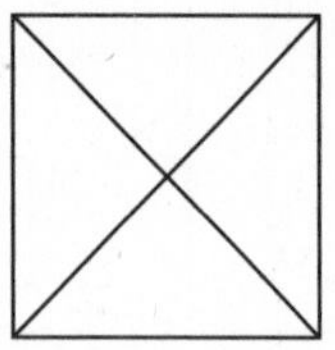 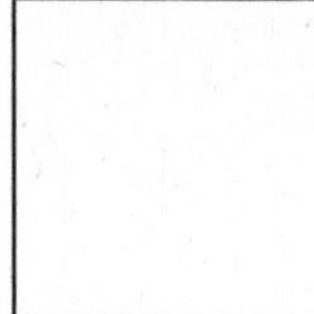

7. GO DEEPER Mrs. Lee has two sandwiches that are the same size. She cuts each sandwich into halves. How many equal parts does she have in all?

_______ equal parts

8. THINK SMARTER Emma wants to cut a piece of paper into fourths. Fill in the bubble next to all the ways she could cut the paper.

○ 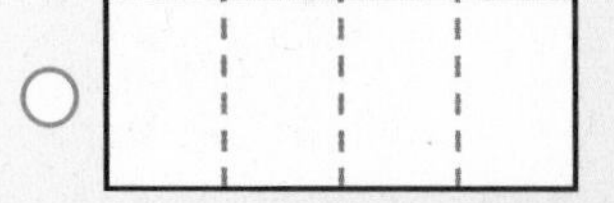 ○ 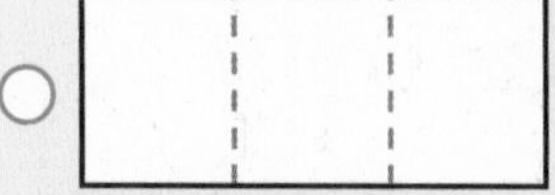 ○ 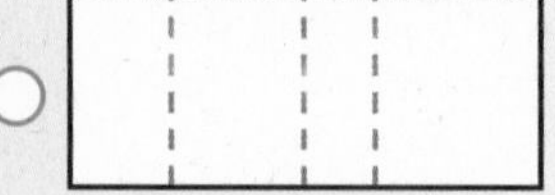 ○ 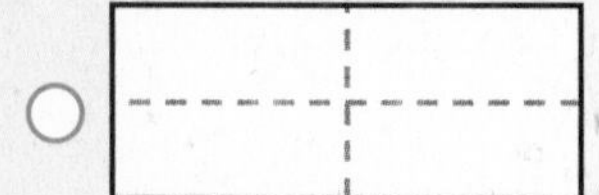

TAKE HOME ACTIVITY • Ask your child to draw two rectangles and show two different ways to divide them into fourths.

Name ____________________

Problem Solving • Equal Shares

Learning Objective You will use the strategy *draw a diagram* to solve problems about equal shares by drawing two different ways to divide a shape.

Draw to show your answer.

1. Max has square pizzas that are the same size. What are two different ways he can divide the pizzas into fourths?

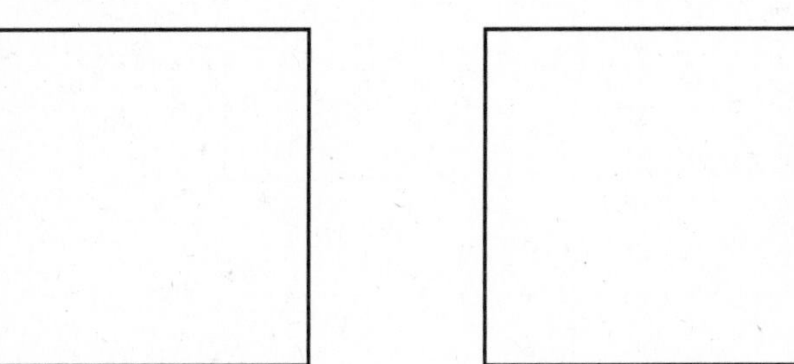

2. Lia has two pieces of paper that are the same size. What are two different ways she can divide the pieces of paper into halves?

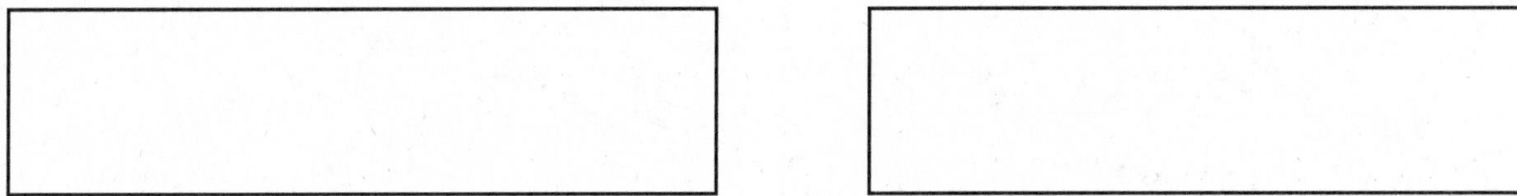

3. WRITE Math Draw and write to explain how you can divide a rectangle into thirds in two different ways.

____

Lesson Check

1. Bree cut a piece of cardboard into thirds like this.

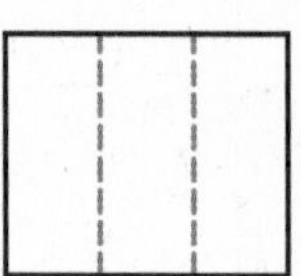

Circle the other shape that is divided into thirds.

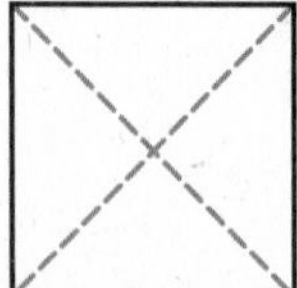
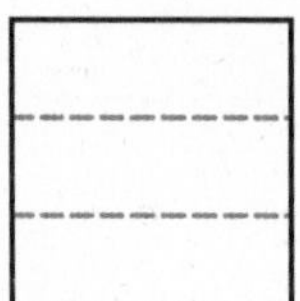
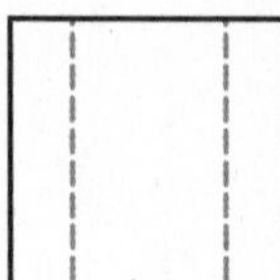
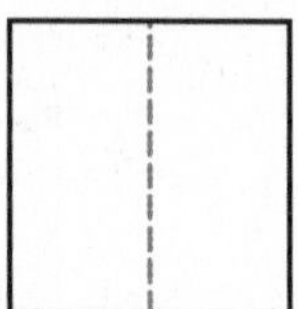

Spiral Review

2. Circle the shape with three equal parts.

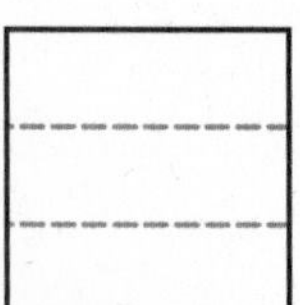
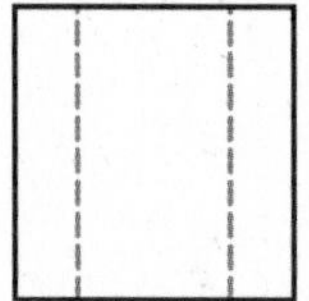
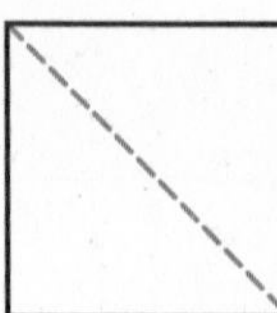
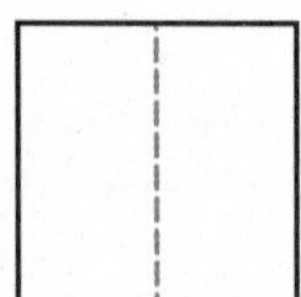

3. How many angles does this shape have?

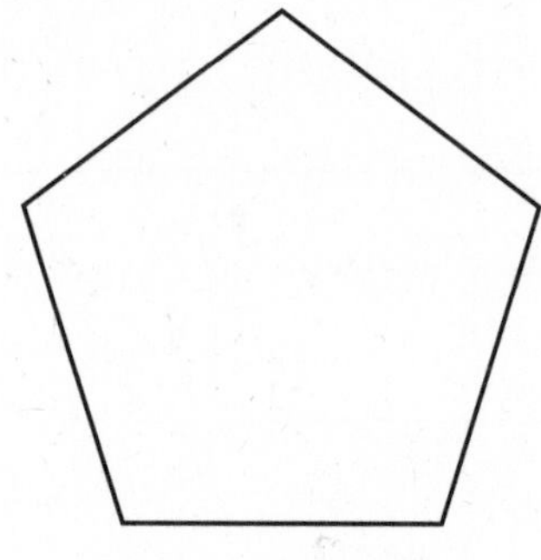

____ angles

4. What is the best estimate for the length of a baseball bat?

____ feet

5. Which is another way to write 10 minutes after 9?

____ : ____

Name ______________________________

Chapter 11 Review/Test

1. Match the shapes.

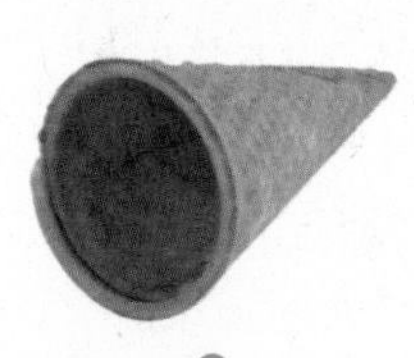

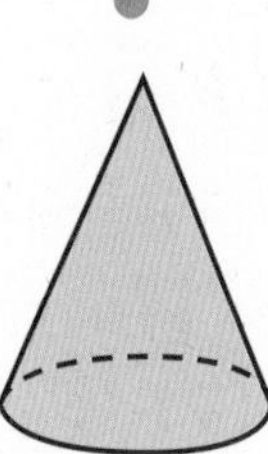

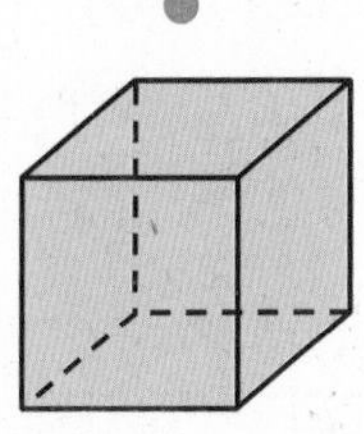

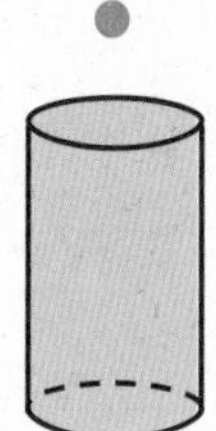

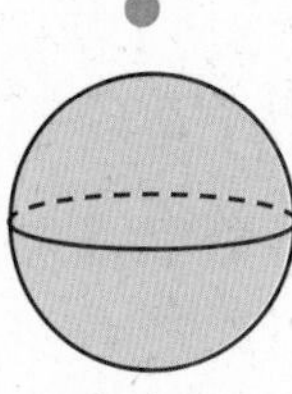

2. Do the sentences describe a cube?
Choose Yes or No.

A cube has 4 faces.	○ Yes	○ No
A cube has 8 vertices.	○ Yes	○ No
A cube has 14 edges.	○ Yes	○ No
Each face of a cube is a square.	○ Yes	○ No

Rewrite each sentence that is not true to make it a true sentence.

____

____

GO DIGITAL Assessment Options Chapter Test

3. Draw lines to show thirds.

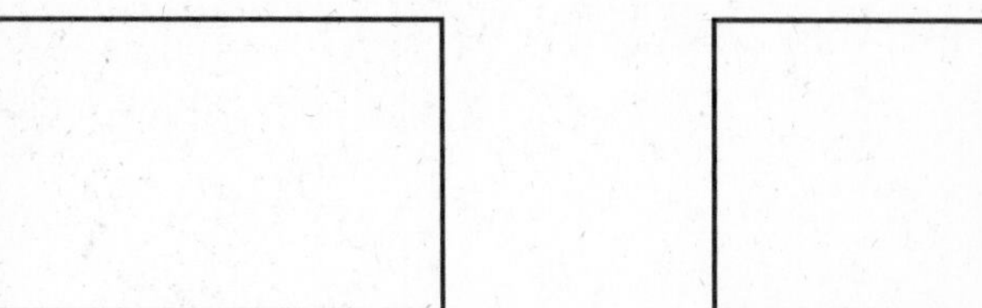

Explain how you know that the parts are thirds.

____

____

4. Will and Ana have gardens that are the same size. They each divide their gardens into fourths. What are two different ways they can divide the gardens? Draw to show your answer.

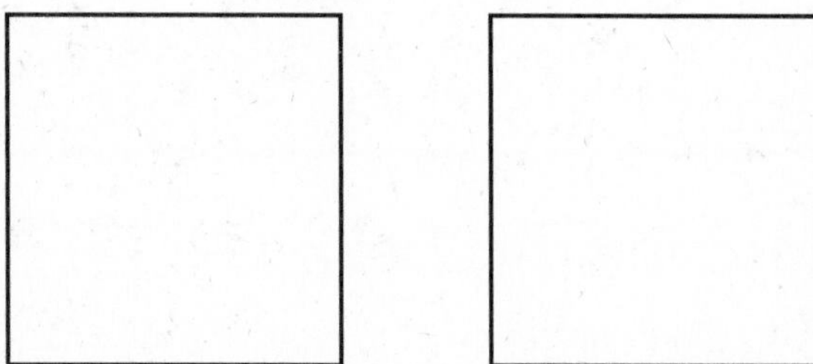

5. Draw to show halves, thirds, and fourths. Color a half of, a third of, and a fourth of the shape.

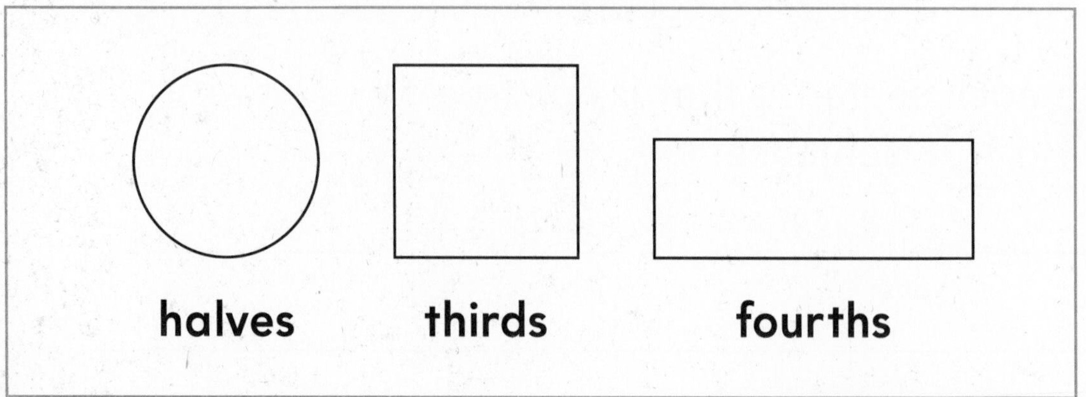

Name ________________________________

6. Max wants to cover the rectangle with color tiles. Explain how you would estimate the number of square tiles he would need to cover the rectangle.

____

____

7. THINK SMARTER + Jenna built this rectangular prism. Circle the number of unit cubes Jenna used.

Personal Math Trainer

8. Rachel makes a pentagon and a quadrilateral with toothpicks. She uses one toothpick for each side of a shape. How many toothpicks does Rachel need?

_______ toothpicks

9. Kevin drew 2 two-dimensional shapes that had 9 angles in all. Draw the shapes Kevin could have drawn.

10. Fill in the bubble next to the shapes that show fourths.

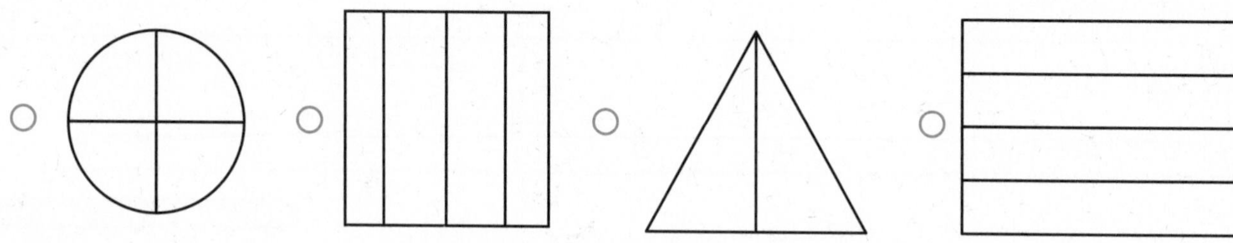

11. GO DEEPER Draw each shape where it belongs in the chart.

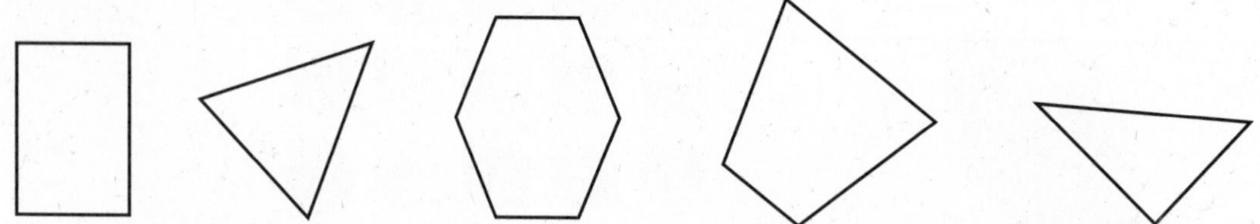

Shapes with fewer than 4 angles	Shapes with more than 3 Angles

Name ______________________________

Magnets Everywhere

Use with *ScienceFusion* pages 152–153.

Develop Vocabulary

1. Write the definition using your own words.

   magnet:

   ____
   ____
   ____
   ____
   ____

Develop Concepts

2. Look at the bottom of the Maglev train where it sits around the train tracks. How is it different than other trains?

   ____
   ____
   ____
   ____
   ____

3. Why do you think the Maglev train can go faster than other trains?

   ____
   ____
   ____
   ____
   ____

Do the Math!

4. It can take up to 45 minutes to do an MRI scan of the head. What is the value of the digit 4 in 45?

5. What is the value of the digit 5 in 45?

6. One Maglev train has gone 361 miles per hour. Write 361 in expanded form.

7. What is the value of the digit 3 in 361? What is the value of the digit 6? What is the value of the digit 1?

Summarize

8. Give examples of ways that magnets are used.

Name ______________________

Rock Resources

Develop Vocabulary

Use with *ScienceFusion* pages 172–173.

1. Write the definition using your own words.

rock:

____

____

____

Develop Concepts

2. Jared used 355 rocks to build a rock wall. Ellie used 372 rocks to build a rock wall. Who used more rocks?

____

____

____

3. Would you rather use rock or wood to build a wall? Why?

____

____

____

4. How many hours do you think it takes for the artist to create a sculpture from rock? Do you think it takes more than 10 hours or less than 10 hours? Why?

____

____

____

Do the Math!

Complete the table with the weights of the two rocks.

Rock	Weight in Pounds
Brown	
Gray	

5. Which rock is heavier? Which rock is lighter?

6. Write two statements comparing the weights of the rocks.

> <

Summarize

7. What material would you most like to use for a sculpture? Why? Make a list of ways people can use rocks.

Name ______________________________

It's in the Air!

Use with *ScienceFusion* pages 304–305.

Develop Vocabulary

1. Write the definition using your own words.

lungs:

____

____

____

gills:

____

____

____

Develop Concepts

2. What would the boy have to do if he dove all the way underwater? Why?

____

____

____

3. Which animal in the table takes the most breaths per minute? Which animal takes the fewest breaths per minute?

How many more breaths per minute does the sparrow take than the horse?

____

____

____

Do the Math!

5. How many more breaths per minute does a sparrow take than a dog? Write a subtraction sentence to find the answer.

6. How many more breaths per minute does a cat take than a horse? Write a subtraction sentence to find the answer.

7. Devin can hold his breath for 20 seconds and Zoey can hold her breath for 15 seconds.

How many seconds longer can Devin hold his breath than Zoey?

Summarize

7. Describe how two different animals get oxygen. Can they survive without oxygen?

Name ______________________________

Everyday Technology

Use with *ScienceFusion* pages 62–63.

Develop Vocabulary

1. Write the definition using your own words.

technology:

____

____

____

Develop Concepts

2. What are some examples of technology that do not use electricity?

____

____

____

3. What are some examples of technology that do use electricity?

____

____

____

4. What are some foods you might cook in a microwave?

____

____

____

Do the Math!

Complete the table with information about how much water the average person uses at home.

Days	Gallons of Water
1	
2	

5. How would you find the number of gallons an average person uses in 3 days?

____

____

6. How many gallons of water does the average person use in 3 days?

____

____

7. Jasmin heats water in the microwave for 45 seconds. She decides it is not hot enough and heats it for 45 more seconds. How many seconds does she heat the water in all?

____

____

____

Summarize

8. List some ways people use technology in their everyday lives.

____

____

____

Name ____________________

Measure It!

Use with *ScienceFusion* pages 228–229.

Develop Vocabulary

1. Write the definition using your own words.

precipitation:

temperature:

wind:

Develop Concepts

2. How does a weather vane measure wind direction?

3. Which direction is the weather vane in the picture pointing?

Do the Math!

4. Measure the temperature in the morning and in the afternoon. Color the thermometers to show the temperatures. What is the morning temperature in degrees Fahrenheit? Celsius? What is the afternoon temperature in degrees Fahrenheit? Celsius?

5. If it is 65°F in the morning and 80°F in the afternoon, how many degrees warmer is it in the afternoon? Write a subtraction sentence to find the answer.

6. If it is 75°F in the morning and 55°F in the afternoon, how many degrees warmer is it in the morning? Write a subtraction sentence to find the answer.

Summarize

7. Describe the three ways we measure weather.

Name ______________________________

At the Beach

Use with *ScienceFusion* pages 340–341.

Develop Vocabulary

1. Write the definition using your own words.

   food chain:

   ____

Develop Concepts

2. From where do plant-like living things get energy?

   ____

3. What do you think might happen after the rockfish eat the krill? Where does the energy in a rockfish go?

   ____

   ____

   ____

4. Draw a food chain that includes an owl, a mouse, a grasshopper, and grass.

5. How does this food chain compare to the food chain with the krill and rockfish?

   ____

   ____

Do the Math!

6. A copper rockfish can grow as long as 55 centimeters. A tiger rockfish can grow as long as 30 centimeters. How much longer can a copper rockfish grow than a tiger rockfish? Write a subtraction sentence to find the answer.

____

____

7. Rockfish can live for many years. One rockfish found in Alaska was 205 years old. How many years older is the Alaska rockfish than one that is 102 years old?

____

____

8. Rockfish swim together in schools. There are 257 rockfish in one school and 412 rockfish in another school. How many rockfish are there in both schools?

____

____

Summarize

9. How do living things depend on each other in a food chain?

____

____

____

Name ____

Turn, Turn, Turn

Develop Vocabulary

Use with *ScienceFusion* pages 280–281.

1. Write the definition using your own words.

rotate:

____

____

____

Develop Concepts

2. Why does the sun appear to always rise in the east and set in the west?

____

____

3. The sun appears highest in the sky at noon each day. How many hours pass between when the sun appears highest in the sky each day?

____

____

4. For about how many hours a day do we see the sun? Is it always the same every day?

____

____

____

Do the Math!

5. How many hours are in a day? How many hours are shown on a clock?

6. If it is 6:00, what time will it be 24 hours later? How do you know? Draw your answer on the clock.

7. How many hours of daylight are there if the sun rises at 6:00 AM and sets at 7:00 PM?

8. Suppose there are 8 hours of darkness and the sun sets at 10:00 PM. What time will the sun rise?

Summarize

9. Why does the sun seem to rise and set?

Name ___________________________

Let's Check Again!

Use with *ScienceFusion* pages 32–33.

Develop Vocabulary

1. Write the definition using your own words.

   investigation:

____

____

____

____

Develop Concepts

2. Why do scientists want results of a test to be the same each time?

____

____

____

____

3. Why is it important that the children included words in their pictures to communicate their results?

____

____

____

____

Do the Math!

4. Choose an object to measure. Use a ruler to measure its length three times in inches.

Length of ___________	
Measure 1	
Measure 2	
Measure 3	

5. How do your numbers compare? Why do you think so?

6. If the results of a test are the same every time, but are not the results you expected, what can you learn?

Summarize

7. Why do scientists redo a test and check it again?

Name ______________________________

Units to Know

Develop Concepts

Use with *ScienceFusion* pages 14–15.

1. How can you use the same ruler to measure with two different units of measure?

2. Which is longer, an inch or a centimeter?

3. About how many centimeters is the same as 1 inch? How can you tell?

Do the Math!

4. Measure the width of the top of your desk in paper clips. How many paper clips did you use?

5. Measure the paper clip. How many centimeters long is the paper clip?

6. How can measuring with paper clips help you predict the length of an object in centimeters?

7. Why is it important to line up an object with the end of a ruler to measure it?

Summarize

8. Describe the two units you can use to measure length. Explain how to measure accurately.

Name ______________________________

Plant Start-Ups

Use with *ScienceFusion* pages 408–409.

Develop Vocabulary

1. Write the definition using your own words.

seed:

____

____

____

____

Develop Concepts

2. What do you do to start growing a plant from a seed?

____

____

____

____

3. What are some plants you would like to grow? Do you think these plants will grow where we live?

____

____

____

____

Do the Math!

4. How much taller did the corn plant grow than the bean plant?

5. About how much taller did the corn plant grow than the tomato plant?

6. About how much taller did the bean plant grow than the tomato plant?

Summarize

7. What is the main idea of "Plant Start-Ups?" Have these pages changed your ideas about plants?

Name ____________________

Attract Attention

Develop Concepts

Use with *ScienceFusion* pages 150–151.

1. What are some things in our classroom that are attracted to magnets?

____

____

____

2. What are some things in our classroom that are not attracted to magnets?

____

____

____

3. What is a magnetic field?

____

____

____

4. What would happen to things that are attracted to a magnet if the magnetic field did not change as you moved away from the magnet?

____

____

____

Do the Math!

5. How far from a paper clip must a magnet be before it does not attract it? Use a ruler to measure.

Distance	Did the magnet attract the paper clip?
$\frac{1}{2}$ inch	
1 inch	
$1\frac{1}{2}$ inches	
2 inches	

6. Compare the distances. How far from the magnet can you observe the magnetic field? How do you know?

7. Why do you think you should test whether the magnet attracts the paper clip every $\frac{1}{2}$ inch instead of every whole inch?

Summarize

8. What are the main ideas of these pages? Use the words *magnet*, *attract*, and *magnetic field* in your writing.

Picture Glossary

addend sumando

5 + 8 = 13

addends

a.m. a.m.

Times after midnight and before noon are written with **a.m.**

11:00 a.m. is in the morning.

angle ángulo

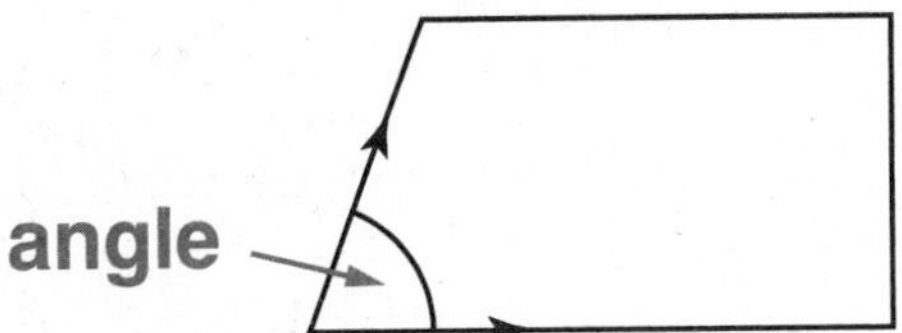

bar graph gráfica de barras

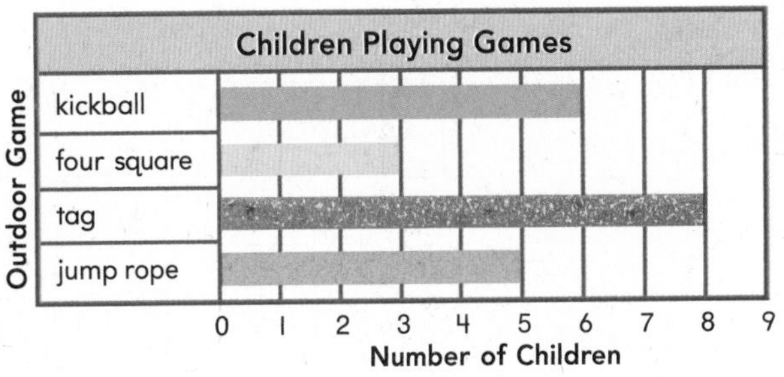

cent sign símbolo de centavo

53¢

cent sign

centimeter centímetro

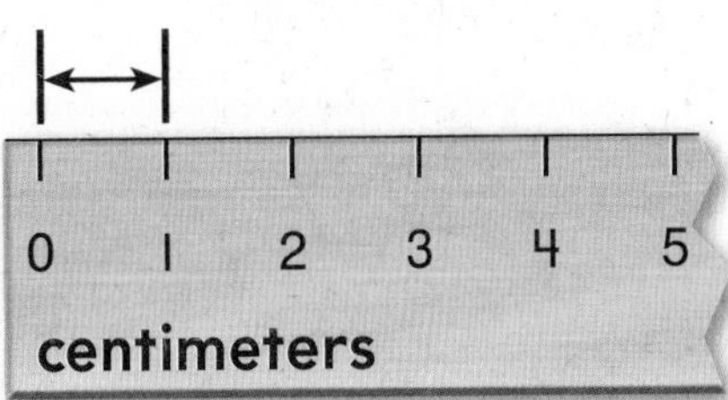

column columna

column

$$\begin{array}{r} 3\,\boxed{3} \\ 3\,\boxed{4} \\ +3\,\boxed{2} \\ \hline \end{array}$$

compare comparar

Use these symbols when you **compare**: $>$, $<$, $=$.

$241 > 234$

$123 < 128$

$247 = 247$

compare comparar

Compare the lengths of the pencil and the crayon.

The pencil is longer than the crayon.

The crayon is shorter than the pencil.

cone cono

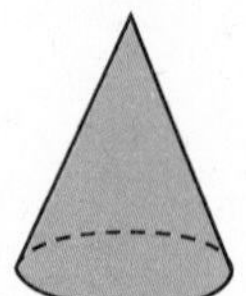

cube cubo

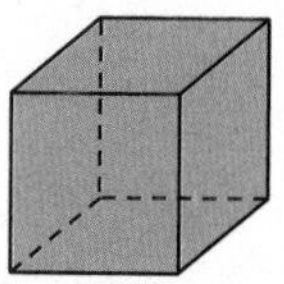

cylinder cilindro

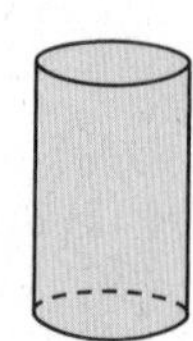

data datos

Favorite Lunch	
Lunch	**Tally**
pizza	||||
sandwich	卌 |
salad	|||
pasta	卌

The information in this chart is called **data**.

decimal point punto decimal

$1.00
↑
decimal point

difference diferencia

9 − 2 = 7
↑
difference

digit dígito

0, 1, 2, 3, 4, 5, 6, 7, 8, and 9 are **digits**.

dime moneda de 10¢

A **dime** has a value of 10 cents.

dollar dólar

One **dollar** is worth 100 cents.

dollar sign símbolo de dólar

$1.00
↑
dollar sign

doubles dobles

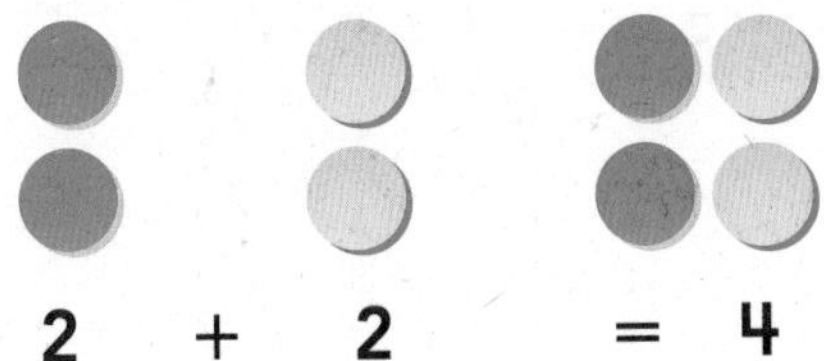

2 + 2 = 4

edge arista

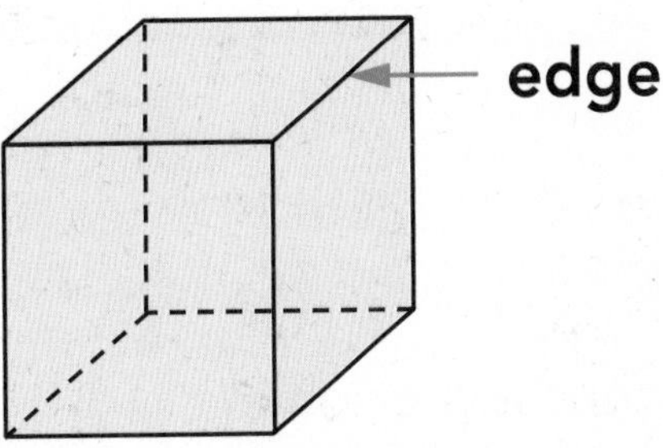

An **edge** is formed where two faces of a three-dimensional shape meet.

estimate estimación

An **estimate** is an amount that tells about how many.

even par

2, 4, 6, 8, 10, . . .

even numbers

face cara

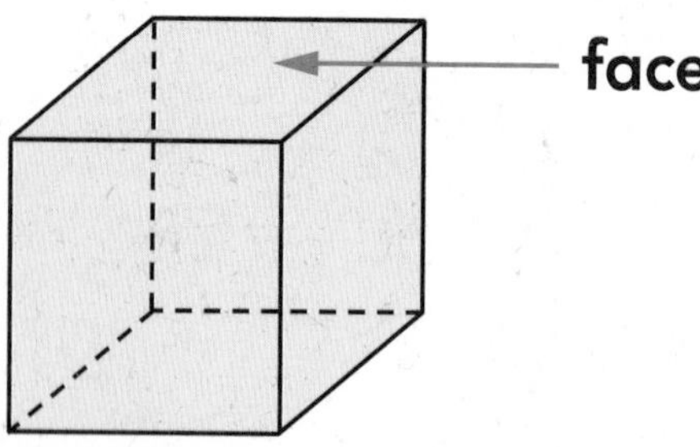

Each flat surface of this cube is a **face**.

foot pie

1 **foot** is the same length as 12 inches.

fourth of cuarto de

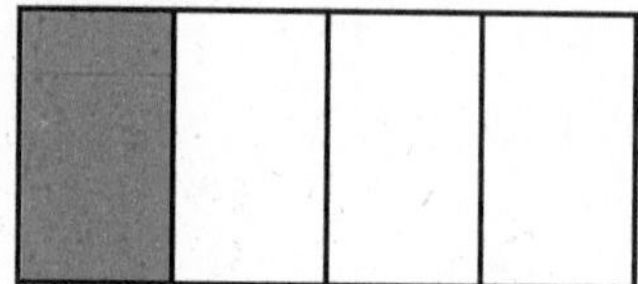

A **fourth of** the shape is green.

fourths cuartos

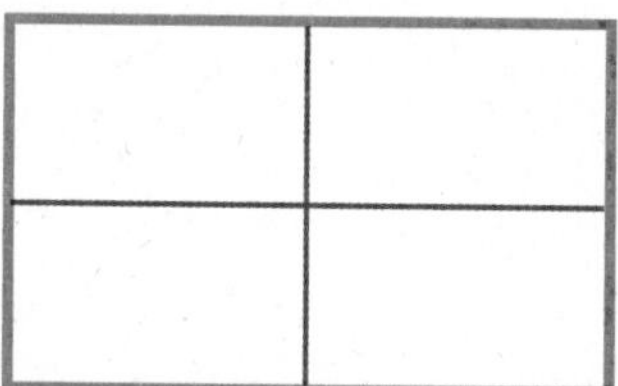

This shape has 4 equal parts. These equal parts are called **fourths**.

half of mitad de

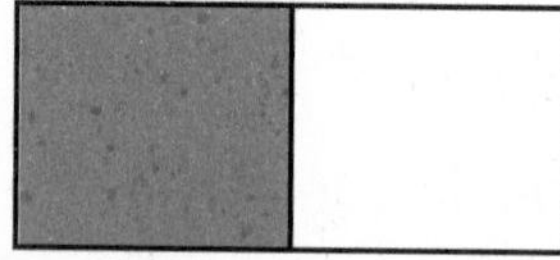

A **half of** the shape is green.

halves mitades

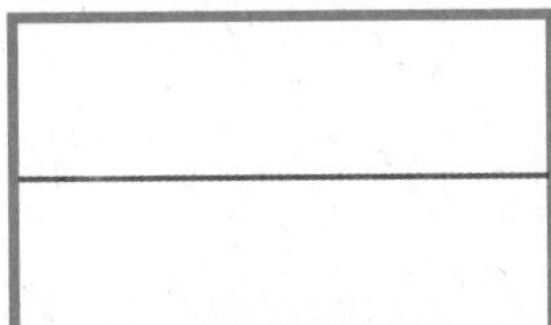

This shape has 2 equal parts. These equal parts are called **halves**.

hexagon hexágono

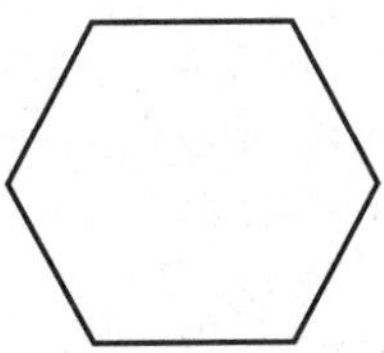

A two-dimensional shape with 6 sides is a **hexagon**.

hour hora

There are 60 minutes in 1 **hour**.

hundred centena

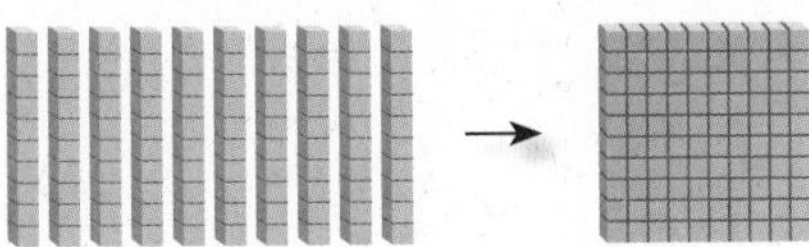

There are 10 tens in 1 **hundred.**

inch pulgada

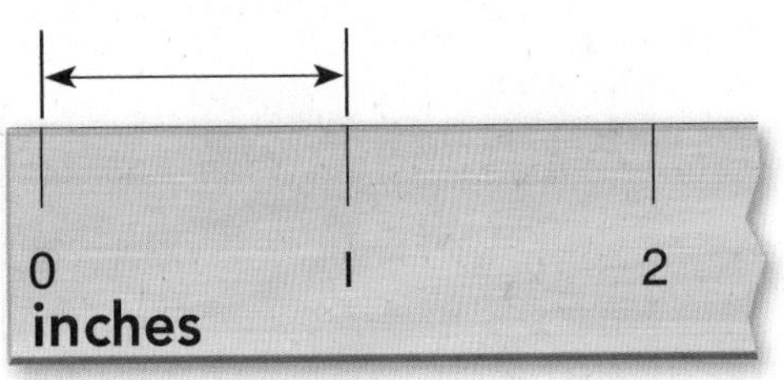

is **equal to** (=) es igual a

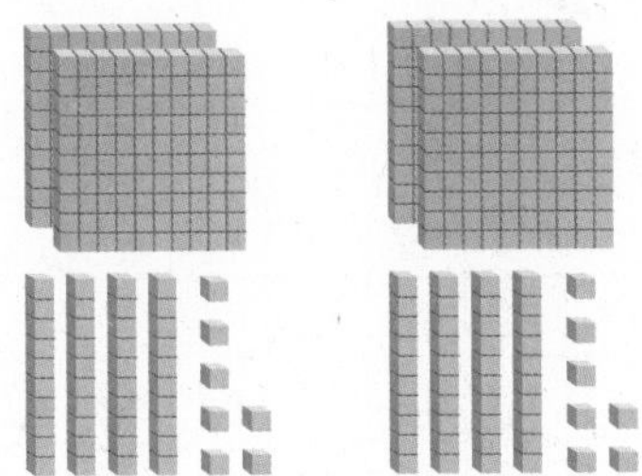

247 **is equal to** 247.
247 = 247

is greater than (>) es mayor que

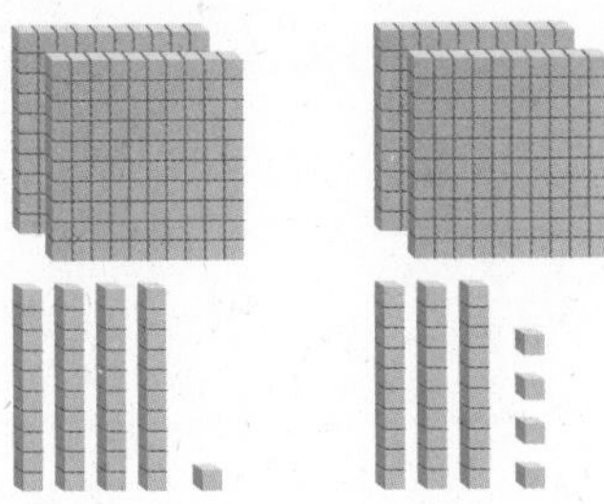

241 **is greater than** 234.
241 > 234

is less than (<) es menor que

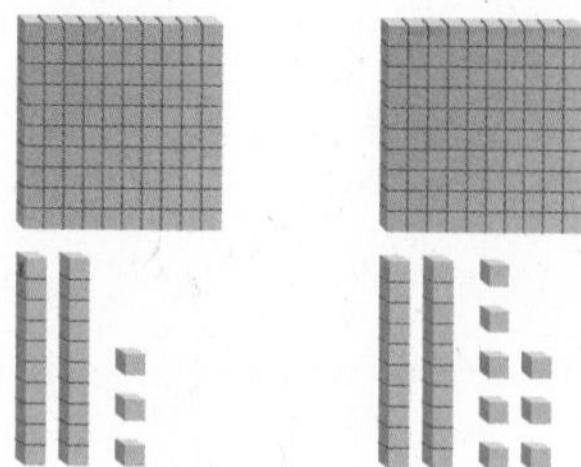

123 **is less than** 128.
123 < 128

key clave

Number of Soccer Games							
March	⚽	⚽	⚽	⚽			
April	⚽	⚽	⚽				
May	⚽	⚽	⚽	⚽	⚽	⚽	
June	⚽	⚽	⚽	⚽	⚽	⚽	⚽

Key: Each ⚽ stands for 1 game.

The **key** tells how many each picture stands for.

line plot diagrama de puntos

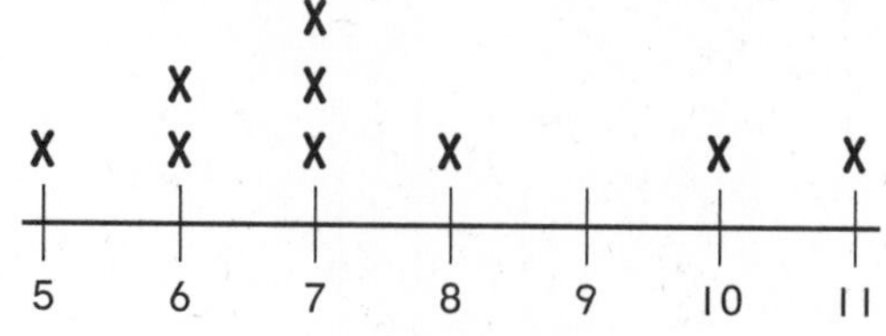

Lengths of Paintbrushes in Inches

measuring tape cinta métrica

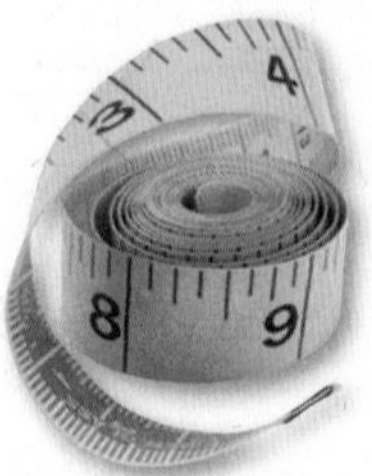

meter metro

1 **meter** is the same length as 100 centimeters.

midnight medianoche

Midnight is 12:00 at night.

minute minuto

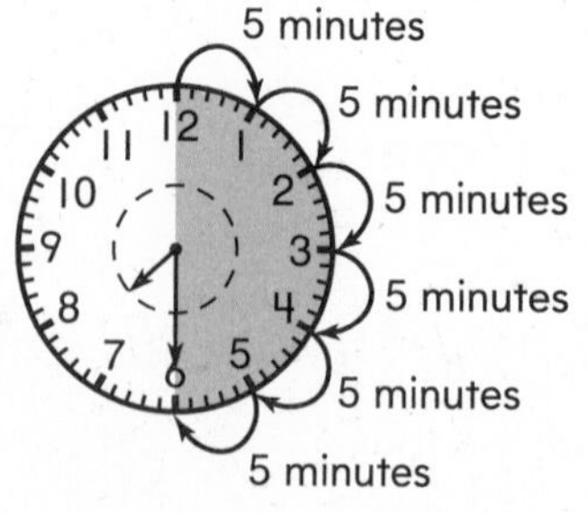

There are 30 **minutes** in a half hour.

nickel moneda de 5¢

A **nickel** has a value of 5 cents.

noon mediodía

Noon is 12:00 in the daytime.

odd impar

1, 3, 5, 7, 9, 11, . . .

odd numbers

ones unidades

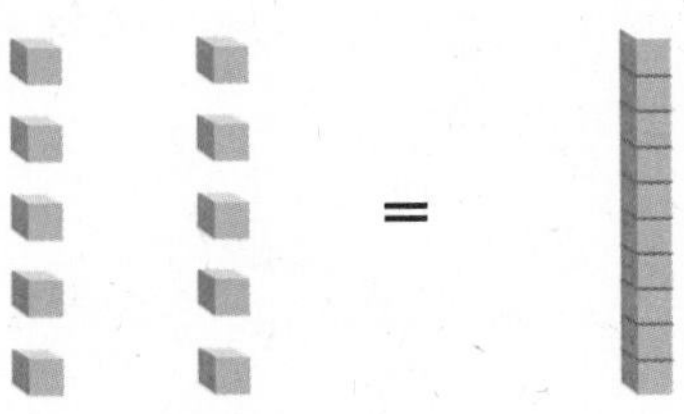

10 ones = 1 ten

penny moneda de 1¢

A **penny** has a value of 1 cent.

pentagon pentágono

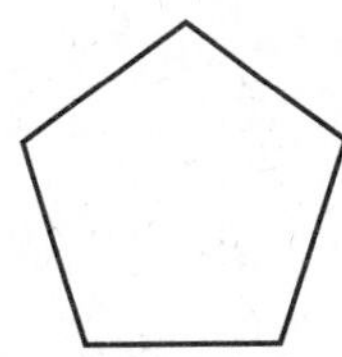

A two-dimensional shape with 5 sides is a **pentagon**.

picture graph gráfica con dibujos

Number of Soccer Games							
March	⚽	⚽	⚽	⚽			
April	⚽	⚽	⚽				
May	⚽	⚽	⚽	⚽	⚽	⚽	
June	⚽	⚽	⚽	⚽	⚽	⚽	⚽

Key: Each ⚽ stands for 1 game.

plus (+) más

2 plus 1 is equal to 3
2 + 1 = 3

p.m. p.m.

Times after noon and before midnight are written with **p.m.**

11:00 p.m. is in the evening.

quadrilateral cuadrilátero

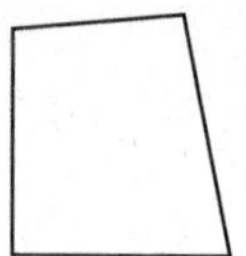

A two-dimensional shape with 4 sides is a **quadrilateral**.

quarter moneda de 25¢

A **quarter** has a value of 25 cents.

quarter of cuarta parte de

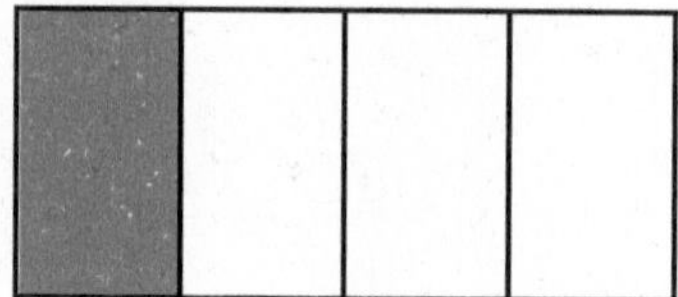

A **quarter of** the shape is green.

quarter past y cuarto

15 minutes after 8
quarter past 8

rectangular prism prisma rectangular

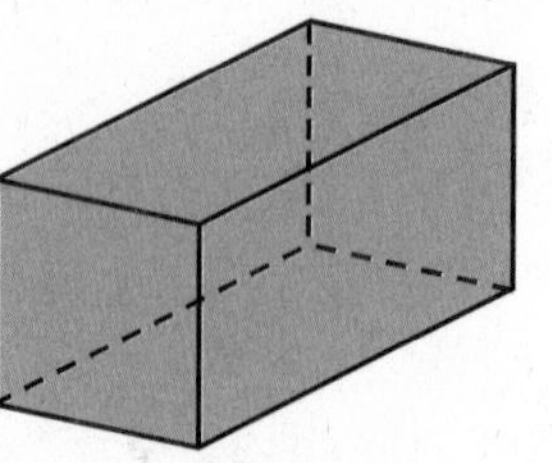

regroup reagrupar

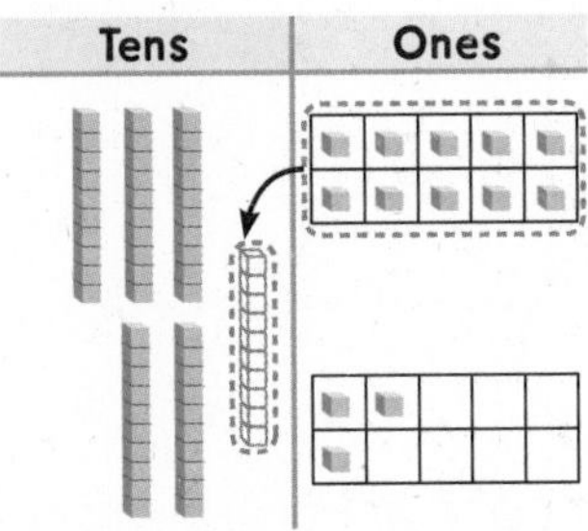

You can trade 10 ones for 1 ten to **regroup**.

side lado

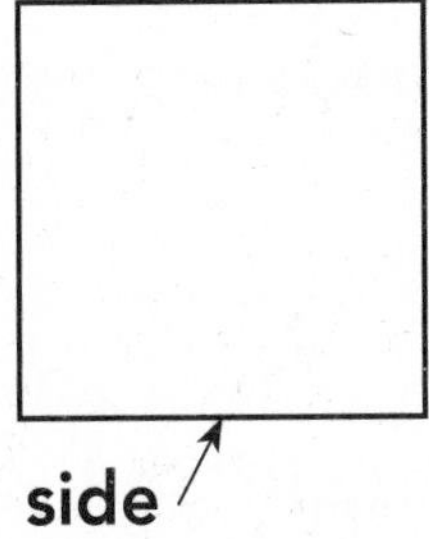

This shape has 4 **sides**.

sphere esfera

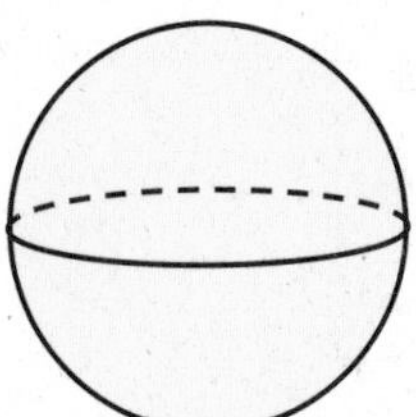

sum suma o total

$9 + 6 = 15$

sum

survey encuesta

Favorite Lunch	
Lunch	**Tally**
pizza	IIII
sandwich	𝍸 I
salad	III
pasta	𝍸

A **survey** is a collection of data from answers to a question.

ten decena

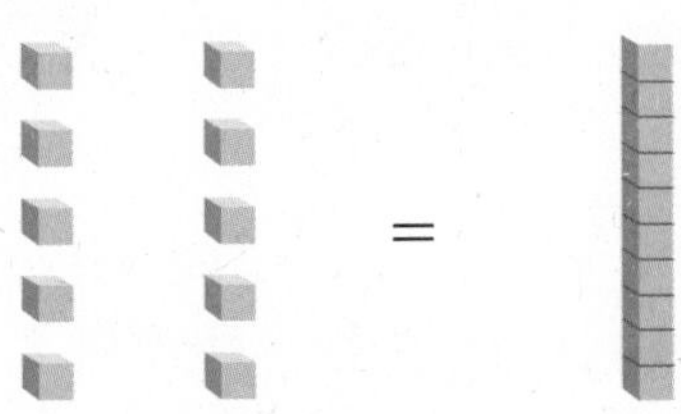

10 ones = 1 ten

third of tercio de

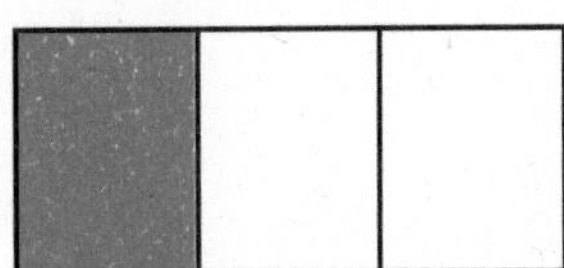

A **third of** the shape is green.

thirds tercios

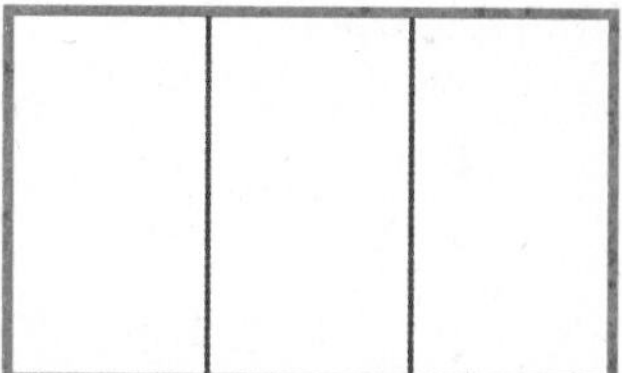

This shape has 3 equal parts. These equal parts are called **thirds**.

thousand millar

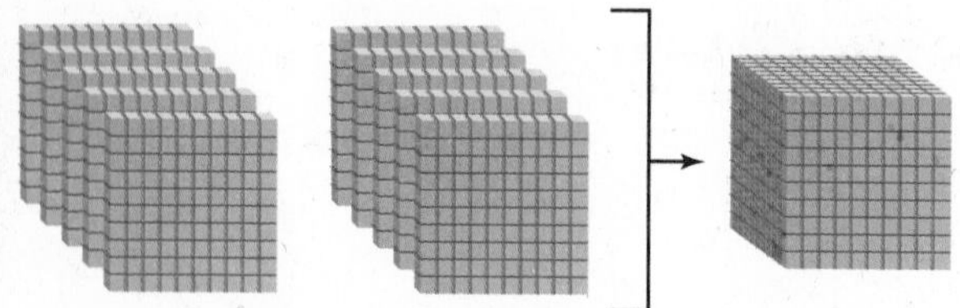

There are 10 hundreds in 1 **thousand**.

vertex/vertices
vértice/vértices

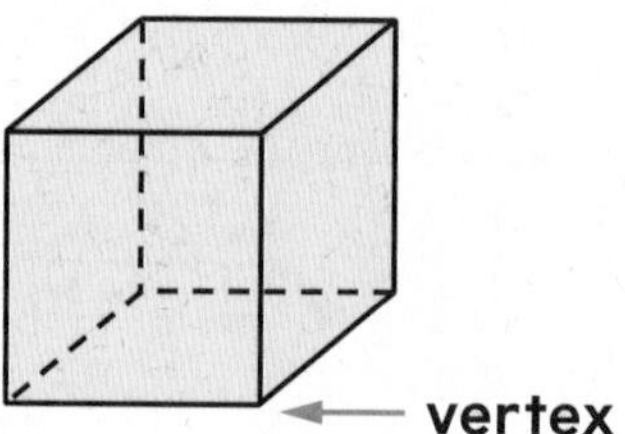

A corner point of a three-dimensional shape is a **vertex**.

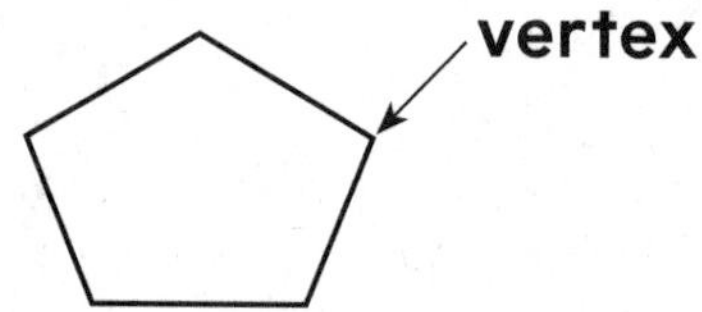

This shape has 5 **vertices**.

yardstick regla de 1 yarda

A **yardstick** is a measuring tool that shows 3 feet.

Index

A

D

E

Q

R

S